T0273972

HIKING
WISCONSIN

HELP US KEEP THIS GUIDE UP TO DATE

Every effort has been made by the author and editors to make this guide as accurate and useful as possible. However, many things can change after a guide is published—trails are rerouted, regulations change, techniques evolve, facilities come under new management, etc.

We appreciate hearing from you concerning your experiences with this guide and how you feel it could be improved and kept up to date. While we may not be able to respond to all comments and suggestions, we'll take them to heart and we'll also make certain to share them with the author. Please send your comments and suggestions to the following address:

Globe Pequot Press
Reader Response/Editorial Department
246 Goose Lane, Suite 200
Guilford, CT 06437

Thanks for your input, and happy trails!

HIKING
WISCONSIN

A GUIDE TO THE STATE'S GREATEST HIKES

THIRD EDITION

Kevin Revolinski
and Eric Hansen

FALCONGUIDES

GUILFORD, CONNECTICUT

To the thousands of men and women
who give so generously of their time
so that Wisconsin remains
a place well worth hiking.
They build and maintain trails,
attend conservation hearings,
and campaign against those
who would turn our rivers
into discharge channels for mines
and our forests into industrial tree farms.

FALCONGUIDES®

An imprint of The Rowman & Littlefield Publishing Group, Inc.
4501 Forbes Blvd., Ste. 200
Lanham, MD 20706
www.rowman.com

Falcon and FalconGuides are registered trademarks and Make Adventure Your Story is a trademark of The Rowman & Littlefield Publishing Group, Inc.

Distributed by NATIONAL BOOK NETWORK

Copyright © 2022 by The Rowman & Littlefield Publishing Group, Inc.
Previous editions of this book were published by Falcon Publishing, Inc., in 2002 and 2016.

Photos by Kevin Revolinski unless otherwise noted
Maps updated by Melissa Baker, © The Rowman & Littlefield Publishing Group, Inc.

British Library Cataloguing in Publication Information available

Library of Congress Cataloging-in-Publication Data available

ISBN 978-1-4930-6332-1 (paper : alk. paper)
ISBN 978-1-4930-6333-8 (electronic)

Printed in India

CONTENTS

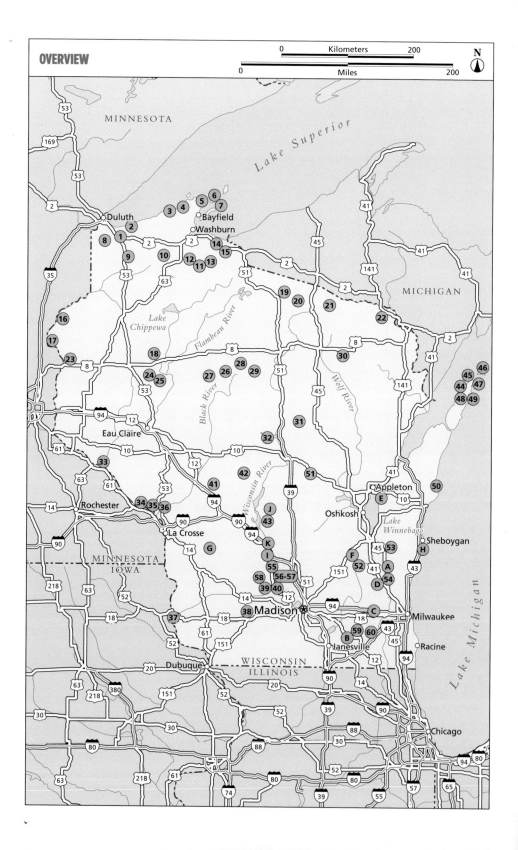

ACKNOWLEDGMENTS

This book would not have been possible without the help of many people. I would like to thank the nearly fifty avid hikers who found time to return my questionnaires and inform me of their favorite routes. Many of those folks are active in the Wisconsin Let's Go Hiking Club, Sierra Club, Milwaukee Nordic Ski Club, North Country Trail Association, or the Ice Age Park and Trail Foundation.

Steve Sorensen, of Ashland, shared his knowledge of many hikes in that area. Drew Hanson, geographer of the Ice Age Park and Trail Foundation, supplied savvy trail data, a steady stream of encouragement, and text review.

Thanks also to the countless land agency personnel who patiently answered my questions.

I am grateful to copy editor Katie Sharp and the rest of the staff at Globe Pequot for their knowledgeable assistance.

Special thanks to my spouse, Anne Steinberg, for frontline editing that kept me on track and a faith in this project that smoothed the rough spots.

Any errors are mine, not theirs.

—Eric Hansen

I am humbled to be providing what amounts to an assist in maintaining such a fantastic collection of Wisconsin hikes. Eric Hansen's work in creating the original edition of this book is impressive, and the trails he chose have not lost their magnificence. Eric Sherman of the Ice Age Trail Alliance deserves my thanks for always keeping me up-to-date on the latest developments of the trail. Jon Jarosh of Door County Visitor Bureau helped me sort out the latest information for the Door County hikes, while Julie Van Stappen of the Apostle Islands National Lakeshore was instrumental in getting me what I needed for the several hikes in the islands and on the lakeshore there. Also, thanks to Marty Swank of the Chequamegon Chapter of the North Country Trail Association. I can't begin to list all the various park personnel, managers, and rangers, and even fellow hikers, who contributed in some fashion to this new edition. Thanks also to David Legere at Globe Pequot/FalconGuides for his guidance and infinite patience. Finally, as always, I am fortunate to have my wife, Preamtip Satasuk, with me literally every step of the way and taking care of so much, from photography to drive navigation to snacks. I couldn't have done this without her.

—Kevin Revolinski

Anderson Lake Trail passes close to Clay Lake (hike 10).

INTRODUCTION

HIKING WISCONSIN

If a foreign visitor were to ask me about hiking in Wisconsin, I would sum it up in three words: *water, woods,* and *wolves*. Bordered by two of the Great Lakes and the Mississippi River, filled with thousands of inland lakes and sparkling streams, the state's abundance of pristine water attracts natives and neighbors alike. A vast second-growth forest of hardwoods and evergreens, concentrated in the Northern Highlands and Central Plain, covers 46 percent of the state. An impeccable authority indicates the quality of that forest's quiet corners: Wild timber wolves, returning of their own free will, have reoccupied much of Wisconsin's forest land, raising pups as far south as the center of the state.

I would tell the visitor that I can leave my Milwaukee home, drive three hours, and walk past the tracks of one of the eight breeding packs of wolves in the central forest. Or I could travel west, to a quiet bluff-top prairie offering broad views of the Mississippi River and the hardwood forests clinging to steep slopes along its shores. Upstream, an hour's drive north of the Twin Cities, I would walk beside one of the cleanest large rivers in the country, the St. Croix, while eagles scan for dinner. There huge glacial potholes, scoured 60 feet deep and 12 feet wide into bedrock, illustrate the epic glacial forces that shaped the St. Croix valley and much of the state.

A little north of there the choices become difficult. Should I walk to the fourth-highest waterfall east of the Rocky Mountains, a stunning 165-foot drop, or opt for solitude at a charming backcountry cascade? Or should I follow part of the North Country Trail's 60-mile passage through a remote forest, passing lakes where the haunting cries of loons echo?

I couldn't leave this part of the state without communing with Lake Superior, possessor of a full eighth, and some of the purest, of the planet's fresh water. Two outings along its shores are classics: a walk along one of the pristine beaches and a hike to one source of that sand, the spectacular wave-carved sandstone sea caves and cliffs east of Cornucopia.

Sometime I would have to head south, but not before making a walking sojourn with another timeless natural wonder, the 17,000 acres of virgin forest, sprinkled with twenty stunningly clear lakes, at Sylvania. A small jog downstate would bring me to another favorite woodland walk, the Ice Age National Scenic Trail near the Yellow River, where fishers and wolf pups romp and the otherworldly Goblin Fern haunts the forest duff. Then memories of the primeval bark of sandhill cranes, nesting osprey, and herons would pull me to a marsh walk along dike roads in the Central Plain.

A detour to Wisconsin's east coast would be in order. I would journey to Door County and roam the rockbound peninsula south of Moonlight Bay, where rare orchids compete with wave washed shores for my attention. Rolling down the coast, Point Beach's 6-mile-long strand would have no trouble getting me out of the car.

Almost home, I would stop in the Kettle Moraine country, grateful that such a treat was near Milwaukee. Miles of Ice Age Trail to follow, shady woods, a tumbled, playful topography, and otter tracks along the streams would persuade me to linger.

I know these places and their rejuvenating powers, and I would gladly return to them. However, this book, and the hiking choices within it, is for you. Whatever your tastes, whichever corner of the state you find yourself in, there is a path waiting for you, a way to reconnect with the natural world. The directions are here. —*E.H.*

ICE AGE NATIONAL SCENIC TRAIL

Not that long ago, 15,000 years back, massive glaciers covered most of the land we know today as Wisconsin. Vast sheets of ice, led by six lobes, scoured rock debris across much of the state, bulldozing everything in their path. It was an era when ice covered wide areas of the northern part of North America, but nowhere else on the continent is the glaciers' path as clear as it is here. Wisconsin's glacial landscape is a renowned showcase for that era.

Terminal moraines, rock rubble from the glaciers' front, are one of their most prominent relics. In the early 1950s an idea surfaced to create a linear ice age park and trail along the moraine's 1,200-mile-long line across the state, the mark of the glaciers' last advance. Today, major parts of that dream are a reality. More than 650 miles of trail are now open along the proposed path.

Four long segments of the Ice Age Trail are noteworthy: the Chippewa Moraine in Chippewa County, the Jerry Lake Segment in Taylor County, and the trail sections in the Northern and Southern Units of the Kettle Moraine State Forest.

Hikers can access trail maps and local chapter contacts as well as a history of Wisconsin's glacial landscape by contacting the foundation's office or website:

Ice Age Trail Alliance, 2110 Main St., Cross Plains, WI 53528; (800) 227-0046; www.iceagetrail.org

NORTH COUNTRY NATIONAL SCENIC TRAIL

In the 1960s the Chequamegon National Forest built a 60-mile-long footpath in northwest Wisconsin and named it the North Country Trail. At the time, there were no great ambitions for it to be more than a trail through Wisconsin's Northwoods.

However, the name caused a stir. In the years that followed, the idea of a North Country Trail stretching across a wide tier of northern states spread, and a movement to build that trail was born.

Today the North Country National Scenic Trail has over 3,160 miles of trail in place on a route that stretches 4,760 miles, from northern New York to North Dakota.

Here in Wisconsin, that first, 60-mile-long trail segment continues to attract hikers looking for long, quiet walks. Its hold on that niche may last, but its claim to fame in the scenery category faces a strong challenge from a stretch of trail in the Penokee Range. Other trail segments are in the Brule River State Forest, Pattison State Park, and Copper Falls State Park.

Trail maps and up-to-date reports on new trail additions are on the North Country Trail Association's website at www.northcountry.org and at the three regional chapters' websites:

Brule–St. Croix Chapter; htg@northcountrytrail.org; www.northcountrytrail.org/trail/wisconsin/bsc

Chequamegon Chapter; che@northcountrytrail.org; www.northcountrytrail.org/trail/wisconsin/che

Heritage Chapter; htg@northcountrytrail.org; www.northcountrytrail.org/trail/wisconsin/htg

LAND ACQUISITION TO PROTECT HIKING TRAILS

Few would argue the point that corridors of natural habitat are essential to a healthy wildlife population. It is time to apply that logic to the spiritual health of our species. When it comes to the habitat of hiking trails, all too often fragmentation takes hold. For a hiker, coming around a corner to find 100 acres of 4-year-old aspen, an obvious remnant of a clear-cut, is a disheartening experience. A fair number of linear hiking trails in the state cross land that is subject to commercial pressure to show a profit by logging. One solution is for hikers to lobby land managers. Conservation easements is another. Land acquisition to protect trail corridors solves the problem.

The State of Wisconsin has a plan, the Knowles-Nelson Stewardship Program, to acquire and preserve green acres. It is important that land acquisition for hiking trails be a priority for that program. To find out how you and other hikers can effectively advocate for trail corridors, contact the Ice Age Trail Alliance or the North Country Trail Association.

SAVING THIS PLACE WE CALL WISCONSIN

"For the strength of the pack is the wolf and the strength of the wolf is the pack."

You, and others like you, can make the critical difference in whether the places we enjoy today are worth visiting in the years to come. Your knowledge of savvy methods to respond to the threats to Wisconsin's wild lands is a key part of the strategy to protect them. Citizen watchdogs are the eyes and ears that blow the whistle on polluters and other illegal activity.

Several threats to our natural landscape loom large. The threat of budget cuts to the Knowles-Nelson Stewardship Program are eternal, shortsighted, self-destructive measures that could damage Wisconsin's natural bounty and, by association, the massive tourism industry. There is also a sustained effort to locate a mine within the Penokee Range, threatening territory and watersheds far beyond its proposed deep cut in the earth. Factory farms, with their ominous "waste lagoons," pose a threat as well.

As drastic as those menaces are, another is even more serious: persistent attempts to weaken the state's environmental protections. You can do a great service for yourself, other hikers, and the community at large by keeping abreast of these issues. Information is power.

In addition, while you are out hiking, watch for questionable activities, like a bulldozer working on the edge of a wetland. Your willingness to make a phone call could save that wetland from illegal filling. "I can list a hundred times that we got non-permitted activities stopped on the weekend because a warden responded quickly to a citizen call," once said John Holmes, a retired conservation warden. "If you see something suspicious, act fast before environmental damage happens."

The Department of Natural Resources maintains a toll-free Violation Hotline so that citizens can confidentially report suspected wildlife, recreational, and environmental violations. You can call (800) 847-9367 or submit a report online at https://dnrx.wisconsin.gov/rav.

WEATHER

The weather in Wisconsin is a source of local pride, often seen as a test of character. At its fiercest, it will challenge you with near hundred-degree heat and below-zero wind chills. Fortunately, there is a lot of fine hiking weather between those extremes. In addition to the obvious seasonal variations, there is often a wide difference between the weather in the north and south of the state. Another, more regional distinction is worth noting: The Great Lakes have moderate temperatures along their shores, resisting heat and cold that may be dominant only a few miles inland.

For hikers more than a casual distance from their vehicle, it pays to know the forecast and be prepared for worst-case scenarios, such as cold rain showers accompanied by strong winds. Several hikes in this book follow Great Lakes shorelines. Be aware that coastline routes are glorious in good conditions but merciless in their exposure to high winds when the weather gets rowdy.

SEASONS

Spring hiking, with its woodland wildflowers, colorful birds, and open sight lines through the leafless forest, can be the best of the year. It is a time when marsh walks along dike routes can lead to extravagant bird migration scenes.

Bug presence is minimal and weather is often temperate and ideal for walking. The weather can be volatile, though; keep track of forecasts and bring appropriate clothing. Right after the snow melts, trails are frequently wet or muddy. A trip to the central sand counties, or a beach walk along Lakes Michigan or Superior, is a good option then. Trails that keep to the top of a moraine, such as the Ice Age Trail in the Northern Kettle Moraine area, drain well and tend to dry before others.

Summer, with its long hours of daylight, lends itself to lengthy hikes, with time to linger at distant destinations. Hot temperatures are a comfort factor directly related to how much of a hike is in the deep shade of the forest canopy. Shady forest trails of the north tend to be reasonably comfortable throughout the summer. Many southern trails weave in and out of the shade and can be warm in the midday heat. Beach walks and open dike routes in marshes can be downright hot during the middle of the day. One way to escape the heat is to walk near the Great Lakes shorelines and enjoy cooler lake-effect temperatures.

Bugs are numerous in early summer and slowly decline as the season progresses. Thunderstorms can soak hikers and expose them to dangerous lightning.

Fall is the favorite season of many hikers. It is hard to disagree with the merits of a forest ablaze with color. Shorter daylight hours dictate an earlier return from hikes. Full rain gear is a good idea for the cooler temperatures and lingering rain showers of fall. Bug season ends, and hikes that would be miserable in June are prime in late September. Hunters are out and about, so wearing some blaze orange is prudent.

Winter snow cover on hiking trails is a sure thing in the central and northern portions of the state. That deep snow may bring an end to the hiking season, but for snowshoe and ski enthusiasts it is a pleasant opportunity to travel the trails in another manner. In the southern part of the state, snow cover is less dominant and hiking is possible at times. Cold weather and the arrival of safe ice offer a unique opportunity there: walking into wetlands and bogs.

CLOTHING

Two truths are the basis of a savvy clothing strategy. First, layer your clothing and you will have options. Temperature, wind, shade, and precipitation can change during a hike. If you have clothing choices, you will be able to add or subtract a layer and be more comfortable when those changes occur. You will be able to walk without becoming overheated, cold, or wet. Second, synthetic thread does not absorb water as cotton thread does. Essentially this means that any moisture in the fabric dries quicker because it is between the threads, not within them. This fundamental advantage of synthetic clothes keeps the hiker drier, with less chance of becoming chilled. In cool temperatures or high winds, that advantage can become a critical safety factor.

The season and length of your hike determine what is essential. A cap and sunblock could be the bottom line for a short warm-weather hike, but consider a long-sleeved shirt and pants for protection from the sun, bugs, and briars.

Rain gear quality should reflect the relative threat of becoming chilled and hypothermic. On a short warm-weather hike, that threat may be low, but in cooler temperatures, and on longer outings, take along full rain gear as well as a sweater and warm hat.

Hiking boots are a basic part of your clothing system. Boots that feature a waterproof and breathable liner will keep your feet toasty in a chilly autumn rain and ease the going when trails are wet.

TICKS AND LYME DISEASE

Wisconsin has its share of insects that can be annoying at times, but one is capable of damage worse than a minor sting: the tiny deer tick. Adults of that species are no larger than one of the letters in the "one dime" imprint on that coin's surface. They inhabit grass and brush, attaching themselves to passing warm bodies. Some deer ticks carry Lyme disease, an illness that affects the nervous system, heart, skin, and joints. It is important to recognize the disease's signs and symptoms, which include skin rash, chills or fever, fatigue, and arthritis-like joint and muscle pains. If the disease is caught in the early stages, antibiotics are usually successful in treating it.

Be sure to do a complete check of your body and clothes for ticks after hiking in tick habitat. Hikers should educate themselves about the disease as well as methods of prevention and treatment. There is a geographical pattern to the occurrence of Lyme disease in Wisconsin. The northwest part of the state has the highest rates, with reported cases tapering off to the southeast. Other tick-borne illnesses have been documented, such as anaplasmosis, babesiosis, ehrlichiosis, Powassan virus infection, and Rocky Mountain spotted fever, but at this time are still rare.

For more information contact the Wisconsin Department of Health Services, 1 West Wilson St., Madison, WI 53703; (608) 266-1865; www.dhs.wisconsin.gov.

BEING PREPARED

Being prepared has its equipment aspects, but in the end mental preparedness is key. We set out on hikes with a set of assumptions in place. We are confident that our physical capabilities and gear can deal with the conditions and terrain we expect to find. In a way we are using a mathematical formula that goes like this: confidence + conditioning + gear + conditions that are reasonable and as expected = successful outing. Trouble arises when one of the factors in this formula changes and the formula no longer computes. That change could be a severe heel blister, twisted ankle, sudden lightning storm, or cold rain squall. At that point, conditions may exceed our capacity to deal with them. There is no warning light on a dashboard, but savvy hikers recognize that moment's approach and trim their sails appropriately.

Even a small fanny pack has room for a small amount of gear that can make a big difference when problems arise. At a minimum, take a compass, energy bar, water, knife, aspirin, bandages, antibacterial ointment, matches, and space blanket emergency bag. Tightly folded garbage bags take up less room than your wallet and can pinch-hit as an emergency shelter or rain gear.

TREADING LIGHTLY ON THE LAND

Zero impact is to hiking and camping what catch-and-release is to fishing. It all boils down to one concept: With a little forethought, we will still be able to enjoy the outing we are taking today in five years.

If you pack it in, pack it out. Leave nothing but footprints. Human sanitation is especially important in the backwoods, away from toilets. Dig a 6-inch-deep hole, well away from any stream or water, relieve yourself, and cover the hole with dirt. Pack out your used toilet paper in a plastic storage bag.

USING THIS GUIDE

The authors' goal framed the research and writing for this book: to find and catalog the best natural ambiance in the state. These are the questions that guided them: Which hikes offer a strong connection with the natural world? Where are the routes that offer outstanding samples of what is unique in our ecosystem? They sought out hikes that were quiet and a pleasure to the eye and offered treats such as waterfalls, wildlife, vistas, and old-growth woodlands.

Deciding not to just take trails at face value, the authors looked for new wrinkles. For example, many of the hikes in this book don't begin at the official trailhead. The hikes may also combine sections of different trails to create the best experience for the hiker. At times they recommend unmarked routes, often in state wildlife areas, and for some hikes the authors have developed off-trail segments.

Field research was done through more than 800 miles of hiking. The authors walked every mile of trail described in this guidebook. The purpose of this guidebook is to organize that pool of knowledge in a way that allows readers to locate outings suitable to their abilities and tastes.

Readers can make an initial screening of the hike chapters by checking the hike finder chart that follows this section. A hike locator map offers a quick scan of which hikes are in a given area.

Hike chapters begin with a summary of the facts readers need to evaluate that hike. "The Hike" offers a brief answer to the question, "Why go?" The nearest town is listed for each hike. The "distance" entry gives the total length of each hike and places it in one of four categories:

1. Loop hike. A loop hike begins and ends at the same point without walking the same stretch of trail more than once. At times, finishing the loop may require a small amount of road walking to return to the starting point.

2. Lollipop hike. A lollipop hike is a loop with a stem. If the loop segment of the lollipop is very small in proportion to the stem, it falls into the category of out-and-back hikes.

3. Shuttle hike. A shuttle hike involves walking from one point to another, using a second vehicle or a bicycle for the return trip.

4. Out-and-back hike. An out-and-back hike involves hiking to a location, then retracing your steps to the point of origin.

Mileage for each hike appears after the heading "Distance." Each hike has an overall difficulty rating:

1. Easy. These are well-marked trails and have reasonably good footing. There are no obstacles worth mentioning, and the length is less than 6 miles.

2. Moderate. These hikes are on marked or obvious trails, old woods roads, or lanes. They are less than 10 miles long, and footing may be rougher in places than on easy hikes.

3. Difficult. This rating reflects either a hike length of more than 10 miles or conditions or navigation that requires considerable skills and/or perseverance. Difficult hikes may be on unmarked trails or old woods roads or involve considerable off-trail travel. The footing may be rough, and there may be steep climbs.

"Best season" lists the time period during which the hike is normally free of snow and reasonable to walk. Early- or late-season snowstorms can change those dates.

Any map listed that is from a land agency or trail organization shows the featured hike or a large portion of it. These maps are often basic but perfectly adequate for easy hikes and some moderate ones. United States Geological Survey (USGS) topographical maps are useful for some moderate and difficult hikes. Unfortunately, it is not unusual for these maps to predate the existence of the hiking trail in question. Topographical maps that show the area but not all of the trail mentioned have "(inc.)," for incomplete, after them. Having both the land agency map and the topographical map is a good idea. Wisconsin's landscape has many attributes, but significant elevation change is not one of them. Therefore, elevation profiles are not included in this book.

A "Fees and permits" section lists items such as state park vehicle stickers or backpacking permits that may be needed for the hike.

Each hike summary also includes a brief description of how to find the trailhead from a nearby town. Finally, there are headings listing any nearby camping and whom to contact for more information.

If there are other aspects of a hike that are important for you to know before your outing, they are listed after the "Special considerations" heading.

TRAIL FINDER

	BEST HIKES WITH KIDS	BEST HIKES WITH DOGS	BEST HIKES FOR WATER LOVERS	BEST HIKES FOR BIRDERS	BEST HIKES FOR GREAT VIEWS	BEST HIKES FOR GEOLOGY BUFFS	BEST HIKES FOR NATURE LOVERS
LAKE SUPERIOR LOWLAND							
1. Amnicon Falls	•		•		•	•	•
2. Superior Shoreline		•	•	•	•		•
3. Lost Creek Falls		•	•	•	•	•	
4. Sea Caves	•				•	•	
5. Oak Island							•
6. Trout Point					•		•
7. Tombolo							•
NORTHERN HIGHLANDS							
8. Manitou Falls	•		•		•	•	•
9. Brule–St. Croix Portage		•	•				
10. Anderson Lake			•	•			
11. Marengo River/Porcupine Lake							•
12. Morgan Falls/St. Peter's Dome	•	•	•		•	•	
13. Copper Falls	•		•	•	•	•	
14. Potato River Falls	•		•		•		
15. Penokee Range					•	•	•
16. Sandrock Cliffs		•	•	•		•	
17. St. Croix			•	•			•
18. Blue Hills/Devils Creek		•	•				•
19. Escanaba Lake			•				

	BEST HIKES WITH KIDS	BEST HIKES WITH DOGS	BEST HIKES FOR WATER LOVERS	BEST HIKES FOR BIRDERS	BEST HIKES FOR GREAT VIEWS	BEST HIKES FOR GEOLOGY BUFFS	BEST HIKES FOR NATURE LOVERS
20. Star Lake	•		•				
21. Hidden Lakes			•	•			•
22. LaSalle Falls			•		•		•
23. Glacial Potholes	•		•		•	•	
24. Chippewa Moraine Circle Trail						•	•
25. Chippewa Moraine/ Plummer Lake		•	•			•	•
26. Jerry Lake		•					•
27. Chippewa Lobe		•					•
28. Timm's Hill					•		
29. Wood Lake		•	•				
30. Ed's Lake			•				
31. Dells of the Eau Claire		•	•	•	•	•	•
32. Mead State Wildlife Area	•		•	•			
WESTERN UPLAND							
33. Chippewa River			•	•			•
34. Trempealeau River	•		•	•	•		•
35. Perrot Ridge			•	•	•		
36. McGilvray Bottoms			•	•			
37. Wyalusing State Park				•	•		•
38. Governor Dodge State Park			•	•			•
39. Ferry Bluff	•		•		•		
40. Black Hawk Ridge				•			
CENTRAL SANDY PLAIN							
41. Wildcat Mound					•		•
42. North Bluff				•	•		
43. Lone Rock		•			•	•	

	BEST HIKES WITH KIDS	BEST HIKES WITH DOGS	BEST HIKES FOR WATER LOVERS	BEST HIKES FOR BIRDERS	BEST HIKES FOR GREAT VIEWS	BEST HIKES FOR GEOLOGY BUFFS	BEST HIKES FOR NATURE LOVERS
EASTERN MORAINES AND LAKE MICHIGAN PLAIN							
44. Eagle Bluff	•		•			•	
45. Door Bluff Headlands Park	•		•		•		
46. Rock Island			•	•		•	
47. Newport State Park			•	•			•
48. The Ridges	•			•		•	•
49. Moonlight Bay			•	•			•
50. Point Beach			•	•			
51. Emmons Creek							•
52. Horicon Marsh	•		•	•	•		
53. North Kettle Moraine		•					
54. Ice Age Trail: Cedar Lakes Loop		•					•
SOUTHERN BLUFFS AND MORAINES							
55. Devil's Lake East Bluff			•		•	•	
56. Devil's Lake to Parfrey's Glen					•	•	
57. Parfrey's Glen	•		•			•	•
58. Natural Bridge	•					•	
59. Lake La Grange		•	•	•			•
60. Beulah Bog			•				•

MAP LEGEND

⬭⬭⬭③⑨⬭⬭⬭	Interstate Highway	⊃⊂	Bridge
⟶⑫⟶	US Highway	■	Building/Point of Interest
⟶⑤⑨⟶	State Highway	◮	Campground
⟶35⟶	County Road	▲	Campsite
⟶⟶⟶	Local Road	⊛	Capitol
= = = = = = :	Unpaved Road	⌒	Cave
⊢ + ⊢ + ⊢	Railroad	†	Cemetery
- - - - - - - -	Featured Trail	▬	Dam
- - - - - - -	Trail	◖◗	Dome
· · · · · · · · ·	Off-Trail Hike	⌶	Gate
‖‖‖‖‖‖‖	Boardwalk/Steps	◣	Hill
- - - - - - -	Ferry Route	⟰	Lighthouse
- · - · - · - ·	State Line	⛰	Mountain
∼∼∼∼	Small River/Creek	🅿	Parking
⬭⬭	Body of Water	▲	Peak/Summit
⸰ ⸰	Marsh/Swamp	⛝	Picnic Area
⬭	Glacier	⬛	Ranger Station
/////////	Sea Caves	⬛	Restrooms
▭	National/State Forest/Park	⬛	Scenic View/Viewpoint
▭	Wilderness Area	⬛	Tower
▭	State/Regional Park	○	Town
▭	Miscellaneous Park	①	Trailhead
▭	Bench	❓	Visitor/Information Center
⌒	Bluffs	≋	Waterfall
⬯	Boat Ramp		

LAKE SUPERIOR LOWLAND

A flat plain, rich in red clay deposits, runs along Wisconsin's Lake Superior shoreline. This level to mildly rolling landscape, once the lake bed of Glacial Lake Duluth, slopes gently upward to the south and ends 5 to 20 miles inland where higher ground rises.

It is a band of boreal forest habitat, with Canada-like flora and fauna. Clay banks border many of the beaches, reaching almost 200 feet in height on Oak Island's north end. That clay bluff is the highest point on Wisconsin's Superior shore, but sandstone sea caves, chiseled by time and waves, are the area's most well-known landscape art.

Lake Superior, an inland sea that possesses a full eighth of the planet's fresh water, as well as some of its purest, is the focus of most hiking trails here. Hikers can expect cold springs, cool summers, and relatively warm autumns in this region, due to the lake-effect climate.

The rocky cliffs and "sea caves" along the Apostle Islands National Lakeshore (hike 4)

1 AMNICON FALLS

Rushing water tumbles over a display of geology that shows evidence of ancient earthquakes, volcanic activity, an ocean and its deposits of sand, and the most recent history of the Ice Age. A short walk takes you past a fine collection of waterfalls and cascades on the Amnicon River, and park literature tells the story in the rock.

Start: From the trailhead at the parking lot
Distance: 0.5-mile lollipop
Hiking time: 30 minutes
Difficulty: Easy
Trail surface: Dirt
Best season: Spring through fall
Other trail users: None
Land status: State park
Nearest town: Superior
Canine compatibility: Pets must be on a leash no longer than 8 feet at all times.
Fees and permits: State park vehicle sticker required

Schedule: Daily, 6 a.m. to 11 p.m.
Maps: Amnicon Falls State Park map or USGS South Range quad (inc.)
Trail contact: Amnicon Falls State Park, 4279 CR U, South Range, 54874; (715) 398-3000; https://dnr .wi.gov
Special considerations: Wet rocks and whitewater are in abundance here, a dangerous combination for the careless or toddlers running loose.
Camping: The park has thirty-six drive-in sites just southwest of the falls.

FINDING THE TRAILHEAD

From the intersection of US 2 and 53 in Superior, drive 13 miles southeast on US 2 to its intersection with CR U. Turn left (north) and drive 0.3 mile to the entrance road for Amnicon Falls State Park. Turn left (west) and proceed west and north 0.4 mile to the falls parking lot. GPS: N46 36.667' / W91 53.453'

THE HIKE

When I think of Amnicon Falls, I think of an art gallery, one with a theme of falling water. Visitors wander from display to display, sampling each for its nuance, then moving on to see what the next exhibit offers. With three waterfalls, and sometimes the aptly named Now and Then Falls as a fourth, there is a lot to contemplate here. This is a compact place, and if you want to choose your own route, you can easily do so without fear of getting lost.

I recommend following the itinerary of the self-guided tour brochure available at the park office for its educational value. This geology booklet explains the complex history of the park's rock. If you follow the tour's numbered posts, you start out going west from the parking lot, past the covered bridge to a view of the Lower Falls and its sandstone cliffs. Next, cross the bridge to the island and turn left (south), facing the thundering cascade of the Upper Falls.

The route continues around the island in a clockwise manner. At the island's southeast corner, turn west, past smaller cascades and a bridge leading to the river's west bank.

This westward turn takes the path downstream along the west branch of the river to Snake Pit Falls, a twisting, turning series of three drops. From there continue west, then north, until you are back at the covered bridge and the Lower Falls.

Upper Falls at Amnicon Falls State Park

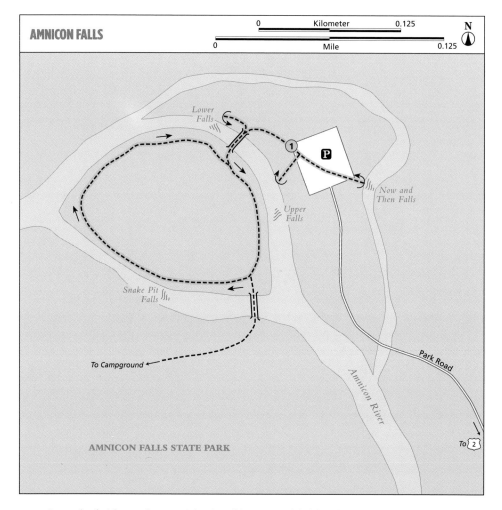

Cross the bridge and turn right (south) to a steel ladder that descends into the mist below the Upper Falls. The parking lot is nearby, but one more treat awaits you if the river flow is not low. Walk to the southeast corner of the parking lot and walk 20 feet south on a broad path to Now and Then Falls. This channel of the river, and the waterfall, goes dry if the river's flow slackens.

Local information: Bayfield Chamber and Visitor Bureau, 42 S. Broad St., Bayfield, 54814; (715) 779-3335; www.bayfield.org

MILES AND DIRECTIONS

0.0 Start from the trailhead.

0.1 Cross the bridge and take the trail to the left.

0.2 Bear right, passing the bridge to the west bank.

0.4 Pass the Lower Falls and take the trail left across the bridge.

0.5 Arrive at the trailhead.

THE GEOLOGY OF WISCONSIN

Wisconsin's history begins long before the arrival of the first humans. It's humbling to stand atop the bluff at Devil's Lake and realize that the rock under your feet is 1.6 *billion* years old, one of the oldest such outcrops in North America. Who cannot marvel at the fact that northern Wisconsin's Penokee Range, now a line of what most would consider merely hills, once stood as imposing as the Alps of today? While Wisconsin is in the center of its continent, at one point it lay at the bottom of the sea. Through the Cambrian, Ordovician, and Silurian Periods (about 540–419 million years ago), these seas laid down the sand and minerals that would become the sandstone and dolomite of today. Reefs flourished, as the fossil record shows.

But around 20,000 years ago this land was nearly completely buried by a layer of glacial ice so thick—up over a mile in some places—that today the earth's crust is still rebounding from its crushing weight. Six lobes of the Laurentide Ice Sheet ground their way across the land, reshaping it, and later sent meltwater rushing over it, exposing the layered sandstone of ancient seas that you see in the Wisconsin Dells area.

Up in Door County and down along Lake Winnebago and Horicon Marsh lies the edge of the Niagara Escarpment, extending from Ontario and New York (and the falls that shares its name). At Door Bluff, its steep carbonate cliffs rise above Lake Michigan waters. Along that same lake you'll find sand dunes, especially at Kohler–Andrae or Whitefish Dunes State Parks.

At Amnicon Falls State Park, you can practically see the entire timeline in rock: Dark basalt at the Upper Falls came from volcanic activity around 1 billion years ago. The Lower Falls runs over sandstone, formed from deposits beneath an ocean about half as old. Glacial drift in the park is from the Ice Age, and you can find potholes worn in the basalt by glacial meltwater rushing by. But perhaps most fascinating here is the Douglas Fault. Around 500 million years ago, this was earthquake zone. A fault line, from Ashland to the Twin Cities, set one layer of rock sliding up against the other so that today you can see the ridge running through the park. Sandstone lies to the north, while south of the fault the sandstone rose up and was worn away to reveal the basalt below.

2 SUPERIOR SHORELINE

The mightiest of the Great Lakes is your companion on this trek, which follows the narrow sandy shoreline preserved from development by the Brule River State Forest. Cross creek outlets and admire driftwood deposits before heading back the way you came.

Start: From the trailhead at Beck's Road
Distance: 6.0-mile out-and-back
Hiking time: 3 hours
Difficulty: Difficult
Trail surface: Sand
Best season: June–September
Other trail users: None
Land status: State forest
Nearest town: Maple
Canine compatibility: Dogs permitted
Fees and permits: None
Schedule: Daily, 6 a.m. to 11 p.m.
Maps: USGS Cloverland quad
Trail contact: Brule River State Forest, 6250 Ranger Rd., Brule, 54820; (715) 372-5678; https://dnr.wi.gov

Special considerations: Moderately difficult, requiring considerable wading in good conditions. Dangerous in poor conditions. An off-trail route along a narrow beach is underwater during periods of high waves or storm surges. A good weather forecast, including moderate wave height, and good judgment are prerequisites for this hike. See cautions in the description of the hike.
Camping: Brule River State Forest maintains the Bois Brule and Copper Range Campgrounds, with twenty-two and fifteen sites, respectively. Backpack camping is also possible with a permit.

FINDING THE TRAILHEAD

From Maple, drive north 4.0 miles on CR F and turn left (west) on WI 13. After 0.5 mile turn right (north) on Beck's Road (graded gravel). Drive 4.9 miles north and park on the side of the road at the top of the lakeside bluff. GPS: N46 42.89952' / W91 43.69932'

THE HIKE

This hike is along a splendid, untamed shoreline, chock-full of solitude and broad lake views. An otter accompanied me when I did this walk, swimming offshore, for half a mile. Ospreys patrolled the coast. A wolf-kill deer, blood not yet congealed, lay just off the beach. Paw prints spoke of a hurried departure. I had seen a blur, and probably had flushed them.

This is a very special place, worthy of thoughtful behavior on your part. In addition to the beauty of the landscape, there is another reason for being careful. Under poor conditions—high waves or storm surges—the beach will be under water. The hike could become a life-and-death epic.

The route is a narrow beach. In benign conditions the only obstacles are the creek mouths and deadfall trees whose limbs cross the beach and reach into the lake. Wading the numerous creek mouths is usually a knee-deep affair if you find the sandbar.

The sandbar is usually C-shaped, with the bulge going out into the lake. Watch for the break of the waves on the bar to locate it. Trekking poles are helpful.

Driftwood along the Lake Superior shoreline

The occasional deadfalls, found once a mile or so, are worse. You can either tunnel through them on the beach or wade around them. On a good day wading is a mere knee-deep affair. However, when the waves come up, knee-deep becomes a waist-high soaking or worse, and hypothermia, becoming seriously chilled, is a concern. The clay banks lining much of the beach tend to discourage any attempt to climb above obstacles.

Before you do this hike, you should check the forecast and be prepared to change your plans if the lake gets rowdy. Exiting from the beach may not be easy.

You should also wear boots that you can wade in. In good conditions you will spend 95 percent of your time strolling down the beach. However, because of the creeks and deadfalls, your feet and shins will be either wet or in the process of drip-drying all the time.

Still interested? If you have a good forecast, begin your outing by descending the lakeside bluff on the steep end of Beck's Road. At the bottom of the slope, you will find yourself alongside the lagoon of Pearson Creek, your first crossing. Mark this spot or memorize it. These creek mouths have a habit of looking similar later in the day, and it is possible to walk right by on your return. Don't ask how I came by that wisdom.

Find the sandbar at the mouth and wade to the east side. Walk the beach eastward, taking in the broad lake views. Fifteen miles to the north, the Minnesota shore, dark and high with forested ridges, looms on the horizon. Far to the west the tall buildings of Duluth are barely visible. At mile 0.5 another creek mouth appears, Haukkala Creek, similar in size to Pearson Creek.

Find the sandbar and wade to the east side. That initial pattern sets the tempo, almost like a rhythmic chant, for this outing. Wade, stroll the beach for a while, then wade again.

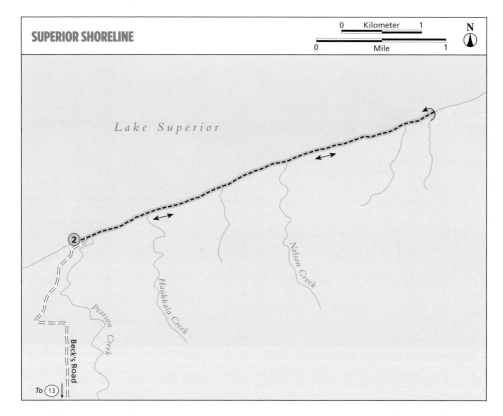

Follow the shoreline east, passing a few minor drainages, and at mile 1.7 you will find Nelson Creek. The exact configuration of the beach at these creek mouths changes with every storm, a study in the dynamics of current, water, waves, and sand.

Cross Nelson Creek and continue walking east. A mile after Nelson Creek, at mile 2.7, a minor, unnamed creek enters from the south. Depending on conditions, there may be no water flowing. A little farther east, at mile 3.0, another drainage enters from the southwest. This is a good turnaround point.

MILES AND DIRECTIONS

0.0. Cross the Pearson Creek mouth (end of Beck's Road and beginning of hike).

0.5 Cross the Haukkala Creek mouth.

1.7 Pass the Nelson Creek mouth.

2.7 Cross another creek mouth.

3.0 Turn around at the second unnamed creek mouth.

6.0 Arrive back at the trailhead.

3 LOST CREEK FALLS

A spot only a local might know about, this hidden waterfall tumbles over a sandstone edge in the heart of the forest. The path rises and falls gently but demands some instinct in the last 100 yards as it follows along the rough banks above Lost Creek Number One. Expect plenty of birds and other wildlife to be observing you.

Start: From the trailhead at a small parking area
Distance: 3.4-mile out-and-back
Hiking time: 1.5 hours
Difficulty: Moderate
Trail surface: Dirt, grass
Best season: Spring through fall
Other trail users: None
Land status: County forest
Nearest town: Cornucopia
Canine compatibility: Leashed dogs permitted
Fees and permits: None
Schedule: Daily

Maps: USGS Bark Bay (inc.) and Cornucopia (inc.) quads
Trail contact: Bayfield County Forestry Department, 117 E. 5th St., Washburn, 54891; (715) 373-6114; www.bayfieldcounty.org
Special considerations: The trails around the falls are narrow dirt paths that are often mildly precarious, thus the moderate rating.
Camping: There are thirty-five drive-in sites at Herbster Township Park, 7.0 miles west of trailhead.

FINDING THE TRAILHEAD

From Cornucopia, drive 1.8 miles west on WI 13. Turn left (south) on Klemik Road (dirt) and go 0.6 mile to small sandy parking area on the east side of the road, room enough for two cars. The trail begins here. GPS: N46 50.202' / W91 08.074'

THE HIKE

Follow these directions and you will find yourself at an unmarked trailhead in an area whose major geographical features bear the names Lost Creek Number One, Lost Creek Number Two, and Lost Creek Number Three. Persevere. After an inauspicious beginning the route finding is straightforward, the walking pleasant, and the woods gain ambiance. Your reward is a charming waterfall set in a sandstone glen where solitude is a reasonable expectation.

From the small parking area, walk east on a grassy trail, possibly waist-high with weeds in June. The route curves gently at about 0.25 mile and at the 0.5-mile mark reaches a junction with a wider snowmobile trail. Follow this to the left and cross a steel-framed bridge over Lost Creek Number Two. (It's worth noting that if you go left on the snowmobile trail, the path leads back to a point on Klemik Road 0.6 mile south of the trailhead.) The surrounding woods change to older aspen, hardwoods, and pines. Continue east on what is now a well-worn woods road. The road swings north before turning south and descending to the bridge (with wood railings) over Lost Creek Number One.

Follow the road southeast some 600 yards and watch for a trail on the west side of the woods road where the road ascends and starts to turn eastward toward a gate up the hill ahead. At this point you should be able to hear the sound of falling water. Before the gate look for some trees that may bear blue paint marks on them, and here you follow a dirt

Lost Creek Falls

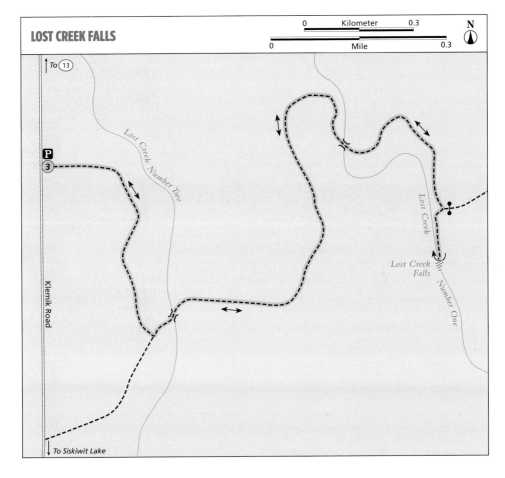

To (13)

Lost Creek Number Two

P
3

Klemik Road

Lost Creek

Lost Creek Falls

Number One

To Siskiwit Lake

0   Kilometer   0.3

0   Mile   0.3

N

path to the right. Just as all roads lead to Rome, at this point all paths seek the waterfall. The waterfall is about 100 yards southwest of this junction, but you will end up walking somewhat indirectly as the rocky path twists and turns through the woods.

Lost Creek Falls, a small, delicate gem, plunges 15 feet over a sandstone ledge in a mossy glen. When the water is low, visitors may find their way atop stones to get near the falls. After taking in the beauty—and perhaps cooling your feet in the stream—backtrack to the trailhead, remembering to take the trail to the right at the juncture after the last bridge.

MILES AND DIRECTIONS

0.5   Turn left at the trail juncture and cross bridge over Lost Creek Number Two.

1.2   Cross bridge over Lost Creek Number One.

1.6   Follow the blue-marked trees on a dirt path.

1.7   Arrive at Lost Creek Falls.

3.4   Arrive back at the trailhead.

4 SEA CAVES

A nearly 2.0-mile hike through the forest of the Apostle Islands National Lakeshore—partly on boardwalk and across a few intermittent streams—takes you to the spectacular mainland sea caves carved from the sandstone cliffs overlooking Lake Superior. Another half mile of trail skirts the edge, granting overlooks of caves, cliffs, and crevices.

Start: From the trailhead at the parking lot
Distance: 4.8-mile out-and-back
Hiking time: About 2 hours
Difficulty: Moderate
Trail surface: Boardwalk, dirt
Best season: Spring through fall (winter when the lake freezes)
Other trail users: None
Land status: National park
Nearest town: Cornucopia
Canine compatibility: Leashed dogs permitted
Fees and permits: Parking fee at Meyers Beach
Schedule: Daily
Maps: National Geographic/Trails Illustrated Apostle Islands National Lakeshore Map, USGS Squaw Bay (inc.) quad
Trail contact: Apostle Islands National Lakeshore, 415 Washington Ave., Bayfield, 54814; (715) 779-3398; www.nps.gov/apis
Special considerations: Use extreme caution near the edge of the cliffs. Undercut and honeycombed sandstone makes a sea cave what it is, and what you are standing on may not be solid rock. Hiking to the caves is possible on the ice when the lake freezes around January or February. Call the park for ice safety conditions. Be sure to wear appropriate protection from brutal cold, especially warm boots with traction, and follow safety warnings. A per-person visitor fee is in effect only during ice caves season.
Camping: Township parks at Little Sand Bay (10.0 miles east) and Herbster (10.0 miles west) offer thirty-eight and thirty-five drive-in sites, respectively.

FINDING THE TRAILHEAD

From Cornucopia, drive 4.2 miles east on WI 13. Turn left (north) on Meyers Road and drive north 0.3 mile to the trailhead. There are picnic tables and a toilet here. GPS: N46 52.990' / W91 02.847'

THE HIKE

Sandstone sea caves, carved by waves and ice, are the signature landmark of the Apostles Islands area. A mile of shoreline east of Meyers Road offers the only opportunity to view them on the mainland, and the walk in is a minor price to pay. It is an undulating 2.0 miles, crossing several ravines.

From the east side of the parking lot on Meyers Road, take the Lakeshore Trail. This narrow two-plank boardwalk starts in young woods sprinkled with orange hawkweed flowers in June and immediately descends into a small drainage. This is the first of several creek crossings along the route. The trail passes the end of Mawikwe Road, a rough dirt road, at mile 0.8.

For nearly 2.0 miles this trail stays in the woods, with only an occasional glimpse of Lake Superior. Doubts vanish with a bang as you arrive at a spectacular sea chasm

A view from the trail overlooking
the cave area of the lakeshore

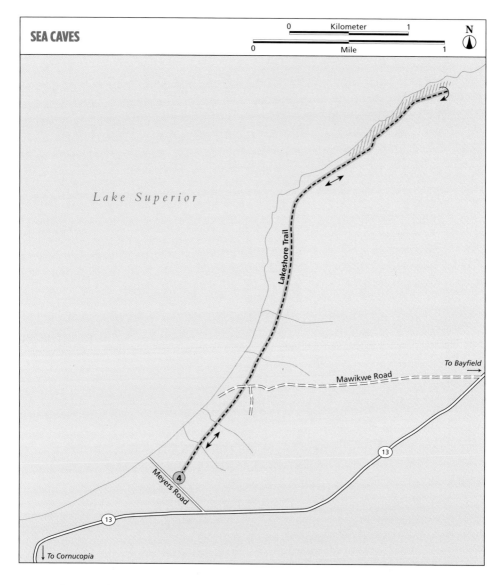

0   Kilometer   1

0   Mile   1

N

Lake Superior

Lakeshore Trail

To Bayfield

Mawikwe Road

13

Meyers Road

4

13

↓ *To Cornucopia*

at mile 1.8, a deep and intricate cleft knifing into the shoreline. A sign warns of the dangers and a lifesaver ring hangs from it. Two separate arches of chockstones, soil, and small birch trees bridge the small canyon, and below you may see kayakers venturing in as far as they can go. A wooden fence keeps visitors from venturing too close to the edge in some places.

This spectacular chasm begins a 0.5-mile-long parade of sea caves, cliffs, and a small dripping waterfall. Several promontories offer vantage points for long views of the shoreline. At mile 2.4 the trail moves inland, a logical place to turn around and retrace your steps to Meyers Road.

Local information: Bayfield Chamber and Visitor Bureau, 42 S. Broad St., Bayfield, 54814; (715) 779-3335; www.bayfield.org

THE CREATION OF THE SEA CAVES

The history of the rock of the Apostle Islands, and the lakeshore they once were part of, goes back over 600 million years ago to the late Precambrian era. At that time braided rivers flowing through the region deposited the sediments that over time became the thick rock we have today. Glaciers came and went more often than people generally think when they use the term Ice Age, but the most recent advance of ice took place about 12,000 years ago. The grinding and depositing of drift had its impact on the land, but the sea caves are another story.

The top and bottom layers of the red-tinted sandstone came from the rivers, while the middle portion, known as the Devils Formation—after Devils Island, where the best caves are—was made when those deposits became sand flats that often lay under shallow waters and were characterized by ripples. The resulting rock layers are thin, soft, and porous. Water gets inside and expands when it freezes. Plus, take a look northward from Meyers Beach and you have anywhere from 60 to 80 miles of open water between the national lakeshore and the North Shore. When winds come down from Canada across that stretch of water, big waves are the result.

Rising and falling lake levels, expanding ice in cracks and fractures, and that constant erosion of wind and water resulted in the various caves, tunnels, and overhangs you see today on the north side of Devils Island, at Swallow Point on Sand Island, and along the mainland. The waves undercut the cliffs, carving what are called reentrants, and over time some of these reentrants become deep enough and widen enough to connect to others, thus creating a tunnel or cave behind parts of the cliff face that haven't worn away as yet.

Bayfield County Tourism, 117 E. Fifth St., Washburn, 54891; (715) 373-6125; www.bayfieldcounty.org

MILES AND DIRECTIONS

0.0 Start from the trailhead at the parking lot.

0.8 Cross the two-track Mawikwe Road.

1.8 Arrive at the sea caves.

2.4 Turn around where the trail bears right and heads inland.

4.8 Arrive back at the trailhead.

5 OAK ISLAND

Come for the day or camp for the night on the highest and driest of the Apostle Islands. Much of the 11.0 miles of trails passes through shady forest, and the middle of the island is the highest point on Wisconsin's Lake Superior shore. Pristine beaches and wildlife viewing await.

Start: From the trailhead near the dock
Distance: 7.8-mile out-and-back base camp backpack or day hike
Hiking time: About 3 hours
Difficulty: Moderate
Trail surface: Dirt
Best season: June–September
Other trail users: None
Land status: National park
Nearest town: Bayfield
Canine compatibility: Leashed dogs permitted
Fees and permits: Camping permit required, available from the park office in Bayfield, and overnight dock fee for boats
Schedule: Daily
Maps: National Geographic/Trails Illustrated Apostle Islands National Lakeshore Map, USGS Oak Island (inc.) and York Island (inc.) quads

Trail contact: Apostle Islands National Lakeshore, 415 Washington Ave., Bayfield, 54814; (715) 779-3398; www.nps.gov/apis
Special considerations: From late June to early September, Apostle Islands Cruise Service has twice-daily service to Oak Island (715-779-3925; www.apostleisland.com). Water taxi service is available at other times. Oak Island, known as the "least buggy" island, is the highest and driest of all the Apostle Islands.
Camping: Five individual campsites and two group campsites are on the island. Campsites are sometimes temporarily closed because of bear activity. Camping permits are obtained at the park office in Bayfield.

FINDING THE TRAILHEAD

If not arriving by private boat, catch the cruise boat (see "Special considerations") at the Bayfield harbor and get off at the dock on the west side of Oak Island. A vault toilet, water pump, two campsites, and a ranger residence are there. GPS: N46 55.743' / W90 45.128'

THE HIKE

When you stand on the clay banks at Oak Island's northern tip, you can't help but wonder who else has stood here or passed by. This spot, known as the Overlook, is a commanding height with a view that takes in ten islands. It is easy to imagine that voyageurs or Native Americans posted lookouts on this strategic location, watching for the canoes of friend or foe. A canoe traveling Lake Superior's south shore would have to pass nearby or risk the open waters of the lake.

Walk north 100 yards from the dock on Oak Island's west side and a trail sign will direct you onto the Loop Trail, a shady path in a pleasant, mature hardwood forest. The trail ascends slowly and gains 400 feet in the next 1.7 miles. After 1.2 miles you pass the junction of the Northwest Beach Trail, and at mile 1.7 you top out near the highest point in the Apostles Islands and turn left (north) on the Overlook Trail.

A hiker on the Oak Island trail
APOSTLE ISLANDS NATIONAL LAKESHORE

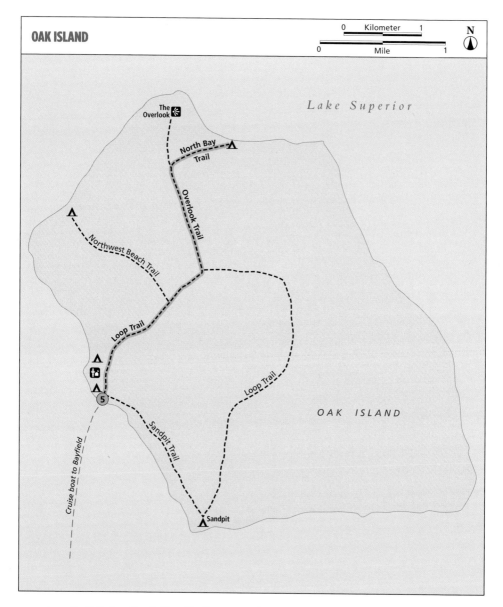

At mile 2.8 the North Bay Trail turns right (east) and drops to the beach. You may want to continue 0.7 mile to the Overlook, but that destination also makes a fine after-dinner hike after you have set up camp. From the viewpoint you can see Hole-in-the-Wall, a sea arch on the island's northeast shore. The North Bay Trail dead-ends at mile 3.9, the designated campsite set in trees just off the beach.

Doubts about the wisdom of passing up campsites closer to the dock tend to vanish within moments of arrival as you look around. There's a broad lake view and a 0.5-mile-long beach perfect for morning or moonlight strolls, and the view through your tent door isn't exactly hard on the eyes, either. Eagles cruise the shoreline and mergansers dot the waves.

You may opt to spend your second day here, looking for a perfect driftwood seat to practice the fine art of Lake Superior gazing. If you would rather roam, opt for a complete tour of the island's trails in a counterclockwise direction.

Walking in that direction leaves you with a choice 2.6 miles from North Beach when the Northwest Beach Trail heads north. It will cost you 3.2 miles round-trip and 300 feet of vertical to take a look at, but the pristine beach and enjoyable trail are worth it. If you took the side trip, at mile 7.0 you will be back at the dock and have a chance to load up on water from the pump. Go south on the Sandspit Trail, crossing numerous small drainages and often staying within sight of the lake. The Sandspit itself at mile 8.5, on the island's southwest corner, offers broad lake views and an artesian well for water.

From the Sandspit, head north on the Loop Trail, steadily ascending 400 feet in the first mile before descending 100 feet as you swing east of the island's summit ridge. In this area, at about mile 10.0, watch for the remains of an old logging camp. An intricately embossed wood stove and other metal artifacts are near the trail. The familiar Overlook Trail junction is at mile 11.0. Turn north, and another 2.2 downhill miles brings you in to camp. To return to the dock on day three, retrace your steps from the first day.

Recommended itinerary: I recommend a base camp backpack trip with two nights at North Bay. Day one would be a 3.9-mile backpack into North Bay, with a 3.8-mile (round-trip) after-dinner walk to the Overlook. The second day would feature a 14.3-mile day hike around the Loop Trail with a side trip to the Northwest Beach. Day three is the 3.9-mile return backpack to the dock.

Options: Day hiking on Oak Island is possible. Backpackers have other choices besides the recommended itinerary. Four locations other than North Beach, one just 50 yards from the dock, have campsites, and all offer easy access to the Loop Trail system described above.

Local information: Bayfield Chamber and Visitor Bureau, 42 S. Broad St., Bayfield, 54814; (715) 779-3335; www.bayfield.org

Bayfield County Tourism, 117 E. Fifth St., Washburn, 54891; (715) 373-6125; www .bayfieldcounty.org

MILES AND DIRECTIONS

0.0 Depart from Oak Island dock.

1.2 Stay right as you pass Northwest Beach Trail junction.

1.7 Take a left at Overlook Trail junction.

2.8 Turn right at the North Bay Trail junction.

3.9 Arrive at North Bay campsite.

5.1 Turn left at the Overlook Trail junction.

6.2 Take a right on the Loop Trail.

7.8 Arrive back at Oak Island dock.

6 TROUT POINT

Leave the more popular and frequented Presque Isle area and cross Stockton Island to its secluded north side at Trout Point. Either as a long day hike or an overnight trip with a stay at the campsite there, this trek offers a wide, private lake view at a sandy beach far from the madding crowd.

Start: From the trailhead of the Quarry Bay Trail
Distance: 12.6-mile out-and-back
Hiking time: About 5 hours
Difficulty: Moderate
Trail surface: Dirt
Best season: June–September
Other trail users: None
Land status: National park
Nearest town: Bayfield
Canine compatibility: Leashed dogs permitted
Fees and permits: Camping permit required, available from Apostle Islands National Lakeshore, and a nightly fee for boat docking
Schedule: Daily
Maps: National Geographic/Trails Illustrated Apostle Islands National

Lakeshore map, USGS Stockton Island (inc.) quad
Trail contact: Apostle Islands National Lakeshore, 415 Washington Ave., Bayfield, 54814; (715) 779-3398; www.nps.gov/apis
Special considerations: From late June to early September, Apostle Islands Cruise Service has daily service to Stockton Island (715-779-3925; www.apostleisland.com). Water taxi service is available at other times.
Camping: Trout Point is an individual campsite. Three group sites and an individual site are at Quarry Bay, and nineteen sites are at Presque Isle. Camping permits are obtained at the park office in Bayfield.

FINDING THE TRAILHEAD

If not arriving by private boat, catch the cruise boat (see "Special considerations") at the Bayfield harbor and get off at the Presque Isle Docks on Stockton Island. Vault toilets, a water pump, nineteen campsites, and a ranger station are there. GPS: N46 54.772' / W90 32.955'

THE HIKE

Trout Point, on Stockton Island's quiet north shore, may be the most remote walk-in campsite in the Apostle Islands. When you sit here, it is easy to feel as if you have inherited an entire private ecosystem. Somehow the view seems both intimate and boundless as your eyes wander from the nearby beach to the watery horizon and far-off shores. Morning and evening shows are spectacular as the changing light turns the water a zillion shades of blue. Groups of loons swim by the campsite, while others join mergansers in the offshore waters. Ospreys and bald eagles scan from treetop perches or cruise the shoreline on dawn patrol.

Comparing Trout Point with Presque Isle, on the opposite side of the island, is a study in contrasts. Presque Isle is the most visited place in the Apostles, and a steady hum of boat traffic is not unusual.

From the Presque Isle Docks, walk north on the broad, well-worn Quarry Bay Trail, passing a long string of shoreline campsites. Stay straight (northwest) at mile 0.6 as the Tombolo Trail goes right. At 1.6 miles turn right (north) on the Trout Point Trail; here

A black bear triggers a camera just off of Trout Point Trail. The national park monitors bear activity closely. APOSTLE ISLANDS NATIONAL LAKESHORE

your transition from front country to backcountry begins in earnest. The Trout Point Trail is a shady, narrow footpath, sparsely used, and a low maintenance priority. It will get you where you want to go, but the next 3.5 miles are notable mostly for the robust insect population.

At mile 5.3 the woods gain ambiance as a northward-flowing brook marks the last mile of the walk. You follow the drainage to the lake, finally emerging at the campsite near a 1917 lumber camp. To return to Presque Isle Docks, retrace the steps of your first day.

Recommended itinerary: This is a perfect destination for a two-night base camp trip. The first day would be a 6.3-mile backpack to Trout Point. Day two would be dedicated to beachcombing, wildlife watching, and relaxation, with a return to Presque Isle Docks on day three.

Options: Staying a third night at Presque Isle would ease the pressure to move quickly on the day you are walking in (or out) to Trout Point. It would also give you a chance to walk the Tombolo Trail. This fascinating trail combines with the Julian Bay Trail to make a 4.0-mile loop that traverses a wetland on a sturdy boardwalk before traveling Julian Bay's long beach.

Local information: Bayfield Chamber and Visitor Bureau, 42 S. Broad St., Bayfield, 54814; (715) 779-3335; www.bayfield.org

Bayfield County Tourism, 117 E. Fifth St., Washburn, 54891; (715) 373-6125; www .bayfieldcounty.org

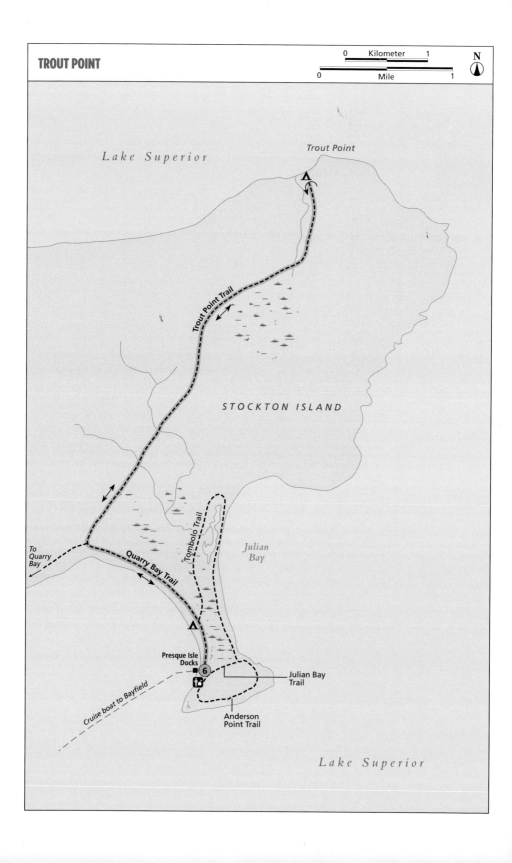

Lake Superior

Trout Point

Trout Point Trail

STOCKTON ISLAND

Tombolo Trail

Julian
Bay

To
Quarry
Bay

Quarry Bay Trail

Presque Isle
Docks

6

Julian Bay
Trail

Anderson
Point Trail

Cruise boat to Bayfield

Lake Superior

N

0   Kilometer   1

0   Mile   1

Trout Point Trail APOSTLE ISLANDS NATIONAL LAKESHORE

MILES AND DIRECTIONS

0.0   Depart from the trailhead of Quarry Bay Trail.

0.6   Stay left at the Tombolo Trail junction.

1.6   Take a right on Trout Point Trail.

6.3   Arrive at Trout Point.

11.0 Stay left at the Trout Point/Quarry Bay Trail junction.

12.6 Arrive back at Presque Isle Docks.

7 TOMBOLO

Take a turn across two islands—Presque and Stockton—which became one over the centuries due to the wear and tear of Lake Superior's waves. A boardwalk crosses a notable dune-and-bog ecosystem and leads to a splendid beach walk that may include a bit of wading.

Start: From the trailhead near the dock
Distance: 3.8-mile loop
Hiking time: About 2 hours
Difficulty: Moderate
Trail surface: Boardwalk, sand, dirt
Best season: June–September
Other trail users: None
Land status: National park
Nearest town: Bayfield
Canine compatibility: Leashed dogs permitted
Fees and permits: Camping permit required, available from the park office in Bayfield, and a nightly fee for boat docking
Schedule: Daily
Maps: Trails Illustrated Apostle Islands, USGS Stockton Island (inc.) quad

Trail contact: Apostle Islands National Lakeshore, 415 Washington Ave., Bayfield, 54814; (715) 779-3398; www.nps.gov/apis
Special considerations: From late June to early September, Apostle Islands Cruise Service has daily service to Stockton Island (715-779-3925; www.apostleisland.com). Water taxi service is available at other times. A lagoon at Julian Bay sometimes requires a brief, shallow wade.
Camping: Nineteen walk-in campsites are at Presque Isle Bay. Obtain a permit from park office in Bayfield.

FINDING THE TRAILHEAD

 If not arriving by private boat, catch the cruise boat (see "Special considerations") at the Bayfield harbor and get off at the Presque Isle Docks on Stockton Island. Vault toilets, a water pump, nineteen campsites, and a ranger station are there. GPS: N46 54.772' / W90 32.955'

THE HIKE

Ask most visitors to the Apostle Islands how the lake shapes the shoreline and they would point to the sea caves. Those sandstone caverns are a clear example of waves, ice, and time nibbling away at rock with grains of sand washing away. Waterborne sand, perhaps even the same grains, is also an element in the landscape of this hike. Here, however, the process adds to the shoreline, forming sandbars that mature into vegetated dunes as the lake recedes.

A tombolo, a spectacular example of these creative powers, is a land bridge (connection) that forms between two previously isolated bodies of land. In this case rocky Presque Isle, once a mile offshore, became a part of Stockton Island. The story of that transformation unfolds as you walk this short loop hike.

From the Presque Isle Docks, walk north past tall pines and waterfront campsites on the broad Quarry Bay Trail, 0.6 mile to the beginning of the Tombolo Trail. Turn right (north) on the smooth, well-defined, but narrow footpath.

Fall colors on Tombolo Trail
APOSTLE ISLANDS NATIONAL LAKESHORE

At Tombolo Trail's juncture with Julian Bay Trail
APOSTLE ISLANDS NATIONAL LAKESHORE

JULIAN BAY TRAIL
Presque Isle Dock .4 mi.

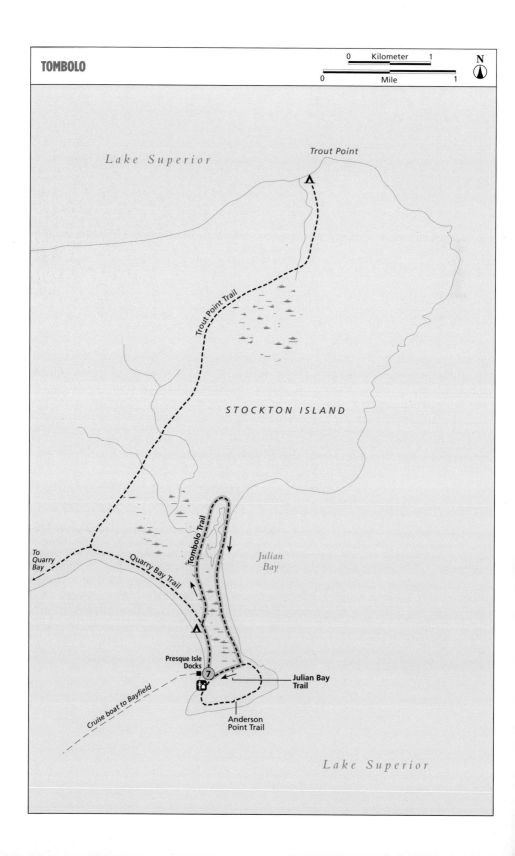

TOMBOLO

0   Kilometer   1
0   Mile   1

N

Lake Superior

Trout Point

Trout Point Trail

STOCKTON ISLAND

Tombolo Trail

Julian Bay

To Quarry Bay

Quarry Bay Trail

Presque Isle Docks

7

Julian Bay Trail

Cruise boat to Bayfield

Anderson Point Trail

Lake Superior

A trail sign along Tombolo Trail APOSTLE ISLANDS NATIONAL LAKESHORE

After passing through open, piney woods for 0.5 mile, a lagoon/bog complex appears to your east, dry land ends, and the trail becomes a sturdy boardwalk. A pattern of alternating sand ridges and linear bogs emerges from the wetland. In aerial photos these ridges appear as a series of broad arcs, each the mark of a shoreline of the past. The boardwalk crosses a small stream and a portion of the bog before reentering the woods.

The trail rounds the north end of the lagoon area and at mile 2.1 emerges on the youngest of the sand ridges, Julian Bay's beautiful beach. Follow the waterline south; at mile 2.7 the mouth of the lagoon sometimes requires a brief wade. I found a pleasant, knee-deep channel 50 feet wide.

Continue south on the beach. When the grassy dunes and sand end and shady woods begin at mile 3.4, the route leaves the topography of the tombolo for that of Presque Isle. Turn right (east) on the wide Julian Bay Trail where it meets Anderson Point Trail and take that 0.4 mile to the Presque Isle Docks, where the hike began.

Local information: Bayfield Chamber and Visitor Bureau, 42 S. Broad St., Bayfield, 54814; (715) 779-3335; www.bayfield.org

Bayfield County Tourism, 117 E. Fifth St., Washburn, 54891; (715) 373-6125; www .bayfieldcounty.org

MILES AND DIRECTIONS

0.0 Start from the trailhead at Presque Isle Docks.

0.6 At Tombolo Trail junction with Quarry Bay Trail, go right.

2.1 Tombolo Trail turns south on Julian Bay's beach.

2.7 Cross the creek at the lagoon (intermittent, may be either open water or sand).

3.4 At the Julian Bay Trail/Anderson Point juncture, turn right.

3.8 Arrive back at Presque Isle Docks and the trailhead.

NORTHERN HIGHLANDS

Wisconsin's largest region, the Northern Highlands, covers the third of the state south of the Lake Superior lowlands. Heavily forested and sprinkled with thousands of lakes, it is a broad upland sitting on a granite base, sloping slightly to the south. That bedrock base shows up often in the region's waterfalls, including the fourth highest east of the Rocky Mountains. The glaciers passed this way, and many Ice Age landforms, from moraines to potholes, are visible today.

Large breeding populations of bald eagles, ospreys, and loons nest on the lakeshores, while black bear and fisher roam the woodlands. Some two hundred timber wolves call the Northern Highland forest home.

Hiking trails here cross vast forests, border clear streams and lakes, and skirt wildlife-rich marshes. Hikers can find relief from summer heat under the shady forest canopy.

The view of Spruce Lake from the Escanaba Lake Trail (hike 19)

8 MANITOU FALLS

Most will come to this state park to enjoy the view of the 165-foot-high Big Manitou Falls, the tallest waterfall east of the Mississippi. But stay on the trail and it takes you along a scenic river and a lakeshore to get to Little Manitou Falls as well.

Start: At the trailhead in the parking lot near the park office
Distance: 4.4-mile lollipop with two stems
Hiking time: About 1.5–2 hours
Difficulty: Easy
Trail surface: Packed dirt, some asphalt
Best season: Spring through fall
Other trail users: None
Land status: State park
Nearest town: Superior
Canine compatibility: Dogs are allowed only on the Logging Camp Trail and the Big Falls Hiking Trail and in designated picnic areas, and must be on a leash no longer than 8 feet at all times.
Fees and permits: State park vehicle sticker required
Schedule: Daily, 6 a.m. to 11 p.m.
Maps: Park handout or USGS Sunnyside (inc.) and Borea (inc.) quads
Trail contact: Pattison State Park, 6294 S. SR 35, Superior, 54880; (715) 399-3111; https://dnr.wi.gov
Camping: Pattison State Park has fifty-nine drive-in campsites 0.25 mile south of the trailhead, as well as three walk-in backpacking sites.

FINDING THE TRAILHEAD

From the intersection of US 2 and WI 35 in Superior, drive south 12.9 miles on WI 35 and turn left (east) into Pattison State Park. Drive 500 feet east, past the park office, and park in the west end of the large parking lot there. GPS: N46 32.229' / W92 7.097'

THE HIKE

Big Manitou Falls is more than just big; it is a giant. A vertical drop of 165 feet makes it Wisconsin's highest and the fourth-tallest waterfall east of the Rocky Mountains. Better yet, another waterfall, the state's eighth highest at 31 feet, is 1.5 miles upstream on the Black River. Combining visits to both these falls with a hike along the park's riverside paths makes a memorable outing.

First decide if you want to pick up a copy of the self-guided tour brochure from the park office. Then walk west to the entrance of the pedestrian tunnel under WI 35. As you emerge from the tunnel's west end, a fork in the trail offers a choice. Take the path on the right (west); 100 feet farther on a chasm of air, mist, and falling water appears beyond the railing of the first viewpoint. This is Big Manitou Falls. Several more observation points, one a platform, offer spectacular views of the waterfall before you reach the west end of this spur and turn around to retrace your steps back to the tunnel.

Just before the tunnel, turn right (southwest) and cross the pedestrian bridge to the southwest shore of the river. Turn right (north) again on a paved path where a series of constructed lookouts stretch along the gorge's crest. The second one in, marked with a #5 to correspond with the self-guided tour, offers a good vantage point for viewing the complete top-to-bottom sweep of the waterfall.

Big Manitou Falls

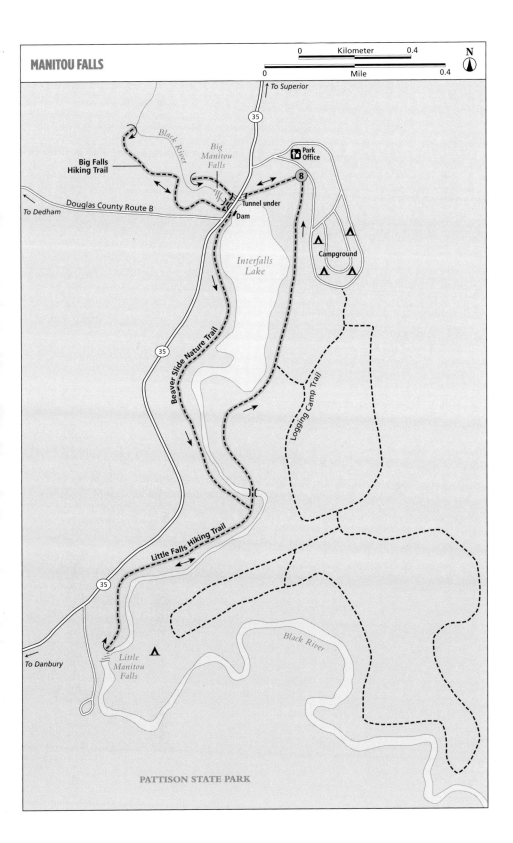

MANITOU FALLS

Kilometer
0   0.4

Mile
0   0.4

N

↑ To Superior

35

Black River

Big Manitou Falls

Park Office

Big Falls Hiking Trail

8

Tunnel under Dam

Douglas County Route B

To Dedham

Campground

Interfalls Lake

35

Beaver Slide Nature Trail

Logging Camp Trail

Little Falls Hiking Trail

35

To Danbury

Little Manitou Falls

Black River

PATTISON STATE PARK

Continue west, leaving the constructed viewpoints behind on what is now a broad, gravel path (park maps refer to this as the "Big Falls Hiking Trail") that slowly descends past pines and aspens to the river. Here it is a gently gurgling stream, and a trailside bench makes a fine place for a break.

The maintained trail ends at the river. Turn around and walk back to the pedestrian tunnel under the highway and cross to the southeast side. As you emerge from the tunnel, turn right (south) and cross a walkway over the dam that creates Interfalls Lake. This leads to a dirt and gravel path, shown as the "Beaver Slide Nature Trail" on park maps, that follows the lakeshore south.

Follow that path, first along the lake, then along the Black River, to a junction and bridge over the river at mile 2.4. Turn right (southeast), not crossing the bridge, and continue upstream along a charming streamside path, to Little Manitou Falls at mile 3.0. Pause to enjoy the twin torrents of Little Manitou Falls, then return downstream to the bridge junction at mile 3.6. Turn right (north), cross the bridge, and walk north on the east shore segment of the Beaver Slide Nature Trail.

The marshy upper end of the lake appears to your west; at mile 4.0 bear straight (north) as the Logging Camp Trail enters from the right. Follow the path north along the shore of the lake to the park's bathing beach. Continue walking north 200 yards through the picnic area and you will arrive back at the parking lot.

Local information: Superior–Douglas County Area Chamber & Visitors Bureau, 205 Belknap St., Superior, 54880; (800) 942-5313; www.superiorchamber.org

MILES AND DIRECTIONS

0.0 Start from the trailhead at the parking lot.

0.2 Pass under WI 35.

0.3 Stop at the west end of viewing areas north of Big Manitou Falls.

0.4 Cross the bridge over Black River.

0.9 Arrive at the north end of Big Falls Hiking Trail.

1.4 Cross the bridge over Black River and pass under WI 35.

1.5 Turn right on the Beaver Slide Nature Trail.

2.4 Go right at the junction with Little Falls Hiking Trail.

3.0 Arrive at Little Manitou Falls.

3.6 Stay right at the Beaver Slide Nature Trail and cross the bridge.

4.0 Stay left at the junction with Logging Camp Trail.

4.4 Arrive back at the trailhead.

9 BRULE–ST. CROIX PORTAGE

For centuries humans have sought this passage between two rivers flowing opposite directions, north to Superior and south to the Mississippi. Consider the Native Americans, and the European explorers who followed, as you hike through woods and wetlands to find this historical portage point.

Start: From the trailhead at the road
Distance: 4.0-mile out-and-back
Hiking time: About 2 hours
Difficulty: Easy
Trail surface: Dirt, grass
Best season: Spring through fall
Other trail users: None
Land status: State land
Nearest town: Solon Springs
Canine compatibility: Leashed dogs permitted
Fees and permits: State park car sticker required for DNR boat landing parking lot

Schedule: Daily, 6 a.m. to 11 a.m.
Maps: Brule River State Forest trail map, North Country Trail Segment Map, USGS Bennett (inc.) quad
Trail contact: North Country Trail Association, Brule–St. Croix Chapter, www.northcountrytrail.org/trail/wisconsin/bsc
Camping: Lucius Woods County Park in Solon Springs has twenty-nine sites.

FINDING THE TRAILHEAD

From Solon Springs, take CR A northeast 3.9 miles. After it turns south, you will notice a historical marker and sign on the west side of the road. The trailhead is opposite on the east side of the road, next to a boulder with a memorial plaque. Farther down the road 100 yards is the entrance road for a DNR boat launch and picnic area, a good place to park. GPS: N46 22.882' / W91 46.571'

THE HIKE

French explorer Daniel Greysolon Sieur du Lhut, Duluth's namesake, was the first to make a record of his passage over this trail in 1680. His story mentions cutting through one hundred beaver dams on the Bois Brule River. He may have been the first to leave a written account, but it seems reasonable to believe that he learned of the route from Native Americans who had used it for some time.

A clear-cut from over a decade ago is slowly growing back in. But what is lost in older growth trees is made up for by the sense of place here. Standing at the Brule end of the historical portage, there is a powerful sense of place permeating that marshy landing. Consider the many travelers and explorers who had passed this way, spotted the open water, and happily dropped their loads.

Several stone markers along the trail mention early European pioneers, including another Frenchman, Pierre-Charles Le Sueur, in 1693, and Henry Schoolcraft, discoverer of the source of the Mississippi, in 1820. But long before these travelers came, the Native Americans who left no written records challenge the imagination. Who were they? Where did they come from, and where were they going?

The trailhead begins next to a large boulder with a marker on it, on the east side of the road opposite the larger marker and vehicle turnout on the west side. Follow the trail

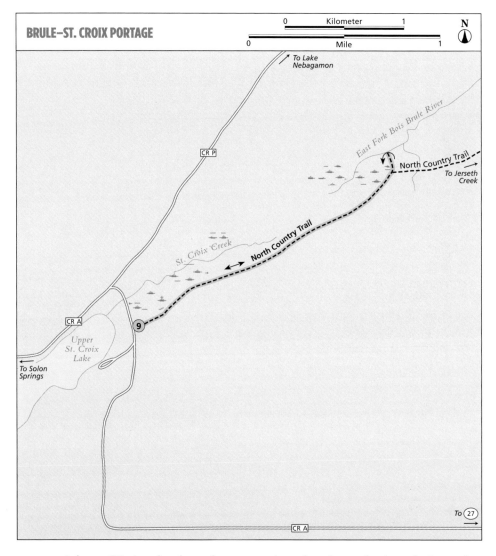

east as it leaves CR A and makes a short ascent through a pleasant hardwood, pine, and aspen forest in an eroded gully. The North Country Trail continues through the woods on a plateau-like hilltop before entering the previously cut-over area after 0.5 mile. That clearing offers views north across the wetland bottom that is the headwaters of both the St. Croix and Brule Rivers.

After crossing this area, the trail reenters woods on a sidehill traverse 15 vertical feet above the wetland. At mile 2.0 a worn path leads left (north) 100 yards, out of the woods and onto grass hummocks. A stream, barely large enough to float a canoe, floats northeast. This is the Brule end of the portage and the hike's turnaround point.

Local information: Superior–Douglas County Area Chamber & Visitors Bureau, 205 Belknap St., Superior, 54880; (800) 942-5313; www.superiorchamber.org

The portage lies along the North Country National Scenic Trail PREAMTIP SATASUK

MILES AND DIRECTIONS

0.0   Start from the CR A trailhead.

2.0   Arrive at Brule end of portage.

4.0   Return to CR A trailhead.

10 ANDERSON LAKE

A lovely trek through the federal Rainbow Lake Wilderness, this path crosses the North Country Trail and offers looks at several small lakes along the way.

Start: From the trailhead in the parking area
Distance: 8.2-mile out-and-back
Hiking time: 3 hours
Difficulty: Moderate
Trail surface: Dirt, with soggy areas
Best season: Spring through fall
Other trail users: None
Land status: National forest
Nearest town: Drummond
Canine compatibility: Leashed dogs permitted
Fees and permits: None
Schedule: Daily
Maps: USGS Delta (inc.) quad

Trail contact: Chequamegon-Nicolet National Forest, 113 Bayfield St. E., Washburn, 54891; (715) 373-2667; www.fs.usda.gov
Special considerations: Parts of the trail are soggy from spring water and may require waterproof footwear.
Camping: This hike is within the Rainbow Lake Wilderness of the Chequamegon-Nicolet National Forest, and camping is permitted along the trail. Campsites must be at least 100 feet away from the trail or water's edge.

FINDING THE TRAILHEAD

From Drummond, drive 5.6 miles north on FR 35 and turn left (west) into a small parking area. GPS: N46 24.113' / W91 16.290'

THE HIKE

A first-time visitor to the south end of the Rainbow Lake Wilderness may think the script calls for a mere walk in the woods, but the soundtrack tells another story. The haunting tremolo cry of loons echoes across this pocket-size preserve, and a map check reveals why: There are a dozen small lakes scattered around this route.

The Anderson Grade, an old railroad grade from the logging era, provides easy access to four of those lakes. Combining that route with a short jaunt on the North Country Trail to Rainbow Lake creates a fine outing, with hardly a mile going by without a new lake to contemplate.

Begin by walking west from the trailhead on the Anderson Grade, Forest Service Trail 502. It's level, fast walking. After little more than 100 yards, the trail crosses a low area, often soggy or filled with water from nearby springs. Waterproof footwear is a good idea, although you may cobble together deadfall for a bit of nature's boardwalk, if previous hikers haven't done so already. Clay Lake appears to the south just beyond this, and 0.25 mile after that, Flakefjord Lake peeks through the trees to the north.

The old railroad grade enters the woods and more rolling terrain for a mile before coming to an unmarked spur to Bufo Lake at mile 1.5. That spur runs south a short distance to a piney peninsula protruding into Bufo Lake.

Resume walking west on the Anderson Grade. Go straight (west) where the North Country Trail enters from the left (south) at mile 1.7 and splits off to the right (north) 100 yards later.

The trail passes close to Clay Lake

Follow the Anderson Grade west as it makes a very broad turn to the left around a long wetland. Pay attention as it begins a southwesterly course. At mile 2.8, make a very sharp left turn (east) on a spur of the Anderson Grade and walk east about 100 yards. At that point a path leads south to the north shore of Anderson Lake, a pleasant place for a break.

When you are ready, return to the Anderson Grade and retrace your steps to the North Country Trail intersection at mile 4.1. Turn left (north) and walk north along that narrow trail to Rainbow Lake at mile 5.3.

Rainbow Lake is another turnaround on this route. Walk south on the North Country Trail, reaching the intersection with the Anderson Grade at mile 6.5. Turn left (east) and follow the old railroad grade back to the trailhead at mile 8.2.

Local information: Bayfield County Tourism, 117 E. Fifth St., Washburn, 54891; (715) 373-6125; www.bayfieldcounty.org

Restaurant: Delta Diner, 14385 CR H, Delta; (715) 372-6666; www.deltadiner.com. An outstanding roadside eatery 7.0 miles north of the trailhead. People drive hours just to eat here.

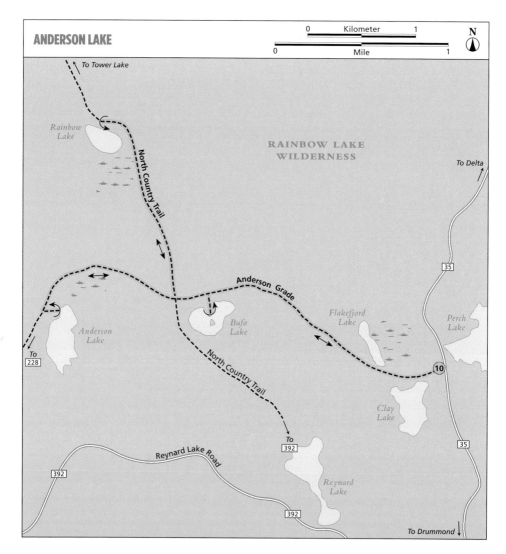

ANDERSON LAKE

Kilometer
0   1

Mile
0   1

N

To Tower Lake

Rainbow Lake

RAINBOW LAKE
WILDERNESS

To Delta

North Country Trail

35

Anderson Grade

Flakefjord
Lake

Perch
Lake

Bufo
Lake

Anderson
Lake

To
228

North Country Trail

10

Clay
Lake

To
392

35

Reynard Lake Road

392

Reynard
Lake

392

To Drummond

MILES AND DIRECTIONS

0.0 Depart from the trailhead on the Anderson Grade.

1.5 Pass the Bufo Lake spur on the left.

1.7 Go straight across the North Country Trail intersection.

2.8 Turn east for Anderson Lake.

2.9 Arrive at Anderson Lake.

4.1 Backtrack and at the North Country Trail intersection, turn left.

5.3 Arrive at Rainbow Lake.

6.5 Return to Anderson Grade intersection and go left (east).

8.2 Arrive back at the trailhead.

11 MARENGO RIVER/ PORCUPINE LAKE

If you are looking for a long hike in the wilderness, this segment of the North Country Trail passes through the Chequamegon National Forest, passing the ruins of a historic settlement, crossing rivers and creeks, and offering three scenic overlooks and glimpses of six lakes. This works best as an overnight excursion.

Start: From the trailhead on the west side of FR 187
Distance: 22.6-mile point-to-point shuttle hike
Hiking time: About 11 hours/2 days
Difficulty: Difficult
Trail surface: Dirt
Best season: Spring through fall
Other trail users: None
Land status: National forest
Nearest town: Mellen
Canine compatibility: Leashed dogs allowed
Fees and permits: Parking fees may apply in some national forest parking areas.
Schedule: Daily
Maps: USFS "The North Country National Scenic Trail," USGS Mineral Lake, Marengo River, Grandview (inc.), and Diamond Lake (inc.) quads

Trail contact: North Country Trail Association, Chequamegon Chapter, che@northcountrytrail.org or www.northcountrytrail.org/trail/wisconsin/che. Chequamegon-Nicolet National Forest, Great Divide Ranger Office, 10650 Nyman Ave., Hayward, 54843; (715) 634-4821; www.fs.usda.gov
Camping: This part of the North Country Trail is in the Chequamegon National Forest, and camping is permitted along the trail without a permit (though National Forest parking areas may demand a daily fee). Campsites must be at least 100 feet away from the trail or water's edge. The Beaver Lake Campground, with ten drive-in sites, is 2.4 miles west of the trailhead.

FINDING THE TRAILHEAD

From Mellen, drive west 8.7 miles on CR GG. Turn right (north) on FR 187 (Mineral Lake Road). Follow FR 187 north and west about 4 miles to the North Country Trail, just south of the Lake Three Recreation Area. GPS: N46 19.058' / W90 51.600'

THE HIKE

This hike is a story about woods, very big woods. Along the way there are a few lakes, as well as a handful of viewpoints from rock outcrops, but the overwhelming theme here is the forest. It is a beautiful forest of large, relatively old hardwoods, with a scattering of pines.

Begin your hike by walking west from the small trailside parking area on FR 187. The trail is usually a footpath, but with a design that leaves enough space between trees for an ATV to pass for maintenance purposes. Occasionally the trail follows an old woods road.

Seitz Lake and its marshy borders come into sight to the north at mile 1.3. The trail continues its run to the west, and at mile 3.0 a sign marks a spur leading south to the Beaver Lake Campground. Stay right (west) at that junction as the trail runs close to Beaver

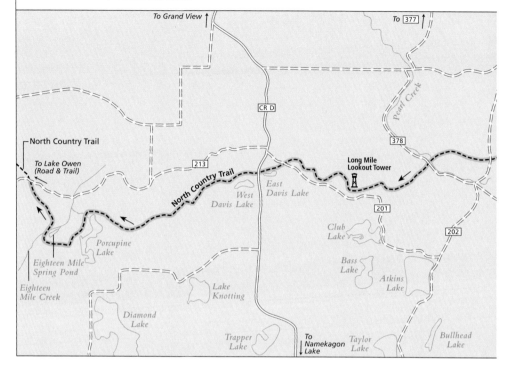

Lake's north shore. Near the lake's northwest corner, you pass an old beaver dam before the trail rises into the wooded hills.

The North Country Trail rolls west, bisecting the small drainages that run north–south in this area. Despite that "cross grain" travel, the vertical relief in this section is in the moderate neighborhood of 100-foot gains and losses.

After the trail crosses FR 383 at mile 6.1, the topography becomes more dramatic and the forest notably pleasant. At mile 7.3 the trail reaches the first of three overlooks that mark a 2.0-mile stretch of trail. A signed spur trail leads 100 feet north where a rock outcrop emerges from the trees, offering long views north to Mount Ashwabay, north of Washburn.

Continue walking west to mile 7.8, where another sign marks another side trail to a viewpoint. This time it is a 140-yard walk to the north to the rock ledge. The views here are northward again but broader than the first overlook. This is the best of the three lookouts in this section.

Resume walking west. As the trail enters a small pine plantation, a marker noting the Swedish settlement appears. To investigate, walk south through the pines to a clearing where old walls and other remains of the settlement endure.

After leaving the settlement area, the trail begins to drop in earnest, some 300 feet, to the Marengo River below. At mile 8.5 a short side trail leads to a three-sided Adirondack-style trail shelter. The trail reaches the Marengo River at mile 8.6, crosses on a wide, sturdy bridge, and ascends steeply on the river valley's west slope.

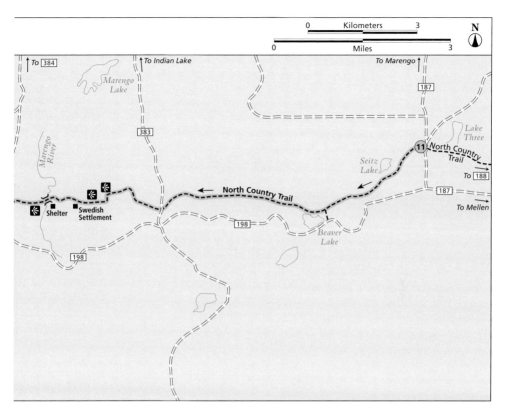

At the top of that climb, a broad dome of rock rises south of the trail, the third over-look at mile 9.1. This is a pleasant break spot, offering wide views of the upper part of the Marengo River watershed and the wooded hills that line the river valley.

The trail resumes its westward march, passing FR 202 at mile 9.7 and crossing Pearl Creek at mile 11.2 on a bridge. Just after that stream, FR 378 is at mile 11.3.

The next landmark is the Long Mile Lookout Tower at mile 13.2, bordering a stretch of trail where the path takes a northward jog. To the east of the trail, past the closed tower, there is a cluttered but worthwhile view to the east toward St. Peter's Dome. From the tower area, the trail meanders west, roughly paralleling FR 201, before crossing it at mile 15.2. It then runs along the north shore of charming East Davis Lake at mile 15.5 and crosses CR D (paved) at mile 15.7.

CR D marks the eastern boundary of the Porcupine Lakes Wilderness Area, and a sign there offers a map of the area. The trail shrinks to a narrow footpath and traverses a thick, shrubby forest, a "green tunnel." At mile 16.9 the trail makes a memorable crossing of a beaver dam. This 50-foot-long crossing puts a premium on slow, precise footwork.

The trail continues west through thick, mixed forest. When the woods open into pleasant glades, you are within a mile of Porcupine Lake. The path reaches the north-ern end of the lake, which loons frequent, at mile 19.7, and proceeds south along its western shore.

Cross Porcupine Creek and walk south, watching for trail signs, ignoring two paths that lead west. Continue walking south and southwest, catching a last glimpse of Porcu-pine Lake to the east.

TRAIL

Along with North Country Trail signs, mileage markers are spread along the hike to help you keep track of your progress.
PREAMTIP SATASUK

The trail is high on a ridge here, and to your northwest another body of water appears, the pond of Eighteen Mile Creek. Your path rounds the south and west side of this marsh, crossing small Eighteen Mile Creek at mile 21.3 and turning north. At mile 21.6 bear left (northwest) as the trail forks. At mile 22.1 turn right (north) at a T intersection. At mile 22.6 the North Country Trail intersects FR 213, marking the end of the hike.

This is a long, excellent segment of the North Country Trail, but unless you are a hardcore trekker, probably not something you are going to do in one day. One option that works well is a two-night backpacking trip, with the first night near the Marengo River and the second at Porcupine Lake. This would mean 8.6 miles of hiking the first day and 11.1 miles the second. The Marengo River offers brook trout fishing. Nearby are several overlooks and the historic Swedish settlement ruins.

Local information: Northern Great Lakes Visitor Center, 29270 CR G, Ashland, 54806; (715) 685-9983; www.nglvc.org

Bayfield County Tourism, 117 E. Fifth St., Washburn, 54891; (715) 373-6125; www .bayfieldcounty.org

MILES AND DIRECTIONS

0.0 Start from the FR 187 trailhead.

1.3 Skirt Seitz Lake on your right.

3.0 Pass the trail to Beaver Lake Campground.

6.1 Cross FR 383.

7.3 Stop at the first overlook.

7.8 Come to the second overlook.

8.1 See the remains of the Swedish settlement.

8.5 Continue past an Adirondack shelter.

8.6 Cross the Marengo River.

9.1 Arrive at the third overlook.

9.7 Cross FR 202.

11.2 Cross Pearl Creek.

11.3 Cross FR 378.

13.2 Come to Long Mile Lookout Tower.

15.2 Cross FR 201.

15.5 Pass East Davis Lake on your left.

15.7 Cross CR D, east boundary of Porcupine Lake Wilderness.

19.7 Cross Porcupine Creek with Porcupine Lake on your left.

21.3 Cross Eighteen Mile Creek.

22.6 Finish at FR 213, north boundary of Porcupine Lake Wilderness.

12 MORGAN FALLS/ ST. PETER'S DOME

This popular hike enters the Chequamegon National Forest and takes you to an unusual and scenic waterfall, tumbling 80 feet down a narrow channel in a gorge. From there the trail rises to the highest point in the county with a view all the way to Lake Superior and the Bayfield Peninsula.

Start: From the trailhead at the parking lot
Distance: 3.2-mile out-and-back
Hiking time: About 1.5 hours
Difficulty: Moderate
Trail surface: Dirt
Best season: Spring through fall
Other trail users: None
Land status: National forest
Nearest town: Mellen
Canine compatibility: Leashed dogs allowed
Fees and permits: USFS parking fee
Schedule: Open daily

Maps: USFS Morgan Falls and St. Peter's Dome, USGS Marengo Lake (inc.) quad
Trail contact: Chequamegon-Nicolet National Forest, Great Divide Ranger Office, 10650 Nyman Ave., Hayward, 54843; (715) 634-4821; www.fs.usda .gov
Special considerations: Parts of this trail have rough footing.
Camping: There are ten drive-in sites at Beaver Lake, 7.9 miles south of the trailhead.

FINDING THE TRAILHEAD

From Mellen, drive 8.7 miles west on CR GG and turn right (north) on FR 187. Drive north and west 4.7 miles and turn left (west) on FR 199. Drive 5.0 miles and turn right (east) into the trailhead parking area. GPS: N46 21.037' / W90 55.416'

THE HIKE

Morgan Falls, plummeting 80 feet down a granite slab, earns mention as the prettiest waterfall in the state. That cascade combines with a notable viewpoint, St. Peter's Dome, to make this an outstanding hike. This trail has its rough spots, but the attractions are worth it. Much of the route, particularly past Morgan Falls, is an eroded jumble, with roots and rocks waiting to trip the careless.

Begin your tour from the southeast corner of the trailhead parking lot, where a well-worn trail leads east. Follow that route through a forest of maples and birches to a small stream at mile 0.4, Morgan Creek. Turn right (south) and follow the marked path along the west side of the creek.

Soon the sound of the falls drifts through the woods, and as the valley walls close in, you catch a glimpse through the trees of falling water. The drop begins high above you, at the same level as the canopy of the trees, plummets to a pool in a ledge, then descends another 6 feet to the creek bed.

When you are ready, retrace your steps north along the creek to the main trail. Turn right (east), cross the creek on logs, and begin a slow ascent to the southeast. Old

The view from St. Peter's Dome reaches all the way to Lake Superior.

foundations, the remains of a Civilian Conservation Corps camp from the 1930s, come into view on the left and shortly after that a spring, encircled in a cistern of stone and mortar. Water, part of a mile-long beaver pond on Canyon Creek, is sometimes visible through the trees to the north.

The trail continues to run east, crossing a charming brook, a miniature Morgan Falls lined with moss and ferns. You will pass another creek, smaller and quieter, as well as a bench. At mile 1.4 stay straight (east) as the path crosses a snowmobile trail. Shortly after the trail hits a T intersection with an old woods road. Turn right (south). A moment later turn left (east) off the old road, following the obvious wear marks up the slope.

Switchbacks ease the trail's ascent as it makes its way to the top of St. Peter's Dome at mile 1.8. A grassy glade appears as the slope levels out, and the trail runs a final 100 yards to the viewpoint, a broad granite dome. Fine views open up to the west and north.

To the west the Chequamegon Forest seems to stretch forever. Morgan Creek's lake-like beaver pond marks the hike's beginning. As you look north, patches of farms toward Ashland interrupt the woodlands. On a clear day you can pick out Madeline Island and Mount Ashwabay near Bayfield. While this land is federally owned, it is also a designated State Natural Area for its variety of plant life, including some rare species of fern.

Local information: Northern Great Lakes Visitor Center, 29270 CR G, Ashland, 54806; (715) 685-9983; www.nglvc.org

MORGAN FALLS/ST. PETER'S DOME

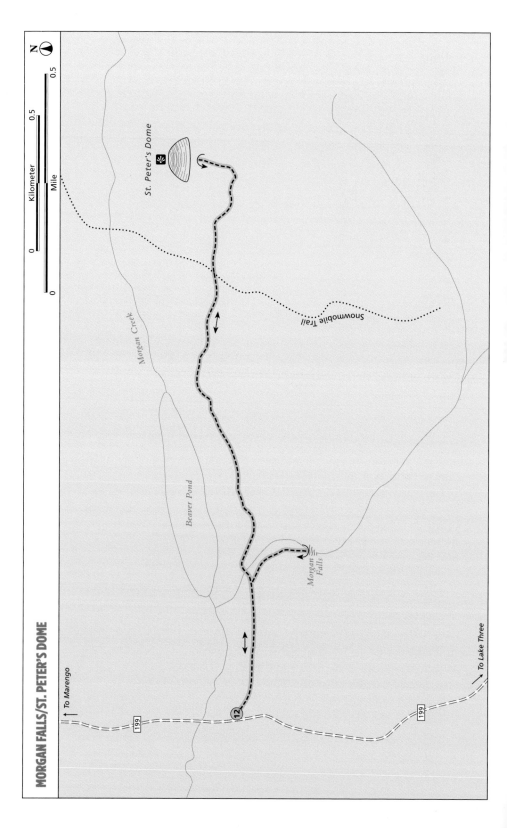

St. Peter's Dome

Morgan Creek

Beaver Pond

Morgan Falls

Snowmobile Trail

To Marengo

199

12

To Lake Three

199

Kilometer

Mile

N

Morgan Falls tumbles down a chute and collects in a shaded pool. PREAMTIP SATASUK

MILES AND DIRECTIONS

0.0 Start from the trailhead.

0.4 Go right at the junction of Morgan Falls Trail and St. Peter's Dome Trail.

0.6 Arrive at Morgan Falls, then backtrack.

0.8 At the junction of St. Peter's Dome Trail and Morgan Falls Trail, go right.

1.4 Cross a snowmobile trail.

1.8 Arrive at St. Peter's Dome.

3.2 Arrive back at the trailhead.

13 COPPER FALLS

One of northern Wisconsin's most beautiful state parks, Copper Falls has two impressive waterfalls where the Bad River meets Tyler Forks River. The North Country Trail passes through the park, and an observation tower gives you a bird's-eye view of a richly forested terrain with impressive geological sights along the river gorge.

Start: From trailhead at the parking lot
Distance: 1.8-mile loop
Hiking time: About 1 hour
Difficulty: Easy
Trail surface: Dirt
Best season: Spring through fall
Other trail users: None
Land status: State park
Nearest town: Mellen
Canine compatibility: Leashed dogs permitted

Fees and permits: State park vehicle fee
Schedule: Daily, 6 a.m. to 11 p.m.
Maps: Copper Falls State Park trail map, USGS Mellen (inc.) and Highbridge (inc.) quads
Trail contact: Copper Falls State Park, 36764 Copper Falls Rd., Mellen, 54546; (715) 274-5123; https://dnr.wi.gov
Camping: Copper Falls State Park has fifty-one drive-in campsites and four backpacking sites.

FINDING THE TRAILHEAD

From Mellen, drive north 0.5 mile on WI 13 and turn right (east) on WI 169. Take that road north, and at mile 2.2 turn left (northwest) into the park entrance road. Get a map and park newspaper at the entrance station. Follow the park road north to the trailhead at the northeast side of the picnic area parking lot. GPS: N46 22.309' / W90 38.572'

THE HIKE

It is difficult to maintain a brisk pace on Copper Falls' Three Bridges Trail; too many distractions line the path's route. Its well-constructed 1.8 miles offers a constant parade of falling water, charming nooks, and rock canyons. Those canyon walls are part of the rich geological history described in the park's newspaper.

Walk east from the parking lot past the concession building and turn left (north) to cross a sturdy bridge over the Bad River. On the other side you have an option to go left a short distance uphill to reach the observation tower. Otherwise, continue to the right, following the broad, constructed trail north to the viewpoint overlooking Copper Falls at mile 0.3. Old pictures show a 30-foot drop, but today the falls is eroding into a rapids, with its largest drop 12 feet.

The path follows the top of the gorge to where Brownstone Falls comes into sight on the other side of the 100-foot-deep chasm. It is a stunner, a 30-foot drop on the Tyler Forks River, a tributary of the Bad River that then joins the main stream directly below.

Your route turns west and follows the top of the sheer canyon called Devil's Gate before dropping down stone steps to a bridge over the Bad River. On the north side of the river the trail swings east and ascends stone and wood steps to an intersection with a spur trail leading north at mile 0.9. Ignore the spur trail, a segment of the North Country Trail, and continue straight (east) to a spur to the right (south) at mile 1.0.

The CCC-built trail to the Copper and Brownstone Falls

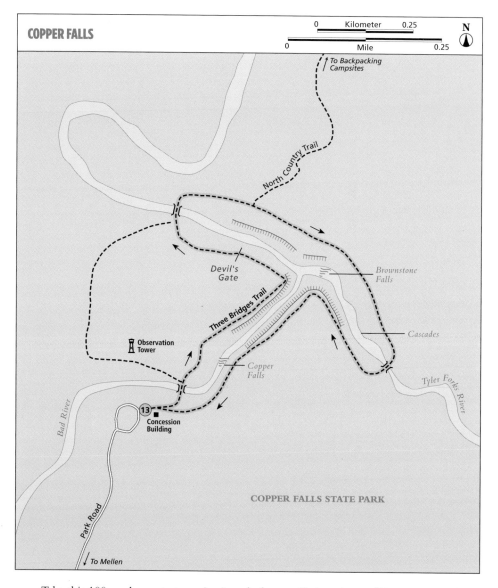

Take this 100-yard spur to two viewing platforms offering views of Brownstone Falls from above as well as the Tyler Forks Cascades upstream. When you're ready, return to the main trail and continue east to a bridge that crosses the Tyler Forks River. After that crossing, the path swings west and at mile 1.2 comes to the final viewing platforms. Again, there are views of Brownstone Falls, but the real treat is a view straight down the length of Devil's Gate, a hidden world of rock and water.

The trail swings south and soon the first bridge and concession building come into sight. The parking lot is just beyond.

Local information: Northern Great Lakes Visitor Center, 29270 CR G, Ashland, 54806; (715) 685-9983; www.nglvc.org

Copper Falls

MILES AND DIRECTIONS

0.0 Start from the trailhead in the picnic area parking lot.

0.1 Cross the bridge over the Bad River.

0.3 Stop to view Copper Falls.

0.6 Cross another bridge over Bad River.

0.9 Follow the North Country Trail east.

1.0 Take a spur to the viewing platform above Brownstone Falls.

1.1 Cross the bridge over Tyler Forks River.

1.2 Pass the viewing platform for Brownstone Falls and the Devil's Gate gorge.

1.8 Arrive back at the trailhead at the parking lot.

14 POTATO RIVER FALLS

This is a bit of a short hike, but the steps may make you break a sweat. The three out-and-back trails take you to viewing platforms where you can see an impressive series of waterfalls. One trail ends at the river's edge a short distance downstream from the Lower Falls.

Start: From the first of three trailheads at the parking lot
Distance: 0.8-mile out-and-back
Hiking time: About 30 minutes
Difficulty: Easy
Trail surface: Dirt, wood steps
Best season: Spring through fall
Other trail users: None
Land status: County park land
Nearest town: Gurney
Canine compatibility: Leashed dogs allowed

Fees and permits: None
Schedule: Daily
Map: USGS Gurney (inc.) quad
Trail contact: Iron County Forestry Department, 607 3rd Ave. N., #2, Hurley, 54534; (715) 561-2697; ironcountyforest.org
Camping: This county park has five free rustic campsites located along the lane heading south from the parking lot.

FINDING THE TRAILHEAD

From Mellen, drive 15.9 miles northeast on WI 169 and turn left on Potato River Falls Road. Take that road west and south 1.7 miles to the parking area. GPS: N46 27.786' / W90 31.774'

THE HIKE

Potato River Falls, a compact series of drops, has two named features, the Upper Falls and the Lower Falls. The Upper Falls has two 20-foot drops. That cascade starts with a plunge down a bedrock chute, bounces off boulders, and drops again. A few hundred feet downstream, the river spreads out across a black lava shelf and drops another 30 feet at the spectacular Lower Falls.

A system of three viewing platforms eases a tour of the 150-foot-deep, red clay gorge. Walk to the southwest side of the parking lot and you will see the first of these platforms, offering a high view of the Lower Falls, directly in front of you.

Next walk to the southeast corner of the parking lot, where a sign directs you along a path to the Upper Falls. That trail quickly turns into a stairway, descending 130 steps to a viewing deck that offers a broad view of the Upper Falls.

When you are ready, walk back toward the parking lot and cross to the northwest corner. There another sign announces a path to a

Steps down to the Lower Falls area
PREAMTIP SATASUK

Potato River Falls
PREAMTIP SATASUK

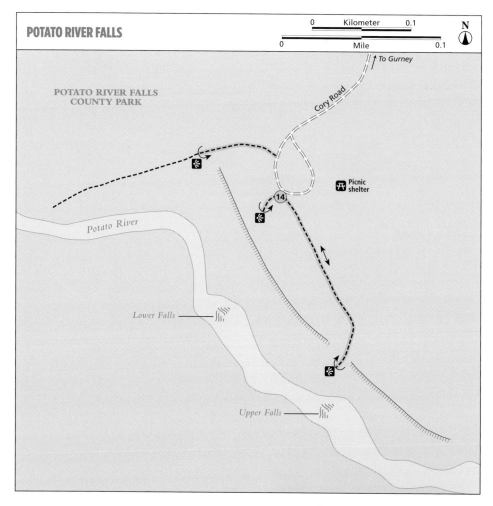

0   Kilometer   0.1

0   Mile   0.1

N

POTATO RIVER FALLS
COUNTY PARK

To Gurney

Cory Road

Picnic
shelter

14

Potato River

Lower Falls

Upper Falls

viewing platform for the Lower Falls. Follow another set of stairs downhill 200 feet, halfway down the slope, to the viewpoint of Lower Falls. Continue past the platform, and a mix of dirt path and a few more steps brings you to the bank of the river downstream around a bend from the Lower Falls. When the water is low enough, you may rock hop through here. Retrace your steps to return to the parking area.

Local information: Iron County Visitor Information, 100 Cary Rd., Hurley, 54534; (715) 561-2922; https://ironcountywi.com

A deer only a few steps off the trail
PREAMTIP SATASUK

15 PENOKEE RANGE

This segment of the North Country National Scenic Trail follows part of a cross-country ski trail system that rises up along the back of a ridge, what used to be part of mountain range that would rival today's Alps. The rugged backcountry trail offers scenic lookouts and trail shelters for thru-hikers and campers.

Start: From the trailhead across from the county park parking lot
Distance: 10.6-mile out-and-back
Hiking time: About 5 hours
Difficulty: Moderate/difficult
Trail surface: Dirt
Best season: Spring through fall
Other trail users: Skiers in winter
Land status: County land
Nearest town: Hurley
Canine compatibility: Leashed dogs permitted
Fees and permits: None
Schedule: Daily
Maps: North Country Trail Heritage Chapter segment map, Uller Ski Trail Map, USGS Saxon (inc.), and Iron Belt (inc.) quads
Trail contact: North Country Trail Association, Heritage Chapter, htg@northcountrytrail.org, www.northcountrytrail.org/trail/wisconsin/htg
Special considerations: Most of this trail segment was originally a ski trail, and footing can occasionally be rough. The two shelters are small cabins built by a local ski club.
Camping: This trail runs through Iron County forestry lands; camping is permitted along the trail. Campsites must be at least 100 feet away from the trail or water's edge.

FINDING THE TRAILHEAD

From Hurley, drive 8.9 miles west on WI 77 and turn right (west) on CR E. After 2.6 miles stay straight as CR E turns left (south). The trailhead is about 100 yards from that intersection on the north side of this unnamed road. Park in the county park on the south side of the road. GPS: N46 24.606' / W90 23.506'

THE HIKE

Perhaps few Wisconsinites outside of this northern area of the state had heard of the Penokee Range until recent open-pit mining proposals made it a household name and sore subject. But the North Country Trail passes through these ancient mountains that once towered as high as the Alps. This segment, following the Uller Ski Trail, traverses a remote ridge while passing fine stands of maple trees, hidden nooks and crannies, and a prime viewpoint.

Begin by walking north from Weber Lake on the North Country Trail. The route ascends steadily for 0.25 mile before leveling out and heading northeast. As the trail begins to skirt a series of rocky knolls on their northern slopes, the ambiance becomes elegant. Hemlocks and oaks accent an open forest of mature maples.

Follow the trail east to Sullivan Creek at mile 1.2 and traverse a series of four bridges across muddy fern gardens. An ascent from the creek brings the trail to a signed intersection for a scenic spur trail at mile 1.9. Turn right (south) on this spur trail, which leads to a worthwhile overlook. Wear marks on this path can be thin, but the trail markings are strong as it jogs southeast and finally west. The last 100 yards merge with an ATV trail before you arrive at the overlook at mile 2.2.

A broad dome of rock offers 180-degree views sweeping from the southeast to the northwest. To the south, the long ridge of the Gogebic Range rises across Alder Creek's valley. Far to the northwest, the Bayfield Peninsula's headlands appear on the horizon.

When you are ready, return to the North Country Trail at mile 2.5 and turn right (east). The trail intersects Tower Road at mile 2.8. Bear left (north) on that old dirt lane

The steep Penokee Ridge rises conspicuously above the terrain

for a short distance, then turn right (northeast) off Tower Road at a well-marked spot. (Some maps may show that Tower Road connects south to CR E, but in fact there is no bridge across Alder Creek and it is a dead end coming from the south.)

Continue northeast on the North Country Trail. About 1.0 mile after Tower Road, a long descent brings you to the Scribner's Meadow shelter, a tiny but functional structure at mile 4.0. Scribner's Meadow is a wetland east of the shelter, along the headwaters of Boomer Creek.

From the shelter, follow the trail south then east as it rounds the meadow and ascends to a low gap in a headland among pleasant, old-growth hardwoods. From that saddle it descends to cross a branch of Alder Creek and arrives at the Smith's Meadow shelter at mile 5.3. That shelter is a good turnaround spot for the hike.

Local information: Hurley Area Chamber of Commerce, 316 Silver St., Hurley, 54534; (866) 340-4334; www.hurleywi.com

Iron County Visitor Information, 100 Cary Rd., Hurley, 54534; (715) 561-2922; https://ironcountywi.com

The origin of these ridges dates back 2.7 billion years to undersea volcanic activity.

MILES AND DIRECTIONS

0.0   Start from the roadside trailhead.

1.2   Cross Sullivan Creek.

1.9   Take the trail to the right at the Vista Spur junction.

2.2   Arrive at the scenic overlook.

2.5   Go right at the Vista Spur junction.

2.8   Cross Tower Road.

4.0   Arrive at Scribner's Meadow shelter.

5.3   Turnaround at Smith's Meadow shelter.

10.0   Arrive back at the trailhead.

16 SANDROCK CLIFFS

This elongated loop follows along the wide St. Croix River, a national scenic riverway, with lovely water views as well as a pass along the upper reaches of some scenic sandstone cliffs on a side channel of the river.

Start: From the trailhead at the parking lot
Distance: 4.4-mile loop
Hiking time: About 2 hours
Difficulty: Easy
Trail surface: Dirt
Best season: May–October
Other trail users: None
Land status: National park
Nearest town: Grantsburg
Canine compatibility: Leashed dogs permitted
Fees and permits: None
Schedule: Daily, 6 a.m. to 10 p.m.

Maps: National Park Service Sandrock Cliff trail map, USGS Bass Creek (inc.) quad
Trail contact: St. Croix National Scenic Riverway, 401 N. Hamilton St., St. Croix Falls, 54024; (715) 483-3284; www.nps.gov/sacn
Camping: Seven walk-in campsites are at Sandrock Cliffs, near the northern end of the trail, while St. Croix Family Campground offers thirty drive-in sites along the trail just south of WI 70.

FINDING THE TRAILHEAD

From Grantsburg, drive 4.7 miles west on WI 70 and turn right (north) into the trailhead parking lot just before the bridge over the St. Croix River. GPS: N45 46.484' / W92 46.750'

THE HIKE

The St. Croix River, running swift, clear, and broad alongside this hike's route, is a pristine marvel. Its clean waters support a notably rich and diverse array of freshwater mussels. Above the river, eagles and ospreys patrol and find this stretch pleasant enough to nest nearby. Wolves use the river as a travel corridor, and two packs are in residence just a few miles north of this hike. Species-wise, this is a happening place.

Sandrock Cliffs, a low sandstone butte bordering a side channel of the river, is near the northern end of a ski and hiking trail system that bears its name. That trail, a very elongated loop with several smaller loops near the cliffs, has its southern terminus at the WI 70 trailhead.

Begin your tour by walking north from the northwest corner of the trailhead parking area on a wood-chip-covered dirt road. Ignore the return path coming in from the right (east) and go due north on the outgoing trail.

The broad trail narrows to a 4-foot width, running pleasantly through pines in the river's floodplain. The water's edge is a steady 30 to 50 feet to your left (west), and every now and then a path invites you over for a river view.

A series of river islands coincides with the trail's ascent up a minor slope and junction with Trail E at mile 1.3. Turn left (north) and follow this path along the top of the Sandrock Cliffs, pausing to scan the waters below for wood ducks and other notables. Continue on Trail E as it rounds the north end of the plateau and then runs along the

Beneath the trail, Sandrock Cliffs stand along an intermittent channel of the St. Croix River.

east side of the butte's top. It returns south and at mile 1.6 intersects Trail B. Turn left (east) onto Trail B. That trail descends to the north, passing the east side of the uplift and reaching a parking lot that services the walk-in campsites in the area. At the northwest corner of the parking lot, at mile 1.9, take the left (north) choice, Trail C, ignoring the trail on the right.

Walk northwest on Trail C. A short distance farther, bear left (north) as the mowed trail splits. You then emerge from the shade and woods you have been in since the start of the hike and for the next 0.75 mile walk through open meadows dotted with young trees. The trail quickly reaches the river at a campsite with a fire ring, then runs northeast through the open floodplain.

The trail then makes a broad swing south and begins to run southwest. At mile 2.4 bear right (west) as Trail D enters from the left. This is the last stretch of open meadow; you may want to scan for raptors before you are again among the short sight lines of the forest. Continue south, turning left (south) at mile 2.7, the junction with the outgoing Trail C, reentering shady woods and reaching the parking lot at mile 2.8.

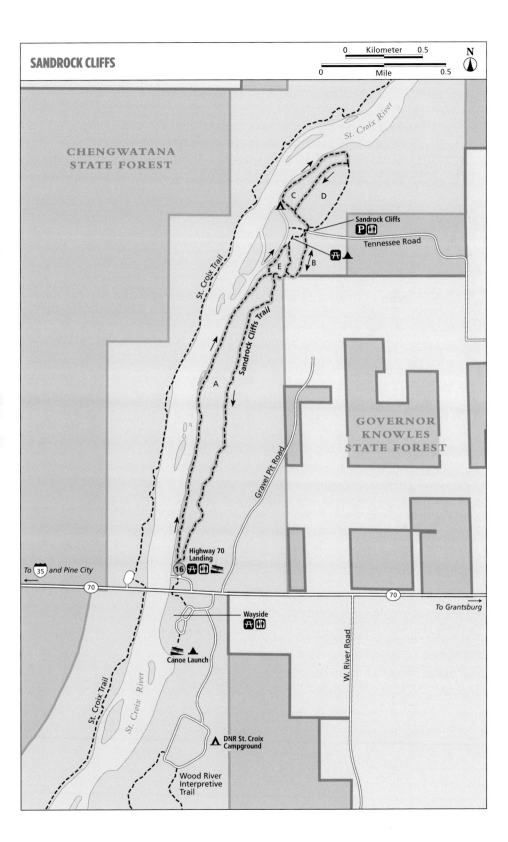

SANDROCK CLIFFS

CHENGWATANA
STATE FOREST

St. Croix River

Sandrock Cliffs
Tennessee Road

C   D

E   B

St. Croix Trail

Sandrock Cliffs Trail

A

GOVERNOR
KNOWLES
STATE FOREST

Gravel Pit Road

To 35 and Pine City

Highway 70
Landing
16

70

70
To Grantsburg

Wayside

W. River Road

Canoe Launch

DNR St. Croix
Campground

Wood River
Interpretive
Trail

St. Croix Trail

St. Croix River

Kilometer
Mile

N

Walk south across the parking lot, pick up Trail B, and follow it southwest to a junction with Trail E, coming in from the right at mile 3.1. Turn left (southwest). One hundred yards later turn left (south) on Trail A's inland return path. That path takes you south through a pleasant woodland setting decorated with giant ferns, to the trailhead at mile 4.4.

Local information: Burnett County Visitors Center (inside The Lodge at Crooked Lake), 24271 WI 35, Siren, 54872; (800) 788-3164; www.burnettcounty.com

Other resources: See FalconGuides *Paddling Wisconsin* to get on the St. Croix River.

Other attractions: Crex Meadows Wildlife Area, 102 E. Crex Ave., Grantsburg, 54840; (715) 463-2739; www.crexmeadows.org

MILES AND DIRECTIONS

0.0   Start at the trailhead at the parking lot.

1.3   Turn left at the Trail E Junction.

1.6   Turn left at the Trail B Junction.

1.9   Cross the parking lot and take Trail C to the left.

2.0   Bear left at the next juncture.

2.4   Bear right at the Trail C and D juncture.

2.7   Turn left on Trail C.

2.8   Cross the parking lot to Trail B.

3.1   Turn left at Trail E junction and left again at Trail A 100 yards later.

4.4   Arrive back at the trailhead on WI 70.

CREX MEADOWS WILDLIFE AREA

Encompassing 30,000 acres, this massive state wildlife area is a mecca for wildlife lovers. Birders have chronicled more than 270 species here, and butterfly species go nearly to triple digits. In fall, in excess of 80,000 sandhill cranes may gather here at Crex Meadows, and many nest here in summer. A boardwalk offers looks into a sedge marsh, and the prairie habitat is complemented by pine barrens. In addition to a couple of 1.0-mile trails, hiking is allowed off trail. The wildlife area has an auto tour as well, similar to the one found at Sandhill Wildlife Area. The wildlife area has no admission fee and is open around the clock and calendar. The Wildlife Education and Visitor Center is open daily from late March to early November. Camping is allowed after September 1. Unlike some wildlife areas, dogs are allowed. Crex Meadows Wildlife Area, 102 E. Crex Ave., Grantsburg, 54840; (715) 463-2739; www.crexmeadows.org.

17 **ST. CROIX**

One of Wisconsin's most impressive rivers and a National Scenic Riverway, the St. Croix is bordered at this point by a state forest. This trail heads north through a pristine river corridor full of wildlife and dozens of lush springs, traversing floodplains and bluffs alike.

Start: From the trailhead at the west end of Evergreen Avenue
Distance: 14.1-mile shuttle hike
Hiking time: About 6 hours
Difficulty: Difficult
Trail surface: Dirt
Best season: April–October
Other trail users: None
Land status: State forest
Nearest town: Grantsburg
Canine compatibility: Leashed dogs permitted
Fees and permits: State park vehicle sticker required
Schedule: Daily, 6 a.m. to 11 p.m.
Maps: Governor Knowles State Forest Trail Map, USGS North Branch, Rush City, and Randall quads
Trail contact: Governor Knowles State Forest, 325 SR 70, Grantsburg, 54840; (715) 463-2898; https://dnr.wi.gov

Special considerations: The difficult rating reflects the hike's length. During periods of high water, portions of the trail, especially in the floodplain, may become wet. Current state forest literature refers to the entire route as the South Trails. State forest maps refer to the segment from Evergreen to Burnett CR O as the Lagoo Creek Route. Those same maps call the trail from CR O to the North Benson trailhead the Benson Brook Route. Older USGS quads refer to the Southern Hiking Trail as the Sunrise Ferry Hiking Trail.
Camping: Backpack camping with free permit. Obtain permit at least seven days in advance from Governor Knowles State Forest.

FINDING THE TRAILHEAD

From Grantsburg, drive south on WI 48. Go straight (south) on WI 87 at mile 4.5 where WI 48 turns east. Drive another 8.4 miles south on WI 87 and turn right (west) on Evergreen Avenue. Drive 11.1 miles west to the trailhead. The last 0.2 mile is a sandy "two track" and the 2.0 miles before that are gravel. GPS: N45 36.008' / W92 52.910'

THE HIKE

Before I hiked this route, I expected the St. Croix River to be impressive. It is. This is a notably pristine large river, and the National Wild and Scenic Rivers Act protects more than 250 miles of its watershed. Eagles nest on the river's shoreline, otters romp on the banks, and rare mussels inhabit the riffles.

Any time spent with this great river is a treat, but it is the dozens of springs that line the base of the river valley bluffs that stand out in my memory. Here, springs are like patches of wildflowers, erupting in shady, mossy nooks.

Begin your journey along the St. Croix by walking north and west from the Evergreen Avenue trailhead of the Lagoo Creek Hiking Trail, following blue blazes through a quarter-mile-long stretch that shows signs of recent logging. Bear with it. The trail enters the woods, and the ambiance improves rapidly as it travels along the crest of the bluff.

Bald eagles are frequently sighted along the St. Croix River.

To the left of the trail, a spring, the first of a series, gushes from a lush, crater-like hole in the escarpment. More springs and spring runs cross the trail as it makes its way down the bluff onto the river's floodplain and across Lagoo Creek on a wood bridge at mile 1.4.

For the next 2.5 miles the trail runs north, sometimes near the river, sometimes slightly back from the water, across a vast floodplain forest drained by Lagoo Creek. The escarpment runs inland for that distance; when it again nears the river at mile 3.9, the trail ascends the bluff.

Barely a quarter mile farther it descends through fern gardens and runs north, past springs and small brooks, just above the floodplain. At about mile 4.7 bear right (north) as a spur trail goes left (west) to a swinging bridge, visible from the junction. That bridge crosses a minor channel of the river to a large grassy island that extends north. Follow the trail north, first traversing the bottom of the slope, then ascending to the top of the bluff. Continue north, walking through hardwood forests, to CR O at mile 6.5.

Cross the road. The trail runs west for a short distance, then north along the top of the escarpment. A parade of verdant springs erupts just below the trail to the left. At about mile 8.9 the trail splits. Turn left (northwest), descending the bluff and making a right (north) turn on an overgrown old road, running due north, at the bottom. Both wear marks and trail signs get a little thin for about a quarter mile here. Continue due north to where, at the edge of the woods and the bottom of the slope, the trail again becomes clear.

At this point the river curves east and the trail ascends the bluff eastward for 0.5 mile before descending beside a small brook. A sturdy bridge takes the trail across Benson Brook; there is a beaver dam just upstream, and the trail moves out onto a broad, open floodplain. For the next mile or so the trail traverses open old fields, nearing the river as it passes the end of Pleasant Prairie Road at mile 11.1.

The route continues east along the river another quarter mile, then turns inland through a stretch of scrubby woods. Pleasant older hardwoods return as the path turns back to the river and runs through elegant, shady fern gardens, with the river 30 feet to the left. A slough creek pushes the path inland just before the trail leaves the floodplain and ascends straight up (steps) the bluff alongside a mossy spring run. At the top, the trail swings northeast and follows the crest to the northern trailhead of the Benson Brook Hiking Trail.

Local information: Burnett County Visitors Center (inside The Lodge at Crooked Lake), 24271 WI 35, Siren, 54872; (800) 788-3164; www.burnettcounty.com

Other resources: See FalconGuides *Paddling Wisconsin* to get on the St. Croix River.

BIRDER'S DELIGHT: THE MISSISSIPPI FLYWAY

Wisconsin is a great state for bird-watching, counting Horicon Marsh and Door County and the Lake Michigan coast as specifically great corridors for birds during migration. Approximately 50 percent of the birds in North America have some relationship with the Mississippi Flyway. This north–south corridor that starts in central Canada and runs to the Gulf of Mexico offers no tall mountains to cross and all the food and water a bird could need. Along the Mississippi River in Wisconsin, eagles are common sights throughout the year. Waterfowl enjoy numerous refuges, backwaters, and dam- and levy-controlled stretches of slower-moving water. A surprise to some is the growing abundance of pelicans as well.

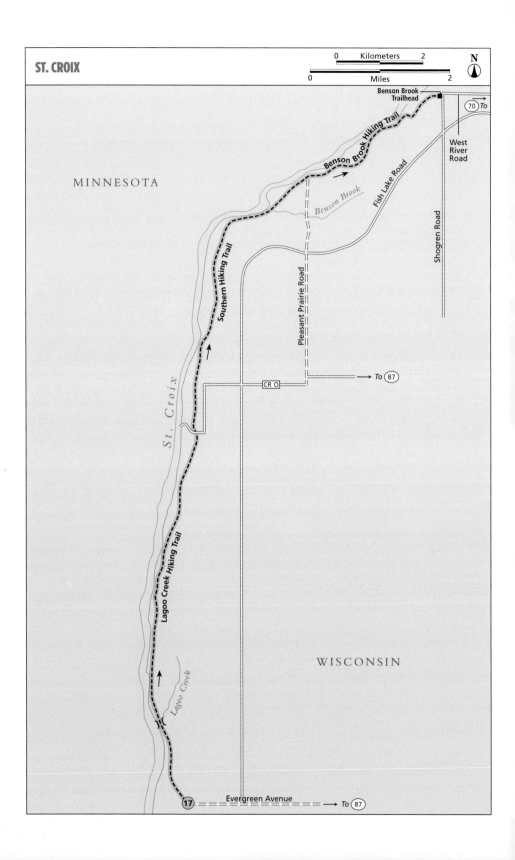

ST. CROIX

Kilometers
0   2
Miles
0   2

N

Benson Brook Trailhead

70 To

West River Road

Benson Brook Hiking Trail

MINNESOTA

Benson Brook

Fish Lake Road

Shogren Road

Southern Hiking Trail

Benson Brook

Pleasant Prairie Road

To 87

CR O

St. Croix

Lagoo Creek Hiking Trail

WISCONSIN

Lagoo Creek

17

Evergreen Avenue

To 87

A bald eagle takes its catch to the river bank.

Other attractions: Crex Meadows Wildlife Area, 102 E. Crex Ave., Grantsburg, 54840; (715) 463-2739; www.crexmeadows.org

MILES AND DIRECTIONS

0.0   Head north from the Evergreen trailhead.

1.4   Cross Lagoo Creek bridge.

3.9   The trail leaves the floodplain.

4.7   Bear right (north) away from a spur trail to a swinging bridge.

6.5   Cross CR O.

8.9   Turn left (northwest) where the trail splits and descends the bluff.

10.3   Cross Benson Brook bridge.

11.1   Pass the end of Pleasant Prairie Road.

13.4   The trail leaves the floodplain and ascends the bluff.

14.1   Arrive at the North Benson trailhead.

18 BLUE HILLS/DEVILS CREEK

This trek along the Northern Blue Hills Segment of the Ice Age National Scenic Trail rises and falls through birch and pine forest, crossing Devils Creek a few times, bringing you to a suggested turn-around point at some wetlands.

Start: From the trailhead on CR F
Distance: 4.6-mile out-and-back
Hiking time: About 2 hours
Difficulty: Easy
Trail surface: Dirt
Best season: April–October
Other trail users: None
Land status: Public easement
Nearest town: Weyerhauser
Canine compatibility: Leashed dogs permitted

Fees and permits: None
Schedule: Daily, 6 a.m. to 11 p.m.
Maps: Ice Age Trail Segment Map #11 or USGS Bucks Lake (inc.) quad
Trail contact: Ice Age Trail Alliance, 2110 Main St., Cross Plains, 53528; (800) 227-0046; www.iceagetrail.org
Camping: Audie and Perch Lake campgrounds have twenty-five drive-in sites, 5.0 miles north of the trailhead.

FINDING THE TRAILHEAD

From Weyerhauser, drive north 6.7 miles on CR F to CR O. Turn left (west) on CR F/O and drive 0.3 mile to the marked trailhead. Park on the side of the road. GPS: N45 30.054' / W91 26.745'

THE HIKE

Two creeks mark the beginning and end of this hike. Each is a gurgling gem, tempting you to stay a while and contemplate its secrets.

Devils Creek running clear below the Ice Age Trail

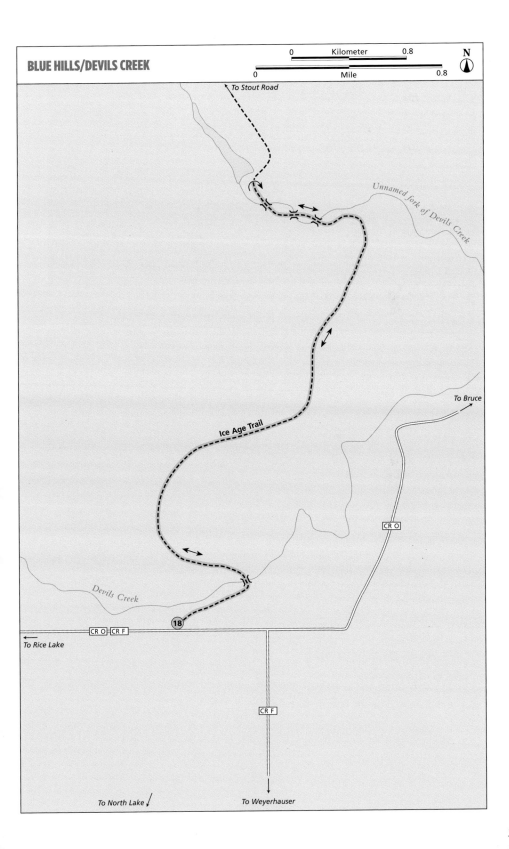

0
Kilometer
0.8

0
Mile
0.8

N

To Stout Road

Unnamed fork of Devils Creek

To Bruce

Ice Age Trail

CR O

Devils Creek

18

CR O CR F

To Rice Lake

CR F

To North Lake

To Weyerhauser

The first bridge across Devils Creek along the Ice Age Trail

Walk north from the trailhead, and a subtle but beautiful scene unfolds. The path follows the crest of a small ridge, 80 feet above Devils Creek, winding among birches and pines before dropping to a bridged crossing. A steep little ascent takes the trail out of the drainage and into a bluff-top grove of birch trees. The trail continues a slow northward ascent and passes into the open hardwood forest that will characterize most of the hike. For the next mile the path swings northeast through rolling hills, until a branch of Devils Creek appears on your right.

This next section, along the creek, is a fine place to pause, picnic, and listen to the stream's song. The creek wanders in a shallow ravine, and the trail reaches the first of a series of three bridges at mile 1.9.

Walk farther upstream; at mile 2.3 the trail nears the outlet of a large wetland, an aging beaver pond. This is a good spot to turn around and retrace your steps south.

To extend this hike, you could continue north through hummocky terrain and hardwood forest, passing occasional logging roads. This entire segment of the Ice Age Trail is 9.6 miles long, ending at CR F again to the north, but exiting the woods briefly to cross Bucks Lake Road at 9.3 miles. Also, 1.1 miles south from the trailhead along CR F, the Southern Blue Hills Segment winds 7.3 miles south to Old 14 Road.

Local information: Rusk County Visitor Center, 205 W. 9th St. S., Ladysmith, 54848; (800) 535-7875; www.ruskcountywi.com

MILES AND DIRECTIONS

0.0   Depart the trailhead at CR F/O.

0.2   Cross the first bridge over Devils Creek.

1.9   Cross the first of three bridges over an unnamed branch of Devils Creek.

2.3   Turn around at the south end of a beaver pond.

4.6   Arrive back at the trailhead.

19 ESCANABA LAKE

Popular with skiers in winter, this color-coded trail system of embedded loops takes you past five lakes tucked in the Northern Highland–American Legion State Forest.

Start: From the trailhead at the parking lot
Distance: 7.7-mile loop
Hiking time: About 3 hours
Difficulty: Moderate
Trail surface: Dirt
Best season: April–October
Other trail users: None
Land status: State forest
Nearest town: Woodruff
Canine compatibility: Leashed dogs permitted
Fees and permits: State park vehicle sticker required
Schedule: Daily, 6 a.m. to 11 p.m.

Maps: DNR "Escanaba Lake Ski Trail" map, USGS White Sand Lake (inc.) quad
Trail contact: Northern Highland–American Legion State Forest, Crystal Lake Visitor Station, 3237 Crystal Lake Rd., Boulder Junction, 54512; (715) 542-3923; https://dnr.wi.gov
Camping: Backcountry camping is allowed throughout the forest with a permit. There are thirty-six drive-in sites and six walk-in sites at Starrett Lake, 3.0 miles south of the trailhead.

FINDING THE TRAILHEAD

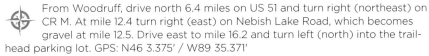

From Woodruff, drive north 6.4 miles on US 51 and turn right (northeast) on CR M. At mile 12.4 turn right (east) on Nebish Lake Road, which becomes gravel at mile 12.5. Drive east to mile 16.2 and turn left (north) into the trailhead parking lot. GPS: N46 3.375' / W89 35.371'

THE HIKE

Cross-country skiers know Escanaba Lake as a well-marked ski trail that might just be the most scenic in the state. It loses none of its charm when the snow melts. Mile after mile of this trail dips and rolls through a forest that seems arranged by an artist: a charming combination of maples, birches, and pines, accented with views of Pallette Lake.

From the northwest corner of the trailhead parking lot, walk north on a broad ski trail. After seventy paces turn left (northwest) on a narrower trail, the beginning of the red, yellow, and blue ski loops. Follow this trail west and at mile 0.7 take the red and green ski trail left (northwest) as the yellow ski loop goes right (north) to Pallette Lake.

From the junction the trail runs west on a low ridgetop and then turns north to round the end of Pallette Lake. Occasional glimpses of the water end as the pathway leaves the lake for 0.5 mile at its northwest corner. After turning east, cross a north–south path at mile 2.7. This is the portage path between Pallette Lake and Lost Canoe Lake, and it is only about 100 yards south to Pallette Lake, a fine spot for a break.

Half a mile east of the portage path are a major intersection and a small trail shelter, complete with fire ring, wood, and a birdfeeder. If for some reason you want to cut your walk short, turn right (south) and the trailhead is 0.8 mile away.

To continue the hike, turn left (northeast) at the intersection and follow the pathway east. At mile 3.9 you cross a small bridge spanning the outlet creek of Escanaba Lake and follow the southeast shore of Lost Canoe Lake. As it leaves that lake, the trail ascends a

The hiking trail is color-coded and open for skiers in winter.
PREAMTIP SATASUK

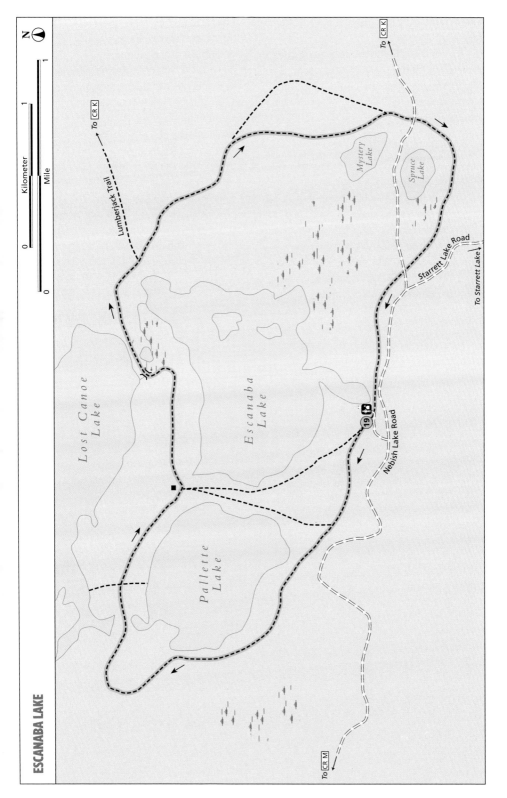

ESCANABA LAKE

N

Kilometer

0 1

Mile

0 1

To CR K

Lumberjack Trail

Lost Canoe Lake

Escanaba Lake

Pallette Lake

Mystery Lake

Spruce Lake

Starrett Lake Road

To Starrett Lake

Nebish Lake Road

19

To CR M

To CR K

piney ridge and a few minutes later descends in a tunnel of thick fir trees to the Lumberjack Trail junction (at mile 4.4). Go straight (south) on the boardwalk and continue to the trail split at mile 5.1. An open, logged area is in sight for a brief moment.

Take the "inside," or "Mystery Lake Trail," to the right (south) at the split and walk south through charming conifers and birch. A bench offers a convenient rest spot and a peek-a-boo look at Mystery Lake through the trees. At mile 5.9 the two trails rejoin and cross Nebish Lake Road at mile 6.0. The trail runs south and then west to round Spruce Lake and its marsh before again crossing Nebish Lake Road at mile 6.9 and reaching the trailhead at mile 7.7.

Options: One alternative would be to turn south from the shelter at mile 3.2, returning to the trailhead for an attractive 4.0-mile loop hike. Another choice would be to go north from the trailhead to the shelter and do the eastern ski loop of 5.5 miles. However, that route leaves out some of the best scenery on this trail system (in the Pallette Lake area). You could also enter the trail system from the north, picking up the Lumberjack Trail at CR K, 1.5 miles from its intersection with the Escanaba Trail. One option I would not recommend is the "outside" choice, as the trail splits at mile 5.1. The "Mystery Lake Trail" has more charm.

Local information: Vilas County Tourism, 330 Court St., Eagle River, 54521; (715) 479-3649; www.vilaswi.com

MILES AND DIRECTIONS

0.0   Start from the Escanaba Lake trailhead.

0.7   Bear left as the Yellow Trail departs right (north).

2.7   Cross the Pallette Lake–Lost Canoe Lake portage trail.

3.2   Pass the trail shelter, and turn left at the junction of Red and Blue Trails.

4.4   Bear right at the junction with the Lumberjack Trail.

5.1   At the trail split, take "inner," "Mystery Lake Trail" to the right.

6.0   Turn right at the trail junction and the trail crosses Nebish Lake Road southward.

6.9   Cross Nebish Lake Road northward.

7.7   Arrive back at the trailhead.

20 STAR LAKE

A pine-covered peninsula juts out into Star Lake, offering a scenic pass partly along the lakeshore but also upon a boardwalk with views into a bog.

Start: From the trailhead at the parking lot
Distance: 2.5-mile loop
Hiking time: About 1 hour
Difficulty: Easy
Trail surface: Dirt
Best season: April–October
Other trail users: None
Land status: State forest
Nearest town: Star Lake
Canine compatibility: Leashed dogs permitted
Fees and permits: State park vehicle sticker required

Schedule: Daily, 6 a.m. to 11 p.m.
Maps: Northern Highland–American Legion State Forest hiking map, USGS Star Lake (inc.) quad
Trail contact: Northern Highland–American Legion State Forest, Crystal Lake Visitor Station, 3237 Crystal Lake Rd., Boulder Junction, 54512; (715) 542-3923; https://dnr.wi.gov
Camping: There are eighteen drive-in sites at West Star Lake Campground just east of the trailhead.

FINDING THE TRAILHEAD

 From the village of Star Lake, go west 0.5 mile on Statehouse Road to the trailhead. GPS: N46 1.969' / W89 28.655'

THE HIKE

Few short trails offer such a strong sense of place as the Star Lake Hiking Trail does. Long stretches of windswept lake views and an intimate bog are part of its tour of a narrow peninsula protruding into Star Lake.

Two paths travel this peninsula, the hiking trail marked with brown signs featuring the figure of a hiker, and a nature trail, with its signs bearing the likeness of a hawk. The hiking trail and the nature trail share the same path for much of the route.

From the southern corner of the trailhead parking lot, pass a water pump and walk south, downhill, on a broad footpath. In this area near the trailhead, a jumble of paths can cause minor confusion. Sixty-five paces downhill from the parking lot, turn right (southwest) where an interpretive sign explains the role of red squirrels in the forest, a pine plantation dating from 1913.

Continue walking southwest. The trail soon turns into a boardwalk through a shady tamarack bog. At mile 0.4 turn left (south) on a 100-foot-long spur of the boardwalk to view the Black Lagoon, a dark, conifer-ringed pond.

Shortly after the Black Lagoon, the boardwalk segment ends. At mile 0.5 a trail junction appears. Stay left (south) on the hiking trail as the nature trail goes right. Soon after this junction the trail emerges onto the lakeshore, first traveling the side of a slope 15 feet above the water, then dropping to the water's edge.

After the confined space of the bog, the vast openness of the lake is an abrupt and pleasing change. The trail weaves its way along the shore, rounds the peninsula's tip, and starts its return to the northeast.

The trail passes through pine plantation near Star Lake.
PREAMTIP SATASUK

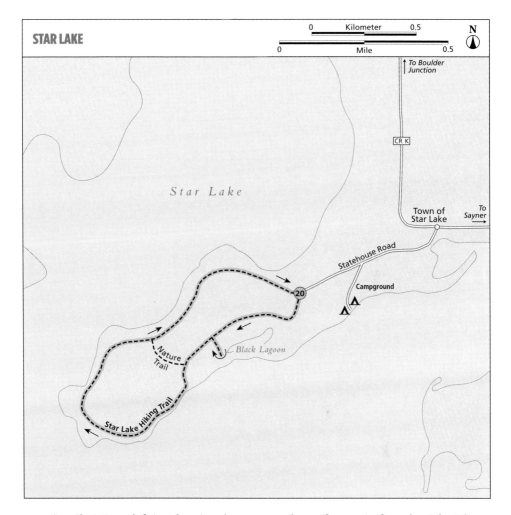

At mile 1.6 stay left (northeast) as the nature trail cutoff comes in from the right. The trail, again the combined route of the nature and hiking paths, continues northeast, near the shoreline. When it finally cuts inland, you are only a few minutes' walk from the trailhead and the end of the hike.

Local information: Vilas County Tourism, 330 Court St., Eagle River, 54521; (715) 479-3649; www.vilaswi.com

MILES AND DIRECTIONS

0.0 Start from the trailhead.

0.4 Take the boardwalk spur to view Black Lagoon.

0.5 Go left at the junction with the Nature Trail.

1.6 Stay left as the Nature Trail rejoins from the right.

2.5 Arrive back at the trailhead.

21 HIDDEN LAKES

This fantastic trek through the Chequamegon-Nicolet National Forest passes ten lakes on its enormous loop, most of them only reachable by hikers. Plan for a full day of hiking or consider staying the night.

Start: From the trailhead in the Franklin Lake Nature Trail parking lot
Distance: 13.3-mile loop
Hiking time: About 6 hours or overnight
Difficulty: Difficult
Trail surface: Dirt
Best season: April–October
Other trail users: None
Land status: National forest
Nearest town: Eagle River
Canine compatibility: Leashed dogs permitted
Fees and permits: Daily parking fee required
Schedule: Daily, 6 a.m. to 11 p.m.
Maps: Chequamegon-Nicolet Hidden Lakes Trail Map, USGS Anvil Lake (inc.) and Alvin Northwest (inc.) quads

Trail contact: Chequamegon-Nicolet National Forest, Eagle River-Florence Ranger District, 1247 E. Wall St., Eagle River, 54521; (715) 479-2827; https://www.fs.usda.gov
Special considerations: Although the trail is a well-marked one, it passes many intersections with old woods roads and other footpaths. Remember that only the Hidden Lakes Trail uses white diamond markings.
Camping: The Hidden Lakes Trail is on national forest land, and camping is permitted along the trail. Campsites must be at least 100 feet away from the trail or water's edge. Franklin Lake Campground, adjacent to the trailhead, has seventy-seven drive-in sites.

FINDING THE TRAILHEAD

From Eagle River, drive 9.3 miles east on WI 70 and turn right (south) on FR 2178, Military Road. After 2.7 miles turn left (east) on FR 2181, Butternut Lake Road. Drive 4.7 miles east and turn right (east) into the trailhead parking area. GPS: N45 55.534' / W88 59.736'

THE HIKE

The Hidden Lakes Trail has no trouble living up to its name. Ten lakes border this route, with eight of them tucked away in quiet corners of the forest. The ambiance is noteworthy. This path meanders past lakes and wanders through hemlock groves with hardly a cabin or building in sight during the entire length of the hike. Its 13.3-mile length makes it a good choice for an energetic day hike or an overnight backpack.

Begin the loop at the Franklin Lake Nature Trail parking lot. Walk south, following the nature trail loop as it swings east through an ancient grove of hemlock trees. The broad trail passes near the shore of Butternut Lake, turns north, and comes to an intersection (featuring a map), with the Hidden Lakes Trail at mile 0.4. Turn right (northeast) on this narrow but well-marked path. The trail runs northeast almost 1.0 mile along a pleasant, low ridge, before rounding the north end of Two Dutchmen Lake. Turning southwest, it runs to the north end of Three Johns Lake, skirts that lake's eastern shore, and crosses FR 2140 at mile 2.7.

Trail bridges span places where hikers once needed to get their feet wet. PREAMTIP SATASUK

Continue walking south, arriving at North Branch Pine River, the outlet of Butternut Lake, at mile 3.8. Cross the bridge and on the south side of the stream, a grassy knoll offers broad views of Butternut Lake and a good break spot.

The trail continues southward and at mile 4.3 intersects the Luna Lake Loop Trail. Bear right (southwest) at this junction as well as at three more in the next mile as your route rounds the northwest shores of scenic Luna and White Deer Lakes.

From the southwest corner of White Deer Lake, the Hidden Lakes Trail runs southwest, passing FR 2179 at mile 6.0. It then passes through spectacular hemlock groves near Four Ducks Lake at mile 6.4 and again near Harriet Lake a quarter mile farther west. Pay attention to the white diamond markers here, because the trail switches from a path to old woods roads several times.

Resuming its westward march, the trail runs through an extensive section of hardwood forest, crosses FR 2179 again at mile 8.1, and doglegs northwest to Pat Shay Lake. Hemlocks sprinkle the slope leading down to the lake to the south.

From the northwest corner of Pat Shay Lake, the trail runs north, following one of the broad ski trails of the Eagle River Nordic system, as it will for the next 3.0 miles. The trail travels a narrow isthmus between wetlands and arrives at a three-sided trail shelter at mile 10.3.

Continuing north, the Hidden Lakes Trail crosses FR 2181 at mile 11.4, turns northeast, and arrives at the Franklin Lake boat ramp at mile 13.2. From there it is little more than 100 yards east along FR 2181 to the trailhead at mile 13.3.

Local information: Vilas County Tourism, 330 Court St., Eagle River, 54521; (715) 479-3649; www.vilaswi.com

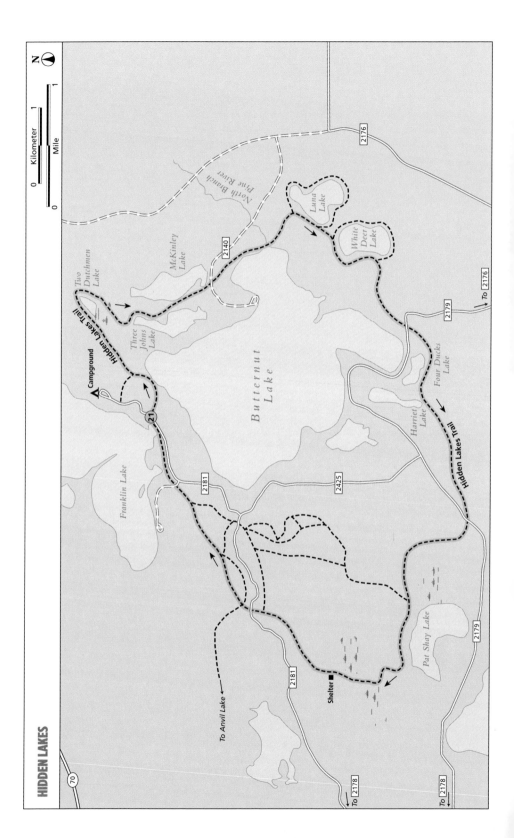

HIDDEN LAKES

N

Two Dutchmen Lake

Hidden Lakes Trail

Campground

Three Johns Lake

McKinley Lake

North Branch Pine River

Luna Lake

White Deer Lake

Butternut Lake

2140

Franklin Lake

2181

2425

Harriet Lake

Four Ducks Lake

2179

To 2176

2176

Hidden Lakes Trail

To Anvil Lake

2181

Shelter

Pat Shay Lake

2179

To 2178

2178

To 2178

0 Kilometer 1

0 Mile 1

A view of Franklin Lake at the beginning and end of the hike

MILES AND DIRECTIONS

0.0   Start from the Franklin Lake Nature Trail trailhead.

0.4   At Hidden Lakes Trail junction, turn right.

1.8   Round the north end of Three Johns Lake.

2.7   Cross FR 2140.

3.8   Take the bridge over North Branch Pine River.

4.3   At Luna Lake Trail junction, bear right.

5.3   Bear right at White Deer Lake Trail junction (southwest).

6.0   Cross FR 2179.

6.4   Pass Four Ducks Lake.

8.1   Cross FR 2179.

10.3 Pass the trail shelter.

11.4 Cross FR 2181.

13.2 Arrive at Franklin Lake boat ramp.

13.3 Cross the park road to arrive back at the trailhead.

22 LASALLE FALLS

A short hike with a moderate climb through some pristine forest leads to a thundering cascade along the wild and scenic Pine River.

Start: From the trailhead in the parking lot
Distance: 2.2-mile out-and-back
Hiking time: 1 hour
Difficulty: Easy
Trail surface: Dirt, crushed rock
Best season: May–October
Other trail users: None
Land status: County and state land
Nearest town: Florence
Canine compatibility: Leashed dogs permitted

Fees and permits: None
Schedule: Daily, 6 a.m. to 11 p.m.
Maps: USGS Florence SE (inc.) quad
Trail contact: Wild River Interpretive Center & Tourism, 5628 Forestry Dr., Florence, 54121; (888) 889-0049; www.exploreflorencecounty.com
Special considerations: Use caution near the waterfall. Be aware that the prime viewing spot is actually an overhang.

FINDING THE TRAILHEAD

From Florence, drive 9.0 miles south on CR N and another quarter mile south on CR U. Turn right (west) on CR C, drive 1.9 miles, and turn right (northwest) on LaSalle Falls Road (dirt). Drive 2.6 miles to a small parking area on the right (north) side of the road. GPS: N45 49.280' / W88 17.236'

LaSalle Falls on the Pine River is longer than it is tall.

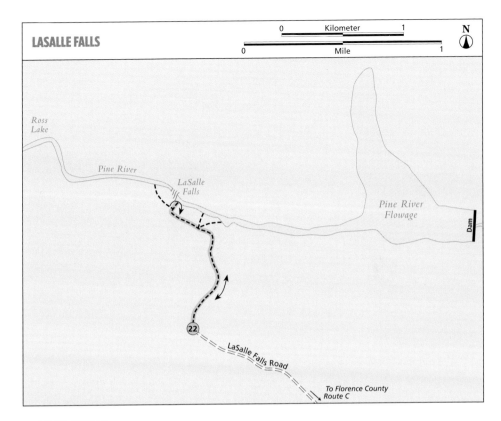

0   Kilometer   1

0   Mile   1

N

Ross Lake

Pine River

LaSalle Falls

Pine River Flowage

Dam

22

LaSalle Falls Road

To Florence County Route C

THE HIKE

As you emerge from your car at the LaSalle Falls trailhead, the first thing you notice is the woods, a mixture of conifers and hardwoods. They are a relief for the eyes after driving in through miles of pine plantations and logging debris. Soon you realize that there is a complete lack of road noise in the background.

This walk takes you through a state-designated Wild and Scenic River Corridor. A sign at the small parking area announces the river project and provides a map of the trail. Begin by walking north from the parking area. Constructed wood-beam steps announce the beginning of a short ascent, and at mile 0.5 you pass a bench and a small creek.

After 0.8 mile you hear the sound of falling water and find yourself at a fork in the trail featuring a sign that reads "End of Designated Trail." Use care near bluffs and waterfalls. A bench and boulder also mark this junction. To your right (northeast) a trail leads to a "gorge overlook" that is not noteworthy. Another trail, the portage trail that allows paddlers to bypass the falls, immediately branches east from the gorge trail. Take the left (northwest) fork of the trail, ascend a small ridge, and proceed another 0.3 mile to the waterfall.

The sound of falling water increases as you descend the ridge and find several paths leading to your right (north) to the top of the cliff above the falls. Careful investigation reveals one that leads to an overlook directly above the foaming cascade. Be aware that this overlook is more than a sheer drop; it is an overhang. Just to the south of this over-hang, a steep scramble down a gully leads you to a spot below the falls' 20-foot drop. A

The view from above LaSalle Falls

few feet back from the overhang, the portage path continues north to the calmer waters above the falls. To return, retrace your steps to the trailhead.

Local information: Wild River Interpretive Center & Tourism, 5628 Forestry Dr., Florence, 54121; (888) 889-0049; www.exploreflorencecounty.com

Other attractions: Paddle the Pine River. See FalconGuides *Paddling Wisconsin*.

MILES AND DIRECTIONS

0.0 Start from the trailhead.

0.5 Pass a bench and small creek.

0.8 Bear left at a fork at "End of Designated Trail" sign.

1.1 Arrive at LaSalle Falls.

2.2 Arrive at the trailhead.

23 GLACIAL POTHOLES

The western terminus of the Ice Age National Scenic Trail appropriately lies within this state park where you can look out over the St. Croix River and find geological features known as "potholes," created by meltwater drainage of a glacial lake. Expect great views of the river, canyon, rock formations, and a waterfall.

Start: From the Pothole Trail trailhead at the parking lot
Distance: 8.9-mile lollipop with two stems
Hiking time: 4 hours
Difficulty: Moderate
Trail surface: Dirt
Best season: April–October
Other trail users: None
Land status: State park
Nearest town: St. Croix Falls
Canine compatibility: Leashed dogs permitted

Fees and permits: State park vehicle sticker required
Schedule: Daily, 6 a.m. to 11 p.m.
Maps: Interstate Park (WI) Hiking Map, Interstate State Park (MN) Map, USGS St. Croix Dalles (inc.) quad
Trail contact: Interstate State Park, WI 35, St. Croix Falls, 54024; (715) 483-3747; https://dnr.wi.gov
Camping: There are eighty-two drive-in sites in Interstate Park.

FINDING THE TRAILHEAD

From the intersection of US 8 and WI 35 (at St. Croix Falls), drive south 0.6 mile, then turn right (west) into Interstate Park. Drive 1.5 miles northwest on the park road (get a trail map at the entrance station), then turn right (north) on the road that leads to the north campground and park at the Pothole Trail trailhead. GPS: N45 24.024' / W92 38.861'

THE HIKE

Ten thousand years ago, glacial Lake Duluth rose hundreds of feet above the present level of Lake Superior. Ice blocked the present eastern drainage of the lake near Sault Ste. Marie. The meltwater of a vast ice field 5,000 feet thick and the size of the state of Minnesota began to flow south past this point.

That incredible current was the source of Interstate Park's famous potholes and rock formations. Giant eddies swirled silt and rocks into the rock in a scouring motion that drilled holes as large as 20 feet in diameter and 60 feet in depth. Riverside cliffs, known as the Dalles of the St. Croix, also owe their shape to the glacial torrent.

For sheer variety this hike's route is hard to beat. It starts with glacial potholes and wanders through the intricate topography of the Dalles before heading south to a quiet waterfall. Returning north, it travels through a classic hardwood forest on the Skyline Trail. It then crosses to the Minnesota side of the river for a dramatic finish, a tour of the largest glacial potholes in the world.

From the Pothole Trail parking lot, turn right (northwest) and begin walking the Pothole Trail loop in a counterclockwise direction. This rock and gravel path, the westernmost segment of the 1,000-mile-long Ice Age Trail, descends to views of the river gorge and pothole-pocked bedrock. It then loops back to your starting point at mile 0.4.

Potholes created by stones whirling in glacial meltwater rushing past thousands of years ago

Walk southeast, crossing the road, and ascend the broad gravel path of the Horizon Rock Trail to the Meadow Valley Trail junction at mile 0.6. Turn right (southwest) on the Meadow Valley Trail and descend rocky switchbacks to the damp hollow below. The transition from a dry, rock-top climate to the moist nook below is striking. Continue walking south, ignoring a spur to the right (west), until you emerge at a picnic area. Turn right (west), walking 100 yards across a grassy lawn to the park road. Turn right (north), walking 70 yards on the road to the Summit Rock Trail at mile 1.0.

Take the rocky Summit Rock Trail due north, past the Echo Canyon Trail that branches off to the left (west), to a rock outcrop offering broad views north along the river. Continue southwest to a junction with the Echo Canyon Trail at mile 1.4 and turn right (west). That path offers more river vistas before heading south to a junction with the Lake O' the Dalles Nature Trail at mile 1.9. Turn right (west) and 20 feet farther turn right (north) again on the River Bluff Trail.

The River Bluff Trail climbs, passing a small pond on the left, to more river views and then descends to the south, emerging onto a grassy flat. Turn east, intersect the Lake O' the Dalles Nature Trail, and turn right (south) on it. At the south end of Lake O' the Dalles, leave the nature trail and continue walking south through picnic areas to the Pines Group Camp and the Silverbrook Trail at mile 3.6.

Follow the Silverbrook Trail, a lane that was the original road from St. Croix Falls to Osceola, as it runs southwest, first on the edge of a marsh, then in woods. A quarter mile before the end, a fork swings left, upslope. Ignore it, and take the right (graveled) fork to the end of the trail. Silverbrook Falls, an 18-foot drop, is visible through the trees at mile 4.8.

A view of the St. Croix River from the cliff top

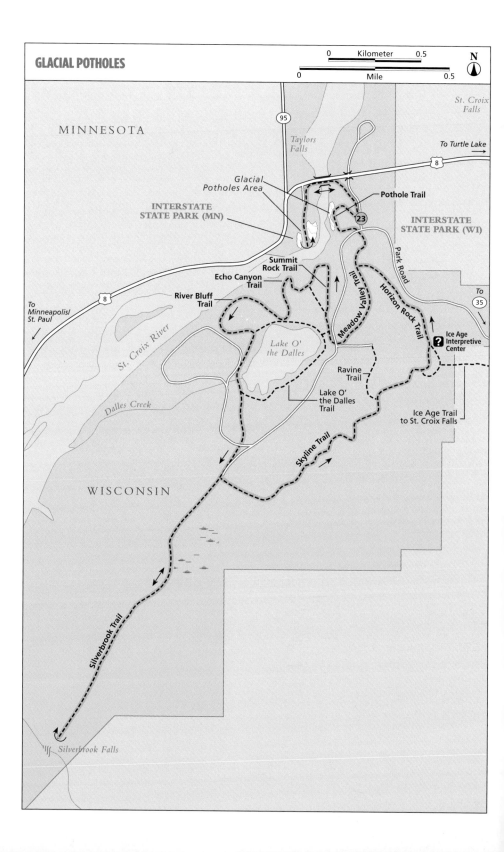

GLACIAL POTHOLES

0 Kilometer 0.5

0 Mile 0.5

N

St. Croix Falls

MINNESOTA

95

Taylors Falls

To Turtle Lake

8

Glacial Potholes Area

Pothole Trail

INTERSTATE STATE PARK (MN)

23

INTERSTATE STATE PARK (WI)

Summit Rock Trail

Echo Canyon Trail

River Bluff Trail

8

To Minneapolis/ St. Paul

St. Croix River

Lake O' the Dalles

Meadow Valley Trail

Horizon Rock Trail

Park Road

To 35

Ice Age Interpretive Center

Ravine Trail

Dalles Creek

Lake O' the Dalles Trail

Ice Age Trail to St. Croix Falls

Skyline Trail

WISCONSIN

Silverbrook Trail

Silverbrook Falls

Retrace your steps to the trailhead for the Silverbrook Trail, mile 6.0, and turn right (east) to begin the Skyline Trail. That path ascends steeply through the glen of a charming brook, your first taste of the pleasant hardwood forest you will sample for 0.5 mile. After climbing to the wooded rim of the valley, the trail winds along the top of the slope. Bear right (north) as the Ravine Trail descends to the left (west) at mile 7.0. In the next half mile bear left (north) as the Skyline Trail and the Ice Age Trail enter from the right. At mile 7.6 the trail arrives at the Ice Age Interpretive Center and the beginning of the Horizon Rock Trail. Follow that path north to your point of origin, the trailhead for Pothole Trail.

From the trailhead it is a mere 400-yard walk to the Minnesota park. Two hundred yards north of this point, the park road goes under US 8, the bridge to the Minnesota side. Walk north on the road and take note of a well-worn path, beginning at the guardrail that goes up the slope to US 8. Being careful to avoid poison ivy in the area, take that unofficial path to the northwest to the sidewalk along US 8. Walk west across the bridge, taking in the fine views of the Dalles downstream.

Bear left (south) as you leave the bridge, pass the entrance to the tour boat dock, and walk south through the parking lot to the building at its south end. Pick up a map of Minnesota's state park there.

South of this point a system of constructed trails winds through a compact, 100-yard-long area containing spectacular glacial potholes. One good choice is to follow the self-guided Pothole Trail, which features a tunnel into one of the largest potholes, Bake Oven, at mile 8.5. When you are ready, retrace your steps to the bridge and return to the Wisconsin side and the start of the hike, the Pothole Trail trailhead.

Options: Any of the numerous small loops that are components of this hike could be eliminated to shorten the distance. Also, cutting out the Silverbrook Falls out-and-back segment would trim off 2.4 miles.

Local information: Polk County Information Center, 710 WI 35 S., St. Croix Falls, 54024; (800) 222-7655; www.polkcountytourism.com

MILES AND DIRECTIONS

0.0 Start northwest from the Pothole Trail parking lot.

0.4 Back at the lot, take the Horizon Rock Trail.

0.6 Turn right on the Meadow Valley Trail.

1.0 Turn right at picnic area and walk the road to Summit Rock Trail.

1.4 Take Echo Canyon Trail to the right.

1.9 Turn right on Lake O' the Dalles Trail and again immediately on River Bluff Trail.

2.6 Take Lake O' the Dalles Nature Trail to the right.

3.6 Cross picnic area to the trailhead of the Silverbrook Trail.

4.8 See Silverbrook Falls.

6.0 Return to the trailhead of the Silverbrook Trail and go right on Skyline Trail.

7.0 Bear right at the Ravine Trail junction.

7.6 At Ice Age Interpretive Center, take Horizon Rock Trail.

8.1 Cross Pothole Trail parking lot and follow park road to US 8.

8.5 Turn around at Bake Oven pothole in Interstate State Park on the Minnesota side.

8.9 Arrive back at the Pothole Trail parking lot.

24 CHIPPEWA MORAINE CIRCLE TRAIL

A shorter hike through Ice Age Trail country, this loop follows the national scenic trail a short distance before following a loop through kettle lakes and along the back of an esker.

Start: From the trailhead near the visitor center
Distance: 4.5-mile loop
Hiking time: About 2 hours
Difficulty: Easy
Trail surface: Dirt
Best season: April–October
Other trail users: None
Land status: State land
Nearest town: New Auburn
Canine compatibility: Leashed dogs permitted
Fees and permits: State park vehicle sticker required. However, Chippewa Moraine State Recreation Area is part of the Ice Age National Scientific Reserve, so federal passes are honored.
Schedule: Daily, 6 a.m. to 11 p.m.

Maps: Chippewa Moraine Interpretive Center Trail Map, Ice Age Trail Atlas Segment Map #15, USGS Marsh-Miller Lake (inc.) quad
Trail contact: Chippewa Moraine State Recreation Area, 13394 CR M, New Auburn, 54757; (715) 967-2800; https://dnr.wi.gov
Special considerations: An excellent "Hiking Field Trip Guide for Glacial Landforms" handout is available from the interpretive center. Check with the staff there for seasonal wildlife-watching opportunities.
Camping: Morris-Erickson County Park, 5.0 miles north, has thirty drive-in sites. Check with the staff at the interpretive center for availability of backpacking sites and designated dispersed camping areas.

FINDING THE TRAILHEAD

From New Auburn, drive 7.0 miles east on Chippewa CR M and turn left (north) into the Chippewa Moraine Interpretive Center drive. Drive 0.2 mile north to the center and park. GPS: N45 13.430' / W91 24.826'

THE HIKE

Wisconsin has no shortage of glacial scenery and place names bearing the word "moraine." The Chippewa Moraine, though, is something special. Here there's an eye-pleasing symmetry to the pattern of rounded hilltops and reflecting lakes. Unlike southeastern Wisconsin's Kettle Moraine, where the glaciers' forward movement formed the moraines, this landscape is a result of glacial ice that stopped moving. After the glacier's horizontal movement ceased, its surface debris flowed into low spots in the ice. Those accumulations of rock debris formed the hills, called hummocks, and depressions formed by large chunks of ice, thicker spots in the ice sheet, melted to become the kettle lakes.

A loop trail of just under 5.0 miles meanders through these jumbled hills, passing seventeen lakes along the way. To take the circle tour, begin by walking northeast from the interpretive center on a short connector trail that drops steeply to a junction with the Circle Trail at mile 0.1. Bear right (north) at that intersection, beginning a clockwise circuit of the loop.

The Circle Trail uses a bit of Ice Age Trail
before breaking off on its own.

CHIPPEWA MORAINE CIRCLE TRAIL

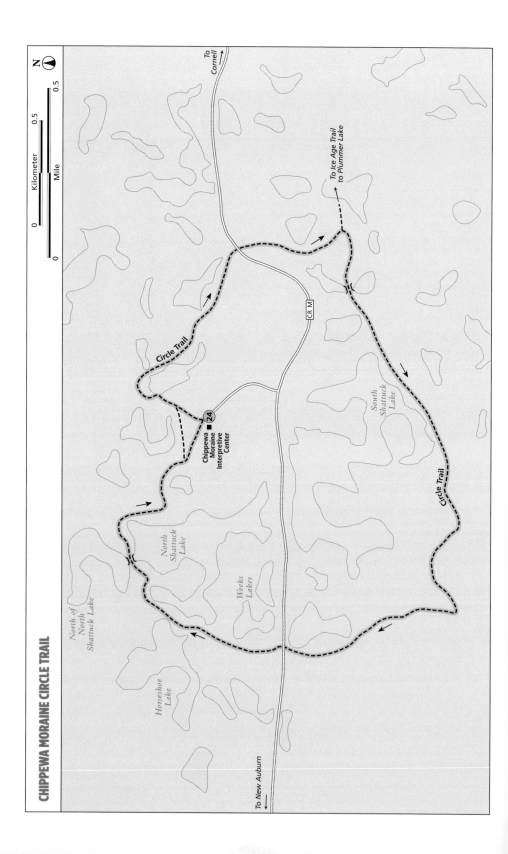

A prairie overlook with abundant wildflowers near the Circle Trail trailhead

As you walk east on the Circle Trail, the land's inherent beauty is apparent. The trail rounds one kettle lake, passes another, and ascends to a scenic bench above a third. It crosses CR M at mile 0.9, climbs to the top of a moraine, and rolls south, passing between two more lakes. Bear right (southwest) at mile 1.4, an intersection with the Ice Age Trail.

The Circle Trail drops from the intersection's knoll, heading west past small lakes, birch trees, and a 0.5-mile-long stretch of South Shattuck Lake's shoreline. After a turn north, the path follows the top of a glacial esker, a low ridge of sediment from a glacial stream, at mile 2.9. Still heading north, it crosses CR M a second time at mile 3.4.

Lakes are seldom out of sight. The Circle Trail heads north, passing two of the Weeks Lakes and along an isthmus between Horseshoe Lake and North Shattuck Lake.

A trail bridge crosses a channel between North Shattuck Lake and a body of water known as North of North Shattuck Lake. Just before the bridge, a bench sits under pine trees, offering a fine view of the lakes. The trail swings south, meeting a connector trail leading to the interpretive center at mile 4.4. Bear right (southeast) at that junction and ascend back to the trailhead at mile 4.5.

Local information: Explore Chippewa County, 1 N. Bridge St., Chippewa Falls, 54729; (715) 723-0331; www.gochippewacounty.com

MILES AND DIRECTIONS

0.0   Start at the trailhead.

0.1   Turn right at the Circle Trail junction.

0.9   Cross Chippewa CR M (east crossing).

1.4   Bear right at the Ice Age Trail junction to stay on the Circle Trail.

2.9   Hike along the back of an esker.

3.4   Cross CR M (west crossing).

4.4   Turn right at the interpretive center spur trail junction.

4.5   Arrive back at the trailhead.

25 CHIPPEWA MORAINE/ PLUMMER LAKE

This section of the Ice Age National Scenic Trail even comes with an interpretive center. Learn about the geological features before you pass them. Along the rising and falling terrain, you will pass no fewer than twenty kettle lakes.

Start: From the Circle Trail trailhead at the interpretive center
Distance: 12.2-mile out-and-back
Hiking time: About 5 hours
Difficulty: Difficult
Trail surface: Dirt
Best season: April–October
Other trail users: None
Land status: State land
Nearest town: New Auburn
Canine compatibility: Leashed dogs permitted
Fees and permits: State park vehicle sticker required. However, Chippewa Moraine State Recreation Area is part of the Ice Age National Scientific Reserve, so federal passes are honored.
Schedule: Daily, 6 a.m. to 11 p.m.
Maps: Chippewa Moraine Interpretive Center Trail Map, Ice Age Trail Atlas Segment Map #15, USGS Marsh-Miller Lake (inc.) and Bob Lake (inc.) quads
Trail contact: Chippewa Moraine State Recreation Area, 13394 CR M, New Auburn, 54757; (715) 967-2800; https://dnr.wi.gov. Ice Age Trail Alliance, 2110 Main St., Cross Plains, 53528; (800) 227-0046; www.iceagetrail.org.
Special considerations: An excellent "Hiking Field Trip Guide for Glacial Landforms" handout is available from the interpretive center.
Camping: Backpack camping on county forest land east of the Circle Trail is allowed as long as you are 100 feet from the trail or water's edge. Check with the interpretive center for current regulations and new designated backpacking sites. Morris-Erickson County Park, 5.0 miles north, has thirty drive-in sites.

FINDING THE TRAILHEAD

 From New Auburn, drive 7.0 miles east on CR M and turn left (north) into the Chippewa Moraine Interpretive Center drive. Drive 0.2 mile north to the center and park. GPS: N45 13.430' / W91 24.826'

THE HIKE

Any short walk on the Chippewa Moraine's Circle Trail offers views full of beautiful rounded hills and kettle lakes. Hike the Ice Age Trail east from there and the scenery never lets up, while the trail just keeps getting quieter.

Start by walking northeast from the interpretive center, descending on a connector trail. Bear right (north) at a junction with the Circle Trail at mile 0.1 and swing around the shoreline of a beautiful kettle lake, a first glimpse of what is to come. The trail runs east, passing a bench above another lake, and crosses Chippewa CR M at mile 0.9.

Turning south, the pathway ascends a moraine, passes between two more kettle lakes, and reaches a junction with the Ice Age Trail on the top of a knoll at mile 1.4. Bear left (east), descending to pass three more lakes and a pine plantation before crossing Ice Age Drive at mile 2.1.

Plummer Lake, the turnaround point for this hike

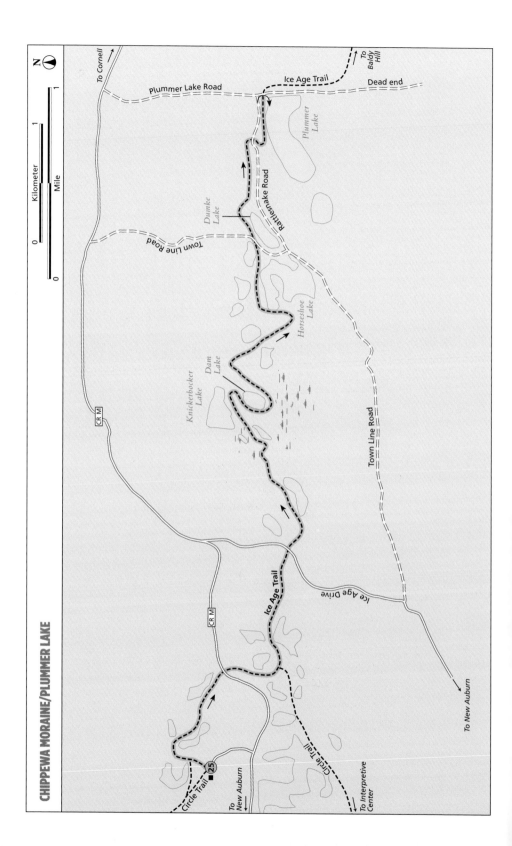

CHIPPEWA MORAINE/PLUMMER LAKE

N

To Cornell

Plummer Lake Road

Ice Age Trail

To Baldy Hill

Dead end

Plummer Lake

Rattlesnake Road

Dunke Lake

Town Line Road

Horseshoe Lake

Knickerbocker Lake

Dam Lake

CR M

CR M

Ice Age Trail

Ice Age Drive

Town Line Road

To New Auburn

Circle Trail

25

Circle Trail

To New Auburn

To Interpretive Center

Kilometer

Mile

1

1

0

0

1

The trail skirts the shore of a fine kettle lake 0.25 mile farther on. A bench under pine trees offers a prime spot for a break and contemplation. Continue walking east as the trail enters a hardwood forest in hilly terrain. A marsh and Knickerbocker Lake are nearby to the north before the trail loops south to Dam Lake, passing the outlet at mile 3.5. Check the marsh south of the outlet for sandhill cranes.

The Ice Age Trail then follows Dam Lake's shore northeast through rolling hills before turning south to Horseshoe Lake, reaching its western end at mile 4.4. This is a quiet and remote stretch of trail.

Follow the trail east along Horseshoe Lake's northern shore to Town Line Road at mile 4.9. Continue hiking east, passing Dumke Lake and ascending to a broad, flat plateau, a glacial feature known as an ice-walled-lake plain. During the glacial era, surface debris covered a rim of stagnant ice surrounding a lake here. Clay and sediment filled the lake, and the ice melted. This left a flat plain, rimmed by the debris and elevated above the surrounding land. A glacial stream drainage, 10 to 40 feet deep, trenches this plain to the northeast.

Resume hiking east. The trail drops from the plateau and follows Rattlesnake Road east for 500 feet. It then parallels the road to its south, following Plummer Lake's shoreline to Plummer Lake Road at mile 6.1. This is a good turnaround spot for the hike.

Options: The Ice Age Trail continues east on the roughly 6.0-mile Harwood Lakes Segment to CR E. Head south about 300 yards on Plummer Lake Road and the trail leaves the road on the east side across from the parking area. Dispersed camping is permitted toward the eastern end of this segment, which would serve overnight hikers well.

Local information: Explore Chippewa County, 1 N. Bridge St., Chippewa Falls, 54729; (715) 723-0331; www.gochippewacounty.com

MILES AND DIRECTIONS

0.0   Start at the trailhead.

0.1   Turn right at Circle Trail junction.

0.9   Cross CR M.

1.4   At Ice Age Trail junction, bear left.

2.1   Cross Ice Age Drive.

3.5   Pass the Dam Lake outlet.

4.4   Pass the western end of Horseshoe Lake.

4.9   Cross Town Line Road.

6.1   Turn around at Plummer Lake Road.

12.2 Arrive back at the trailhead.

26 JERRY LAKE

This woodland hike takes you through national forest without requiring a trip far up north. It's pristine, it's secluded, and the length gives you a full day far from civilization.

Start: From the trailhead on FR 102 west of the parking area
Distance: 13.1-mile shuttle
Hiking time: 5 hours
Difficulty: Difficult
Trail surface: Dirt
Best season: April–October
Other trail users: None
Land status: National forest
Nearest town: Medford
Canine compatibility: Leashed dogs permitted
Fees and permits: None
Schedule: Daily
Maps: Chequamegon-Nicolet National Forest Ice Age National Scenic Trail Map, Ice Age Trail Atlas, Jerry Lake Segment Map #22, USGS Mondeaux Dam (inc.), Jump River Fire Tower (inc.), and Perkinstown (inc.) quads
Trail contact: Chequamegon-Nicolet National Forest, Medford-Park Falls Ranger District, 850 N. 8th, WI 13,

Medford, 54451; (715) 748-4875; www.fs.usda.gov. Ice Age Trail Alliance, 2110 Main St., Cross Plains, 53528; (800) 227-0046; www.iceagetrail.org.
Special considerations: The Ice Age Trail is closed during the gun deer-hunting season. This is usually, but not exclusively, during Thanksgiving week. Waterproof boots and trekking poles come in handy for wet spots.
Camping: You can backpack camp anywhere along the trail as long as you are 200 feet off the trail and 200 feet from water. A designated campsite is at Jerry Lake. Mondeaux Flowage, 5.0 miles east of the trailhead, has three national forest rustic campgrounds with drive-in sites: West Point (thirteen), Eastwood (twelve), and Spearhead Point (twenty-seven), plus four walk-in sites at Picnic Point.

FINDING THE TRAILHEAD

From Medford, drive north 4.9 miles on WI 13 and turn left (west) on CR M. Drive west 7.6 miles and turn right (north) on CR E. Take CR E north 6.4 miles and turn left (west) on FR 102 (also Mondeaux Avenue). Drive 1.6 miles west past the bridge over the North Fork of the Yellow River and turn left (south) at a small parking area for hunters. (Do not confuse this with the White Birch Trail parking area.) Park here, but do not block the gate. GPS: N45 17.585' / W90 29.974'

THE HIKE

This stretch of the Ice Age Trail is an undiscovered gem. If you like quiet, woodland walks on narrow, intimate footpaths, push this hike to the top of your list. Mile after mile of soul-satisfying, deep-woods ambiance rolls by, while the sight of another hiker is a rarity.

Wolves are raising pups in the area. Bald eagles circle over the rivers, otters leave their tracks below, and sandhill cranes trumpet across the marshes. Hemlock groves, birch stands, hardwood forests, verdant wetlands, and clear-running streams border the trail. What's not to like?

The trail comes from the east, crossing North Fork Yellow River with the bridge on FR 102. Begin your hike from the parking area there, heading west on a path marked

The Ice Age Trail's simple footpath
on its way to Jerry Lake
PREAMTIP SATASUK

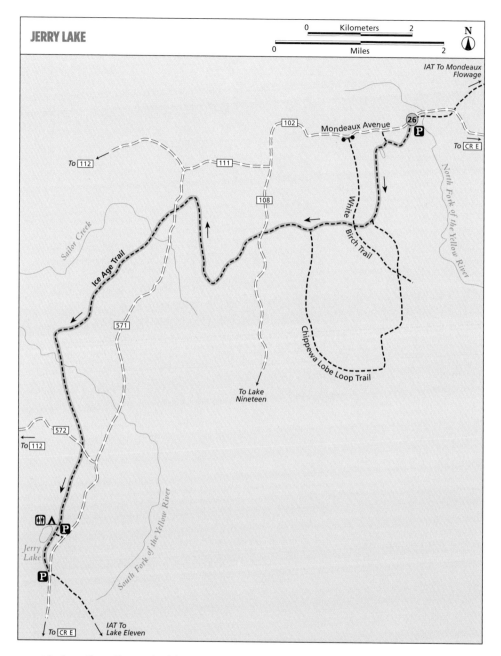

with the yellow diamond of the Ice Age Trail. A wet stretch, decorated with memorable clumps of moss, announces your arrival at a small pond 0.5 mile farther.

The trail rounds the pond—as a spur trail joins from the right (north) directly from FR 102—and enters a hardwood forest as it runs south. At mile 1.4 turn right (southwest) at the junction (eastern) with the Chippewa Lobe Loop Trail. Again a footpath, the trail runs through a pleasant stretch of birches and pines, crossing the grassy lane called the

White Birch Trail, 0.5 mile farther. A section of open hardwood forest follows before the trail arrives at the Chippewa Lobe Loop Trail junction (western) at mile 3.1.

Bear right (west) and follow the Ice Age Trail around the north edge of a wide wetland extending to the south. In June look for orchids on the edge of the bog. On the northwest corner of the swamp, the trail rises into an upland forest and at mile 3.9 arrives at FR 108.

As you walk west from the road, watch for the yellow trail markings if the lack of wear isn't clear enough to mark your way.

The trail meanders southwest for more than a mile before taking a long, nearly mile-long run north along the back of Hemlock Esker, giving you a view of the surrounding forest from 80 feet of elevation. That northward leg begins in a fine birch stand. Dropping off the esker, the Ice Age Trail turns to the southwest and crosses FR 571 at mile 6.9.

Follow the trail southwest from FR 571, and you can see signage for a primitive campsite situated about 150 feet northeast (to the right side of the trail). Soon after, cross Sailor Creek on a small bridge at mile 7.5. The trail continues southwest, passing several grassy but passable roads and an ATV trail before arriving at the South Fork of the Yellow River at mile 10.1. The water is wide but spanned by a 67-foot bridge built by volunteers back in 2012.

After crossing the river, the trail continues south and ascends a low ridge that features the finest hemlock grove of the hike. Continuing a slow rise, the trail meets FR 572 at mile 11.5.

Resuming its southward march, the path ascends slightly through an open hardwood forest and passes a young hemlock grove. A marsh on Jerry Lake's north end appears and then Jerry Lake itself, a pleasant, large pond. A designated campsite and pit toilets are in the woods a short distance in from the lake's northeast corner, at mile 12.9.

Follow the trail south. A spur trail leads 0.2 mile east to a small alternative parking spot on FR 571. Your route, the Ice Age Trail, continues a bit farther but also exits to FR 571 at mile 13.1, the end of the hike.

Local information: Taylor County Tourism, 104 E. Perkins St., Medford, 54451; (715) 748-4729; www.taylorcountytourism.com

MILES AND DIRECTIONS

0.0 Start from FR 102.

1.4 Bear right at the Chippewa Lobe Loop Trail junction (eastern).

3.1 Bear right again at the Chippewa Lobe Loop Trail junction (western).

3.9 Cross FR 108.

6.9 Cross FR 571.

10.1 Cross South Fork of the Yellow River.

11.5 Cross FR 572.

13.0 Pass Jerry Lake on your right and a spur trail on the left.

13.1 Arrive at FR 571 and the end of the hike.

27 **CHIPPEWA LOBE**

Embedded within the outstanding Jerry Lake Segment of the Ice Age National Scenic Trail, this is a shorter option for a day hike and doesn't require a shuttle.

Start: From the trailhead on the east side of FR 108/Lake 19 Road
Distance: 9.3-mile lollipop
Hiking time: About 4 hours
Difficulty: Difficult
Trail surface: Dirt
Best season: April–October
Other trail users: None
Land status: National forest
Nearest town: Medford
Canine compatibility: Leashed dogs permitted
Fees and permits: None
Schedule: Daily
Maps: Chequamegon-Nicolet National Forest Ice Age National Scenic Trail Map, Ice Age Trail Atlas, Jerry Lake Segment Map #22, USGS Mondeaux Dam (inc.), Jump River Fire Tower (inc.), and Perkinstown (inc.) quads
Trail contact: Chequamegon-Nicolet National Forest, Medford-Park Falls Ranger District, 850 N. 8th, WI 13, Medford, 54451; (715) 748-4875; www.fs.usda.gov. Ice Age Trail Alliance, 2110 Main St., Cross Plains, 53528; (800) 227-0046; www.iceagetrail.org.

Special considerations: The Ice Age Trail is closed during the gun deer-hunting season. This is usually, but not exclusively, during Thanksgiving week. Waterproof boots and trekking poles come in handy for wet spots and crossing beaver dams, and during wet periods you can expect those areas to expand. I found this loop very well marked, with blue diamonds at short intervals. Wear marks are often faint, however, and without those markings this loop would be very difficult, if not impossible, to follow.
Camping: A fine designated campsite with pit toilets is at the south end of the loop. You can camp anywhere along the trail as long as you are 200 feet off the trail and 200 feet from water. Mondeaux Flowage, 5.0 miles east of the trailhead, has three national forest rustic campgrounds with drive-in sites: West Point (thirteen), Eastwood (twelve), and Spearhead Point (twenty-seven), plus four walk-in sites at Picnic Point.

FINDING THE TRAILHEAD

From Medford, drive north 4.9 miles on WI 13 and turn left (west) on CR M. Drive west 7.6 miles and turn right (north) on CR E. Take CR E north 6.4 miles and turn left (west) on FR 102. Drive 3.1 miles west and turn left (south) on FR 108. Drive 1.5 miles south on FR 108 and watch for the trail crossing. Park just off the road. GPS: N45 16.323' / W90 32.223'

THE HIKE

If spending a night at a fine backcountry campsite beside a small lake motivates you, this hike is a good choice. Without that inducement, you may find parts of this trail somewhat rough for your tastes, and I recommend the nearby Ice Age Trail as a better choice.

Begin your hike by walking east on the Ice Age Trail from FR 108. This stretch of the trail is a narrow but defined footpath that runs through an upland forest before dropping to round a wetland on its northern border. In June look for orchids on the edge of the bog.

The Chippewa Lobe Trail starts with the yellow blazes of the Ice Age Trail but turns to blue diamonds where it departs to the south.
PREAMTIP SATASUK

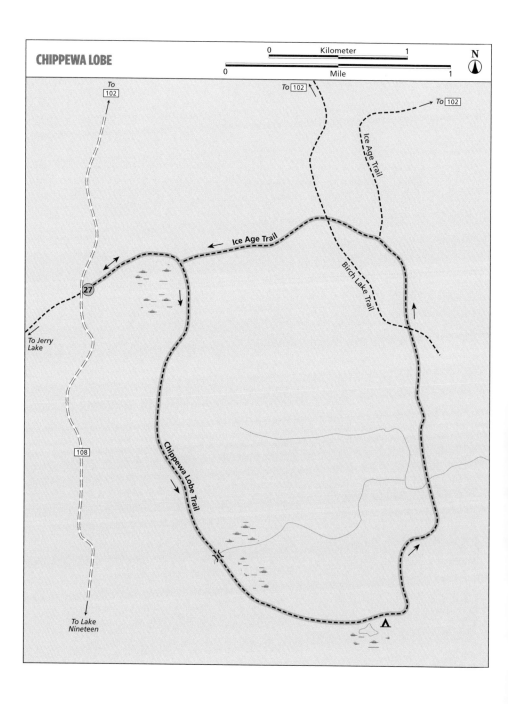

CHIPPEWA LOBE

0 Kilometer 1
0 Mile 1

N

To 102

To 102

To 102

Ice Age Trail

Ice Age Trail

27

Birch Lake Trail

To Jerry Lake

108

Chippewa Lobe Trail

To Lake Nineteen

At mile 0.8 the trail arrives at the Chippewa Lobe Trail junction. A large sign announces the project. Turn right (south), following blue diamond markers along the east side of the wetland.

The trail continues south, always well marked, at times a forest path and sometimes following old roads. A section of old, rotting boardwalk is passable but challenging. Shortly after, at mile 3.0, a sturdy trail bridge crosses over an eastward-flowing stream.

On the south side of the bridge, a narrow ridge carries the trail between the stream's wetlands before the path swings east. Twenty-foot-tall aspen line the trail for a few hundred yards here.

Doubts about the trail's payoff evaporate as you arrive at a small lake. This body of water, at the south end of the loop, appears to be a very large beaver pond. At its outlet, two beaver dams, the product of generations of work, support that theory.

Cross the outlet on a beefy bridge and you will see an improved campsite, complete with benches and a pit toilet. Wood ducks and herons entertain. Beaver come out at dusk, perhaps to avoid the eagles that circle above from time to time. Their tail-slapping antics punctuate the evening hours.

From the campsite, follow the trail east and north through a pleasant forest, a mix of older hardwoods and much younger pines. At mile 4.6 there is a dicey crossing of a small beaver dam, with a knee-deep soaking waiting if you stumble. Shortly after, the trail turns northward, and at mile 4.8 crosses a major, eastward flowing creek. The trail makes a crossing on huge, flattened logs.

Continue north as the trail passes through hemlock groves. At mile 6.0 the route crosses a mowed lane, the Birch Lake Trail, that runs south from FR 102. Resume walking north and you meet the Ice Age Trail at mile 6.8.

Turn left (southwest), following the Ice Age Trail's yellow markers. About 0.5 mile farther you again pass the mowed lane that is the Birch Lake Trail along a charming stretch of pine and birches. A section of open hardwood forest follows before the trail arrives at the Chippewa Lobe Trail junction at mile 8.5, the same spot as mile 0.8 of this hike. This is the end of the loop section of the hike. To return to FR 108, just walk west on the Ice Age Trail, retracing your steps from the beginning of the outing.

Local information: Taylor County Tourism, 104 E. Perkins St., Medford, 54451; (715) 748-4729; www.taylorcountytourism.com

MILES AND DIRECTIONS

0.0 Start east from the FR 108 trailhead.

0.8 Bear right at the Chippewa Lobe Trail junction.

3.0 Cross the trail bridge.

3.9 Pass the designated campsite at large beaver pond.

4.8 Cross a creek.

6.0 Bear right at the junction with Birch Lake Trail.

6.8 Bear left at the Ice Age Trail junction.

8.5 Stay right at the Chippewa Lobe Trail junction.

9.3 Arrive back at the FR 108 trailhead.

28 TIMM'S HILL

This northern portion of this national trail enters a county park to climb Wisconsin's highest natural point. An observation tower there grants a 360-degree view of the horizon. While not part of the Ice Age Trail, this connects to that national scenic trail at the southern end.

Start: From the roadside trailhead at CR C
Distance: 5.8-mile out-and-back
Hiking time: About 3 hours
Difficulty: Moderate
Trail surface: Dirt
Best season: April–October
Other trail users: None
Land status: County park and public easement
Nearest town: Rib Lake
Canine compatibility: Leashed dogs permitted

Fees and permits: None
Schedule: Daily, 6 a.m. to 11 p.m.
Maps: Timm's Hill National Trail Map (Price County Tourism Department), USGS Timm's Hill (inc.) quad
Trail contact: Price County Forestry & Parks, 104 S. Eyder Ave., Phillips, 54555; (715) 339-6371; www.co.price.wi.us. Timm's Hill Trail, www.timmshilltrail.com.
Camping: Wood Lake, 10.0 miles southeast, has eight drive-in sites.

FINDING THE TRAILHEAD

From Rib Lake, drive east 2.0 miles on WI 102 and turn left (north) on CR C. Drive 9.1 miles north. Park on the road's broad shoulder just east of the trail crossing, adjacent to a cemetery. GPS: N45 25.514' / W90 11.217'

The view from the tower up on Timm's Hill, Wisconsin's highest elevation point

THE HIKE

Timm's Hill, at 1,951 feet above sea level, is the highest natural point in Wisconsin. The hill is the namesake of the Timm's Hill National Scenic Trail, a 10.0-mile-long spur connecting to the Ice Age Trail. This hike follows the last 3.0 miles of that path, along roller coaster–like ski trails, past small scenic lakes, to the summit.

Begin your walk where the Timm's Hill National Scenic Trail crosses CR C, just west of the cemetery. Hike north, following red paint blazes, at first along a shallow drainage and then up a slope. At mile 0.2 go straight (north) where the Highway to Heaven ski trail enters from the right.

After that junction the broad trail ascends through a stretch of young aspen. Don't be discouraged, because the scenery improves soon. The trail then enters an older hardwood forest, sprinkled with pine trees, and takes on the character of a rowdy ski trail, not blinking at steep drops and climbs. Bear right (north) at mile 0.9, following the red blazes, at another ski trail intersection. Zillmer Lake appears through the trees to your left as you pull away from the intersection.

The trail ascends and descends a few more hills, passes Otter Lake on your left, and reaches another ski trail junction at mile 1.4. Turn left (northwest) where you see Reuss Lake to the left of the trail and follow the trail as it swings around to the north. At about mile 1.6 bear right (east) as the trail joins a dirt road that runs east for a short distance before swinging north. At mile 1.8 turn left (west) where the trail leaves that road.

Walk west, following the trail as it passes to the south of Little Bass Lake and swings north to meet Rustic Road 62 at mile 2.1. Cross the road and proceed north on a slope above Bass Lake, notably larger than the other lakes along the route. About a quarter mile farther, turn right (north) on a paved park road, part of Timm's Hill County Park.

That road dips to the shores of Bass Lake and passes a fine, small swimming beach. About 150 feet east of the beach, watch for a boardwalk that extends to a small island.

ZILLMER AND THE ICE AGE TRAIL

Raymond T. Zillmer (1887–1960), a graduate of the University of Wisconsin and a lawyer from Milwaukee, was passionate about the natural beauty of Kettle Moraine. As a hiker and naturalist, he understood its importance not only as an area of geological study but also as an object of natural beauty and a destination for outdoor recreation. He was a member of both the Sierra Club and Alpine Club, and at one point was president of the Izaak Walton League, an organization dedicated to the outdoors and protecting natural resources. But most importantly, perhaps, he founded what is now the Ice Age Trail Alliance.

Zillmer pushed to have many of the glacial formations we see today protected as a national scientific reserve. He started with Kettle Moraine, helping to find support for a state forest that now preserves more than 50,000 acres. Then he worked to create a trail that would give residents easy access to this remarkable display of the glaciers' work. Unfortunately, he passed away before that dream came to fruition. In his will he left funds for the creation of the five shelter houses for distance hikers along the trail through Kettle Moraine's Northern Unit. But his passion had spread, and starting with that first trail, an army of volunteers started blazing a trail along the area where the last advance of ice ended. Twenty years after Zillmer's death, President Jimmy Carter signed the law establishing the Ice Age National Scenic Trail, and decades later the Ice Age Trail Alliance and its many volunteers continue the work to complete what will be a 1,000-mile trek through Wisconsin.

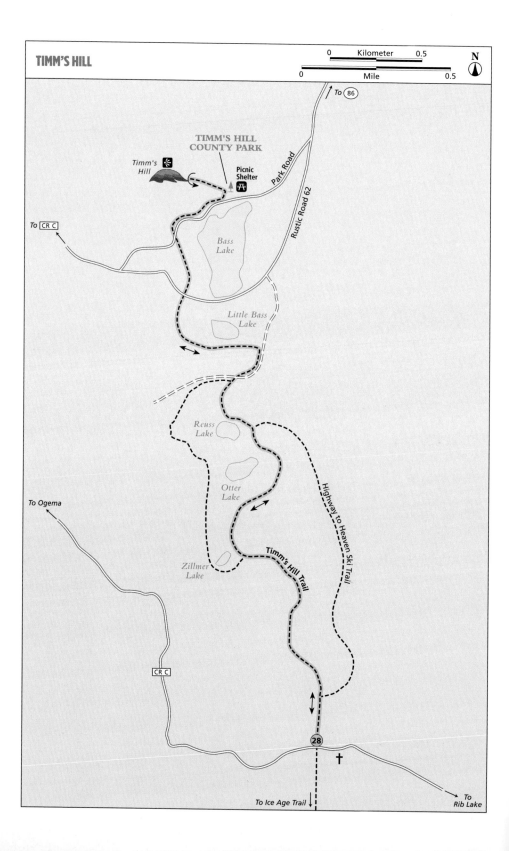

TIMM'S HILL

TIMM'S HILL
COUNTY PARK

Timm's
Hill

Picnic
Shelter

Park Road

Rustic Road 62

To 86

To CR C

Bass
Lake

Little Bass
Lake

Reuss
Lake

Otter
Lake

Highway to Heaven Ski Trail

To Ogema

Zillmer
Lake

Timm's Hill Trail

CR C

28

To Ice Age Trail

To
Rib Lake

Kilometer
Mile

N

Timm's Hill Trail is also a national trail. PREAMTIP SATASUK

The park road swings north from the lake to a parking area and picnic shelter at the eastern base of Timm's Hill. The summit and its observation tower are several hundred yards to the west, 150 feet above the waters of Bass Lake. Ascend steps from the picnic shelter, following white blazes west, up the hill to the tower.

The view from the top is of wooded hills and forest on all sides, with Timm's Lake and Bass Lake nearby in the foreground. Retrace your steps to return to CR C.

Local information: Price County Tourism, 305 S. Lake Ave., Phillips, 54555; (715) 339-4100; www.pricecountywi.net

MILES AND DIRECTIONS

0.0   Head north from the trailhead on CR C.

0.2   Stay left at the juncture with the Highway to Heaven Ski Trail junction.

0.9   Bear right at a ski trail junction.

1.2   Pass Otter Lake on your left.

1.4   Bear left at another ski trail junction.

2.1   Cross Rustic Road 62.

2.9   Arrive at Timm's Hill summit.

5.8   Arrive back at the trailhead.

29 WOOD LAKE

A loop trail in a county park partly follows the Ice Age National Scenic Trail as it rounds a quiet lake and passes through marsh and woods. An old logging camp once operated on the north side of the lake, and its remains are still visible.

Start: From the trailhead in the picnic area
Distance: 2.8-mile loop
Hiking time: About 1 hour
Difficulty: Moderate
Trail surface: Dirt
Best season: April–October
Other trail users: None
Land status: County park
Nearest town: Rib Lake
Canine compatibility: Leashed dogs permitted
Fees and permits: None

Schedule: Daily, 6 a.m. to 11 p.m.
Maps: Ice Age Trail Atlas Wood Lake Segment Map #26, USGS Wood Lake (inc.) quad
Trail contact: Taylor County Forestry & Parks, 224 S. Second St., Medford, 54451; (715) 748-1486; www.co.taylor.wi.us. Ice Age Trail Alliance, 2110 Main St., Cross Plains, 53528; (800) 227-0046; www.iceagetrail.org.
Camping: There are nine drive-in sites, adjacent to the trailhead, at Wood Lake County Park (715-748-1460).

FINDING THE TRAILHEAD

From Rib Lake, drive east and north 4.0 miles on WI 102 and turn right (east) on Wood Lake Avenue. Drive 3.2 miles to Wood Lake County Park and another 0.3 mile to the park's picnic area. GPS: N45 20.245' / W90 4.999'

Trumpeter swans on Wood Lake
PREAMTIP SATASUK

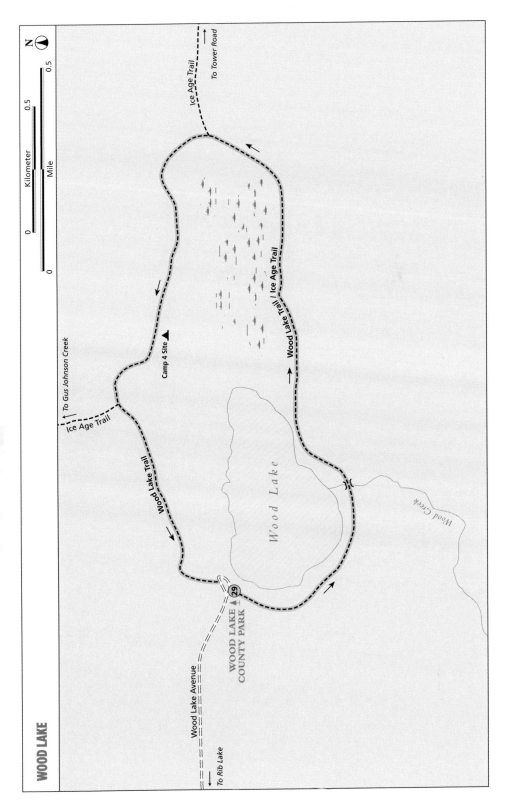

WOOD LAKE

Kilometer

0   0.5   0.5

Mile

N

To Tower Road

Ice Age Trail

Wood Lake Trail / Ice Age Trail

To Gus Johnson Creek

Ice Age Trail

Camp 4 Site

Wood Lake Trail

Wood Lake

Wood Creek

Wood Lake Avenue

To Rib Lake

29

WOOD LAKE
COUNTY PARK

THE HIKE

Wood Lake is one of those quiet, out-of-the-way spots that grow on you. This hike's route begins beside the clear, spring-fed lake waters, continues past an extensive beaver pond, and leads to the remnants of a historic logging camp.

In addition to the trail's attractions, the car campground at the trailhead makes Wood Lake a great choice for families or others looking for a weekend camping spot. It's at the end of a dead-end road, next to a nonmotorized lake, and features a small playground and swimming beach.

The Wood Lake Trail, a loop route, begins on the south side of the picnic area next to the swimming beach, and it is marked here as part of the Ice Age National Scenic Trail. Walk south on the trail, beginning a counterclockwise circuit of the lake. As the trail rounds the lake's south end, it passes stands of birch trees and Wood Creek, the lake's outlet, at mile 0.6.

Continue walking east as the trail follows an old logging railroad grade and begins its run along the south shore of an extensive marsh, enhanced by beavers, east of Wood Lake. Near that marsh's eastern end, the trail swings north on an old woods road. and at the next juncture at mile 1.6, the Ice Age Trail departs to the right. Walk straight (north) at that intersection as the trail rounds the eastern end of the marsh and begins a hilly, up-and-down passage west.

At mile 2.1 the trail arrives at a small clearing, the site of Camp 4. An interpretive sign describes the logging camp as active from 1906 to 1916, with two bunkhouses lodging eighty men apiece. A piece of metal debris, perhaps part of a wood-burning stove, carries the date 1886.

From Camp 4, follow the trail as it heads north, then west, through an open parklike hardwood forest. Turn left (south) at mile 2.4 where the Ice Age Trail comes in from the right (north).

Continue walking west along the Wood Lake Trail, through woods featuring an increasing number of pine trees, arriving back at the trailhead at mile 2.8.

Local information: Taylor County Tourism, 104 E. Perkins St., Medford, 54451; (715) 748-4729; www.taylorcountytourism.com

MILES AND DIRECTIONS

0.0 Head south from the trailhead.

0.6 Cross Wood Lake Creek bridge.

1.6 Bear left at the Ice Age Trail junction (east).

2.1 Pass Camp 4.

2.4 Turn left (south) where the Ice Age Trail comes in from the right.

2.8 Arrive back at the trailhead.

30 ED'S LAKE

A system of cross-country ski trails provides a course through part of the Chequamegon-Nicolet National Forest characterized by birch and hardwoods. A quiet and secluded hike, the trail passes a picnic area along a semi-marshy lake.

Start: From the trailhead at the parking area
Distance: 4.6-mile loop
Hiking time: About 2 hours
Difficulty: Easy
Trail surface: Dirt
Best season: April–October
Other trail users: None
Land status: National forest
Nearest town: Wabeno
Canine compatibility: Leashed dogs permitted
Fees and permits: USFS parking fee
Schedule: Daily, 6 a.m. to 11 p.m.

Maps: Chequamegon-Nicolet National Forest trail map, USGS Roberts Lake (inc.) quad
Trail contact: Chequamegon-Nicolet National Forest, Lakewood-Leona Ranger District, 4978 WI 8 W., Laona, 54541; (715) 674-4481; www.fs.usda.gov
Camping: These trails are on national forest land, and camping is permitted along the trail. Campsites must be at least 100 feet from the trail or the water's edge. Ada Lake, 8.0 miles south of the trailhead, has nineteen drive-in sites.

FINDING THE TRAILHEAD

From Wabeno, drive 0.9 mile west on WI 32 and turn left (west) on WI 52. At mile 3.7 go straight (west) on CR W as WI 52 goes left (south). Take CR W west to mile 9.6 and turn right (north) into a parking area with a signed trailhead. GPS: N45 28.202' / W88 47.482'

THE HIKE

Ed's Lake Trail is a classic walk in the woods on a cross-country ski trail that works well as a hiking trail. Along the way the route passes picturesque hemlock and birch groves, a small lake, and railroad grades left over from the logging era. Note that these trails have directional signs for guiding ski traffic. The first half of this hike will go with the flow of those directional signs on the Birch Trail, and the second half will go "backward" on the Maple Trail.

Begin by walking north from the CR W trailhead to an intersection at mile 0.3 that features a trail map. Ignore the incoming Maple Trail and turn left (north) on the Birch Trail. After a short, winding ascent, a series of birch groves validates the name before the trail heads northwest past a fine stand of hemlocks to Ed's Lake.

A three-sided trail shelter, complete with picnic table and fire ring, sits amid pines near the lake's southeast shore. Ed's Lake, a 0.5-mile-long pond with marshes at either end, fades from sight as the trail swings north and east to an intersection in a small clearing at mile 2.0. Ignore the longer option of the Birch Trail that goes north. Go straight (east) on the shorter version of the Birch Trail along an old railroad grade. Pay attention at mile 2.2 as the ski trail leaves the railroad grade. Bear right (south) here to the next intersection at mile 2.6. Turn left (northeast) on another old railroad grade and your hiking route is now going "backward" on the Maple Trail.

The trails at Ed's Lake are also color-coded and rated for skiers. PREAMTIP SATASUK

About 0.5 mile farther on the railroad grade trail, you are following curves to the east and a compact series of three intersections appears. First, ignore the old railroad grade (actually the same one you left at mile 2.2) that approaches as a sharp left turn (from the west). Second, pass the longer option of the Birch Trail, as it too approaches as a sharp left turn from the west. Take a 90-degree turn to the right (south) at mile 3.1, following the Maple Trail.

This is a pleasant stretch of trail, wandering through a hardwood forest sprinkled with pines and birches. The trail heads steadily south before swinging west to the trailhead. Just before the trailhead the "incoming" ski trail enters from the right. Go straight (south) and soon you will be back at the parking lot.

Local information: Wild River Interpretive Center & Tourism, 5628 Forestry Dr., Florence, 54121; (888) 889-0049; www.exploreflorencecounty.com

MILES AND DIRECTIONS

0.0   Start into the woods at the trailhead.

0.3   Bear left on the Birch Trail.

1.5   Pass the trail shelter near Ed's Lake.

2.0   At the intersection with the Long Birch Ski Trail, go east on an old railroad grade.

2.2   Turn off the old railroad grade on a signed ski trail heading south.

2.6   Turn northeast at the intersection with the Maple Trail.

3.1   Head south (right) at the intersection with the Long Birch Ski Trail.

4.6   Arrive back at the trailhead.

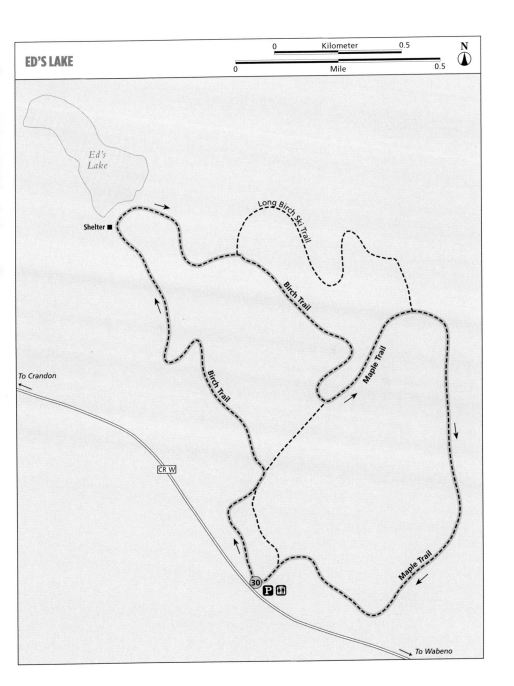

ED'S LAKE

Ed's
Lake

Shelter ■

Long Birch Ski Trail

Birch Trail

Birch Trail

Maple Trail

Maple Trail

To Crandon

CR W

To Wabeno

30 P

Kilometer

Mile

N

0   0.5

0   0.5

31 DELLS OF THE EAU CLAIRE

Wisconsin's other Eau Claire River tumbles and twists through ancient volcanic rock for a stunning display that draws many for the vista. Visitors hop and climb among the rocks and hike along the dells in the namesake county park. But a segment of the Ice Age Trail continues on, offering a more secluded and no less scenic rustic trek along the river as it flows east away from passing park visitors.

Start: From the trailhead at the Ice Age Trail parking area
Distance: 4.7-mile lollipop
Hiking time: About 2.5 hours
Difficulty: Moderate
Trail surface: Dirt, rock, tree roots
Best season: April–October
Other trail users: None
Land status: County park, private
Nearest town: Wausau
Canine compatibility: Leashed dogs permitted
Fees and permits: None
Schedule: Daily, 6 a.m. to 11 p.m.
Maps: Dells of the Eau Claire County Park Map, Ice Age Trail Atlas Dells of the Eau Claire Segment Map #40, USGS Hogarty (inc.) quad
Trail contact: Marathon County Parks, Marathon County Courthouse, 500 Forest St., Wausau, 54403; (715) 261-1000; www.co.marathon.wi.us. Ice Age Trail Alliance, 2110 Main St., Cross Plains, 53528; (800) 227-0046; www.iceagetrail.org.
Special considerations: Use caution along rapids, outcrops, and cliffs.
Camping: Dells of the Eau Claire County Park has twenty-eight drive-in campsites.

FINDING THE TRAILHEAD

From Wausau, take CR Z east 14 miles to where it crosses the Eau Claire River. Find the Ice Age Trail parking lot 0.2 mile east of the river on the left (north). Park at the trailhead. GPS: N44 59.196' / W89 21.421'

THE HIKE

Head north from the trailhead on a packed dirt-and-grass trail with private land and a brushy clearing on your left and mixed forest on the right. In 200 feet the trail enters the woods completely, with several two-plank boardwalks over a few of the commonly soggy areas. The trail takes a hard turn left (west) in front of a gate marking private property.

At 0.3 mile the land descends into thicker hardwood forest, and a stand of pines cushion the trail with needles before the river becomes visible off to the left. More and larger rocks, often moss-covered, rise up from the earth. The sounds of the river accompany you, and a few benches make pleasant perches to pause and admire the river. Listen for chittering kingfishers.

A sign at 0.6 mile marks where the trail enters the Eau Claire River Preserve, and at 1.0 mile cross the first of two footbridges over small spring creeks. Shortly after, you'll pass through a grassy clearing under high-tension wires before the trail returns to shade. At 1.2 miles another sign announces the momentous occasion of crossing the 45th Parallel. There are a couple of places along here where you can step out onto flat rock in the river if water levels allow.

Exposed rock just off the trail along the Eau Claire River

You will see two branches rushing together. This is the southern end of Sandberg Island. At 1.7 miles, not far from where the river first splits around the island, you arrive at the juncture where the county park's Forest Preserve Trail leads to the right and South River Trail continues straight ahead along the river. The latter will be your return trail. Instead, continue along the Ice Age Trail by crossing on the high bridge over the river to your left.

Stone steps take you up along the opposite bank at a higher altitude, and you pass the group campground trail to your left, but keep right on the IAT, which also is marked as leading to the main shelter. A chain-link fence prevents unwary hikers from getting too close to the 60-plus-foot drop-off.

At 1.8 miles a couple of switchbacks bring you lower to the river again on a gravel path. Do you prefer the view from above or below the rock? Because at 1.9 miles a park trail descends to the river level and will reconnect a short distance later. The IAT takes the high road above the river. Follow the yellow blazes. Watch for places to step out for overlooks on the rocks.

The park road is on your left, and the trail briefly touches it then breaks away again to a concrete-and-cobble platform and low wall with a perfect overlook of the dells and the river rushing below. Just past here a short trail and rocky steps grant access to the dells, where you can walk right up to the edge of the rapids, pose on top of rocks, and generally enjoy nature's playground. When you are ready to move on, return to the trail and cross CR Y. The bridge over the river to your right is another nice vista of the dells, and a wide sidewalk keeps you out of traffic.

A park office on your left has a map with the park trails and other information. Cross along the top of the dam and you come to another trail juncture. To the left the Ice

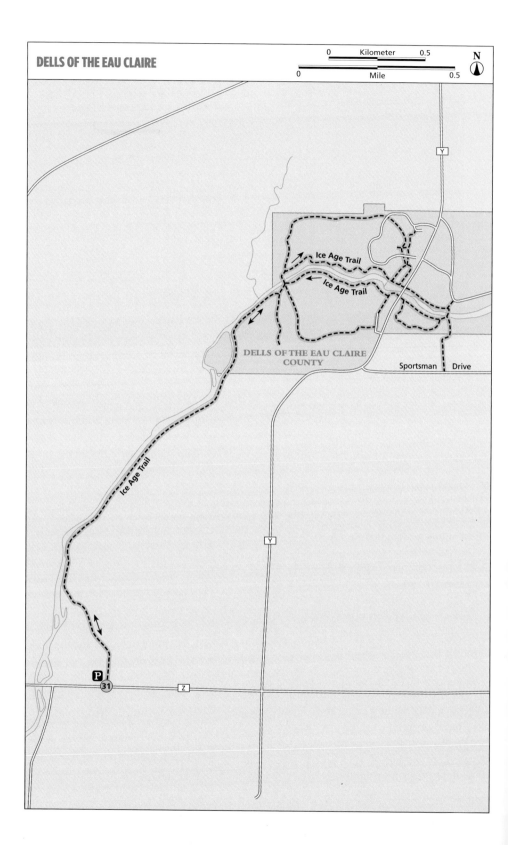

0   Kilometer   0.5

0   Mile   0.5

N

Y

Ice Age Trail

Ice Age Trail

DELLS OF THE EAU CLAIRE
COUNTY

Sportsman   Drive

Ice Age Trail

Y

P
31

Z

A commanding view of the Dells of the Eau Claire River

Age Trail continues another 1,000 feet to Sportsman Drive, where there is no parking, and the next completed trail segment lies 3.5 miles east. For your return here, head right (west) with the river on your right through a corridor of pines. Cross CR Y again and stay right at the next trail junctures. This short segment of the hike isn't as clearly marked as the yellow blazes of the IAT, but as long as you keep the river close on your right, you'll arrive again at the trail bridge at 3 miles. Backtrack along the Ice Age Trail to the trailhead. From the trailhead the Ice Age Trail continues on a 0.9-mile road segment to the Thornapple Creek Segment if you're looking for more. The county park has a trail network totaling 5 miles if you want to extend your hike.

Local information: Visit Wausau, 219 Jefferson St., Wausau, 54403; (715) 355-8788; www.visitwausau.com

MILES AND DIRECTIONS

0.0 Start from the trailhead in the Ice Age Trail parking lot.

1.2 Cross the 45th Parallel.

1.7 Cross the bridge over the Eau Claire River.

2.0 Arrive at the dells.

2.1 Cross CR Y.

2.3 Cross the dam and continue on the county park trail.

2.5 Continue across CR Y.

3.0 Arrive at trail bridge again and backtrack along the river.

4.7 Arrive back at the trailhead.

At 33,000 acres, this state-managed wildlife area is one of the largest in Wisconsin. Wetlands and forest attract migratory birds in spring and fall, delighting birders with a list of identified species surpassing 270. This is easy walking on dikes and two-track roads, and it's ideal for wildlife viewing.

Start: From the trailhead at the parking area on Plum Lane
Distance: 6.1-mile lollipop
Hiking time: 2.5 hours
Difficulty: Moderate
Trail surface: Dirt, grass
Best season: April–August
Other trail users: None
Land status: State wildlife area
Nearest town: Milladore
Canine compatibility: Leashed dogs permitted
Fees and permits: None
Schedule: Daily, 6 a.m. to 11 p.m.
Maps: George W. Mead Wildlife Area map, USGS Big Eau Pleine Reservoir quad (inc.)

Trail contact: George W. Mead Wildlife Area, 201517 CR S, Milladore, 54454; (715) 457-6771; www.meadwildlife.org
Special considerations: This route follows obvious but unmarked lanes and dike roads. Note fall closure dates (September to December) in certain areas of the refuge. Avoid hunting seasons. Bring binoculars, and perhaps a camp chair, to comfortably spend time with the ospreys, herons, and cormorants.
Camping: Big Eau Pleine County Park has forty-six drive-in sites at its West Unit and sixty at its South Unit, about a 20-mile circuitous drive to the north of the trailhead.

FINDING THE TRAILHEAD

From US 10 on the north side of Milladore, drive north 2.7 miles on CR N. Turn right (east) and drive 0.8 mile east on CR H. Then turn left (north) on Plum Lane and take it north 1.2 miles to the trailhead. GPS: N44 40.231' / W89 49.669'

THE HIKE

This is a classic spring bird hike, mixing hardwood forests and open marsh habitat. A wide variety of birds are present here in mid–April, but two features are notable. At the far end of the hike, a dike runs between a heron and cormorant rookery and an active osprey nesting platform. Each of these ongoing shows is about a hundred yards offshore, and parking yourself in between for a sojourn with parents and young is well worthwhile.

From the northeast corner of the Plum Lane trailhead, follow a gated lane northeast through a hardwood forest. This lane shows signs of occasional mowing and has some pea gravel on its surface. It runs north for 0.5 mile before swinging east, arriving at a key intersection I call Junction T at mile 0.9.

A small field borders a grassy lane running due north. Ignore that grassy lane and bear right (east), following the heavier wear marks and pea gravel of the lane you have been following. To the east 0.5 mile, the lane leaves the woods and dry ground, turning north and becoming a dike road traveling among broad wetlands.

While the wetlands are the common attraction at Mead State Wildlife Area, portions of the trail follow two-track through thick forest.

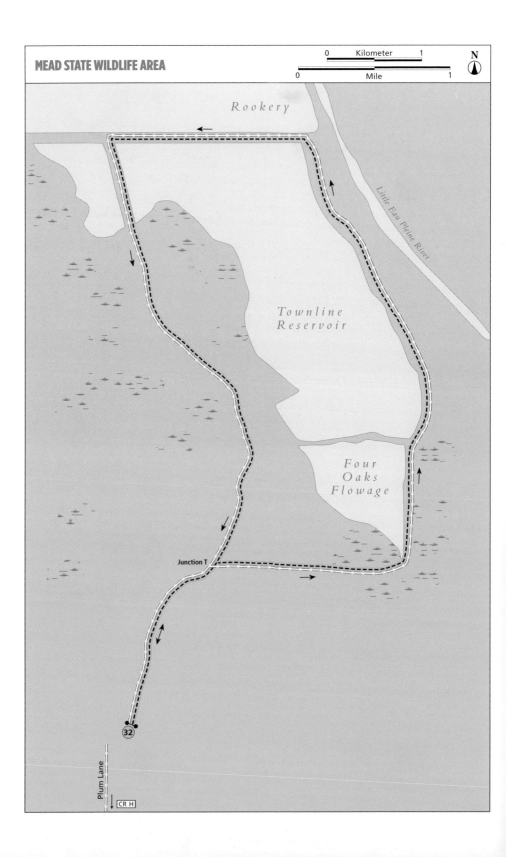

MEAD STATE WILDLIFE AREA

0   Kilometer   1

0   Mile   1

N

Rookery

Little Eau Pleine River

Townline Reservoir

Four Oaks Flowage

Junction T

32

Plum Lane

CR H

Walk north, with the wide pool known as Four Oaks Flowage on your left. In April, herons and ducks seem to be moving in every corner of the marsh. The primeval bark of sandhill cranes reaches across the water.

At mile 1.9 mile you reach the north end of Four Oaks Flowage, a dike running east–west. Go straight (north), continuing on the obvious dike road. A huge expanse of water, the flowage called Townline Reservoir, stretches west and northwest. Swallows swoop for insects near its surface.

Another dike running east–west appears at mile 3.1; this one holds the highlight of the trip. Turn left (west), walk 100 yards or so, and look north. A cormorant and heron rookery thrives on platforms perched on poles emerging from the water, safe from raccoons and other land-based raiders. To the south several active osprey nest platforms are in sight. Parents of all three species come and go constantly, with fresh food for the family. The Little Eau Pleine River runs nearby to the east. During my visit an eagle patrolled the river corridor.

When ready, walk west on the dike to a lone tree at mile 3.6. That tree marks an intersection with another, newer dike that runs south. Turn left (south) and follow that newer dike. The open waters of the flowage give way to more vegetated marsh, and finally, a little more than 0.5 mile south from the lone tree, dry land. The lane, grassy with a few pebbles now and then, runs southeast and then south through young woods.

At mile 5.2 this grassy lane reaches Junction T, the intersection you saw at mile 0.9 of the hike. Turn right (southwest) and retrace your steps from the first part of the hike to arrive back at the trailhead at mile 6.1.

Local information: Stevens Point Area Convention & Visitor Bureau, 1105 Main St., Ste. A, Stevens Point, 54481; (715) 344-2556; www.stevenspointarea.com

MILES AND DIRECTIONS

0.0   Head northeast from the trailhead.

0.9   Turn right (east) at a T intersection.

1.9   Go straight onto the dike at the north end of Four Oaks Flowage.

3.1   Turn left at the north end of Townline Reservoir and see the rookery.

3.6   At a lone tree, the junction of two dike roads, turn left (south).

5.2   Turn right (southwest) at the T intersection again.

6.1   Arrive back at the trailhead.

WESTERN UPLAND

Wisconsin's huge glaciers ground to a halt short of the southwestern portion of the state. As a result, the landscape there shows what the region looked like before the great ice sheets bulldozed it and rounded off the sharp corners. Steep stream valleys dissect the western upland, and the 200-mile-long gorge of the Mississippi River runs the length of it.

That great river is a vital migration route for birds, with tundra swans and pelicans among the notables. Other large rivers—the Chippewa, Black, and Wisconsin—add to the rich web of wildlife habitat here. River otters romp, great blue herons stalk, and eagles nest along the current's flow.

Hiking routes here meander along the rivers, wander through floodplain forests, and climb the steep, wooded hillsides for sweeping views of the river valleys from bluff-top prairies.

The Black River in Van Loon State Wildlife Area

33 CHIPPEWA RIVER

Explore an extensive floodplain along the mighty Chippewa River. The trail passes through oak forest and wetlands on its way upriver. Bird species are abundant, and odds are good you'll see evidence of resident beavers.

Start: From the trailhead at the boat ramp
Distance: 12.4-mile out-and-back
Hiking time: About 5 hours
Difficulty: Moderate
Trail surface: Dirt
Best season: April–October
Other trail users: None
Land status: State wildlife area
Nearest town: Nelson
Canine compatibility: Leashed dogs permitted
Fees and permits: None
Schedule: Daily, 6 a.m. to 11 p.m.
Maps: Tiffany State Wildlife Area map, USGS Wabasha and Ella quads
Trail contact: Wisconsin Department of Natural Resources, P.O. Box 88, Alma, 54610; https://dnr.wi.gov

Special considerations: This hike traverses a floodplain environment. High water levels could be a factor between March 15 and May 1. Depending on conditions, it may be necessary to make a few minor fords to follow this route. Use caution during hunting season.
Camping: A free primitive camping permit is available from Wisconsin DNR. Download the application from the Tiffany Wildlife Area page at https://dnr.wi.gov and email it to the posted address or mail it to P.O. Box 88, Alma, 54610. A copy must be kept with you at the campsite and posted on the dashboard of each vehicle. Drive-in sites available at Holden Park, a county park 17 miles north on Silver Birch Lake.

FINDING THE TRAILHEAD

From Nelson, drive north and west 4.1 miles on WI 35 and turn right (north) into the trailhead, a riverside boat landing on the east bank of the Chippewa River. GPS: N44 26.249' / W92 4.278'

THE HIKE

It takes a while to grasp the size of this place. Tiffany State Wildlife Area, a big chunk of land on a big river, extends 12 miles along the east bank of the Chippewa River, just above its confluence with the Mississippi River. In addition to the east river bank, large sections of the bluff-lined west bank are also state property.

After coming to grips with the scale of the landscape, another impression sinks in. This place feels remote. For almost 7 miles, no road reaches the river on the west bank. On the east bank, WI 25 parallels the river and the hike's route, but it is almost 2 miles away and its presence is hardly noticeable.

This hike's route follows a gated dirt road that shows signs of occasional mowing but is at times grassy and lumpy. It tends to run a little inland from the river but is totally within its floodplain. From time to time narrow paths, some deer trails, some created by hunters, offer an opportunity to approach the riverbank to the west.

Begin your hike by walking north from the trailhead, passing through a floodplain savannah of widely spaced trees and tall grass. A half mile later the road pulls away from the river, enters an oak forest, and at mile 1.2 jogs east slightly and crosses an overgrown

Loose, broken rock along the trail
parallel to the Chippewa River

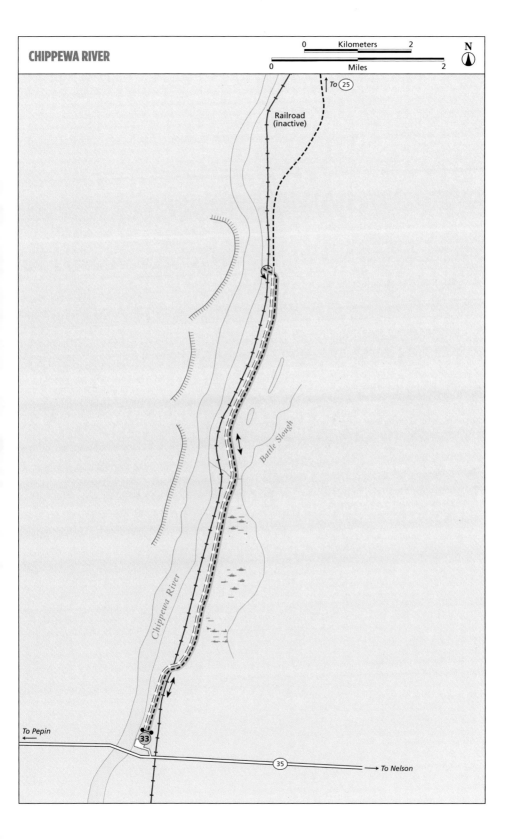

Kilometers

0 2

Miles

0 2

N

To 25

Railroad
(inactive)

Battle Slough

Chippewa River

To Pepin

33

35

To Nelson

The Chippewa River

railroad line. These railroad tracks parallel your route throughout the hike. They offer an alternate route, but the spacing of the track's ties makes it awkward walking.

Continue walking north through a landscape that alternates between oak forest and the open edge of wetlands to the east. At mile 3.4 the lane crosses a side channel that connects the main river with Battle Slough. I saw this spot during dry conditions in the fall and found a dry wash with a sandy bottom. At other times this may be a ford.

After this wash the road swings west for a short stretch before resuming its progress north. The tall bluffs lining the west bank of the river come into view, a vivid contrast to the flat bottomland you are walking.

Beaver sign is abundant. During my visit, ospreys and an eagle cruised the river corridor while turkey vultures rode the thermals rising from the south-facing bluffs. In the woods a flashy pair of pileated woodpeckers entertained. A flock of snow geese passed overhead.

At mile 5.5 the road widens into a small, narrow opening in the woods. This is apparently the turnaround spot for mowing. North of here the lane becomes noticeably more overgrown, but not enough to discourage walking. Watch for a narrow but well-worn path leading west to the river at mile 6.1. Turn left (west) and follow this path 150 yards, first across the railroad tracks, then on to the riverbank. The Chippewa River runs swift and wide here, with 500-foot-tall bluffs rising steeply from the opposite shore. This is a good place to turn around for the hike back to the trailhead.

Local information: Alma Area Chamber of Commerce, 110 N. Main St., Alma, 54610; (608) 685-3303; www.almawisconsin.org

MILES AND DIRECTIONS

0.0   Head north from the trailhead at WI 35 boat ramp.

1.2   Cross the railroad tracks.

3.4   Cross a sandy, dry channel (intermittently dry or wet).

5.5   Cross a small, narrow clearing.

6.1   Take a path left toward the river.

6.2   Turn around at the bank of the river.

12.4   Arrive back at the trailhead.

34 TREMPEALEAU RIVER

Situated at the confluence of the Trempealeau and Mississippi Rivers, the 6,266-acre Trempealeau National Wildlife Refuge is a birding hot spot, especially during migration periods. Hikers trek the dikes and dirt lanes amid the wetlands and bottomland forests.

Start: From the trailhead near the boat landing
Distance: 5.9-mile out-and-back
Hiking time: About 2.5 hours
Difficulty: Easy
Trail surface: Dirt
Best season: March–November
Other trail users: Bicyclists
Land status: National wildlife refuge
Nearest town: Trempealeau
Canine compatibility: Leashed dogs permitted
Fees and permits: None

Schedule: Daily, during daylight hours only
Maps: Trempealeau NWR Map/Brochure, USGS Winona East and Trempealeau quads
Trail contact: Trempealeau National Wildlife Refuge, W28488 Refuge Rd., Trempealeau, 54661; (608) 539-2311; www.fws.gov
Camping: Perrot State Park, 4.0 miles east of the trailhead, has 102 drive-in campsites.

FINDING THE TRAILHEAD

From Centerville, drive west 3.3 miles on WI 35, turn left (south) on West Prairie Road for 1.2 miles, then turn right (south) into the refuge. Continue south on the refuge road for 1.0 mile before turning left (east) on a gravel lane for 0.3 mile. At that point turn right (south) onto another gravel lane where a sign directs you to the boat landing, a mere 0.2 mile farther. Park at the boat landing. GPS: 44 02.532' / W91 31.556'

THE HIKE

Halfway down the Dike Road, a family of otters let me know I was in the right place. All four of them were splashing in a puddle by the riverbank, having such a good time they didn't notice me for ten minutes. Finally spotting me, they ambled up the dike's slope. Each in turn stopped to stare at me for a moment before scooting down the other side and heading for Black Oak Island.

Frolicking otters made my day, but they are only one of many reasons to walk here. This place, a national wildlife refuge established in 1936 by executive order by Franklin D. Roosevelt, offers hikers a pleasant combination of broad sight lines on dike roads and intimate woodland scenes. Three railroads built dikes here in the late 1800s to hold their tracks. Those railroad dikes unintentionally worked to shield the refuge area from siltation and pollution from the two rivers. Today the refuge is an important resting area for migratory birds.

This hike's trailhead, the boat ramp area, is a staging area for bald eagles in early March. They gather there, anticipating the breakup of the upper Mississippi's ice cover and their return to the river's fishing grounds.

Start your walk by continuing south on the dirt road you drove in on, past the gate, onto Kiep's Island, a warbler hot spot during the spring migration. Note the osprey nesting platform to the northeast and continue walking the lane to the island's

Dike-controlled still water offers refuge for water fowl to the west of Trempealeau River where it meets the Mississippi.

southeast corner, at mile 0.4. Look to the southeast and you can see the almost 400-foot rise of Trempealeau Mountain, your walk's next goal. A dike continues south across the lagoon at this point, but it is barren and unattractive, so you will turn around here and walk north.

Continue walking north, past the boat ramp, to the intersection of the boat ramp road and Dike Road at mile 1.1. Turn right (east) and follow Dike Road past the gate and into an area of low, sandy ridges and open oak forest. A mile later the lane emerges into the open near a marshy pond on its north side, turns south, and rises a few feet to run on the crest of a dike.

The broad, open space of the refuge's main lagoon opens to the southwest, with Black Oak Island a quarter mile away. Paralleling the dike to the east, and the reason for its existence, the Trempealeau River runs quiet and brown.

Continue walking south on Dike Road. To the southeast, Brady's Bluff and other heights in Perrot State Park come into view. As the dike doglegs southeast toward Trempealeau Mountain, the sight lines to the west across the lagoon are very long. Pelicans were in the far reaches of the lagoon during my September visit, with a sprinkling of ducks near Black Oak Island. An osprey patrolled the river.

At mile 3.4 Dike Road bumps up against the island of Trempealeau Mountain, a good place to turn around. Retrace your steps on Dike Road to return to the trailhead.

Local information: Trempealeau County Tourism, 36245 Main St., Whitehall, 54773; (608) 538-2311; www. co.trempealeau.wi.us

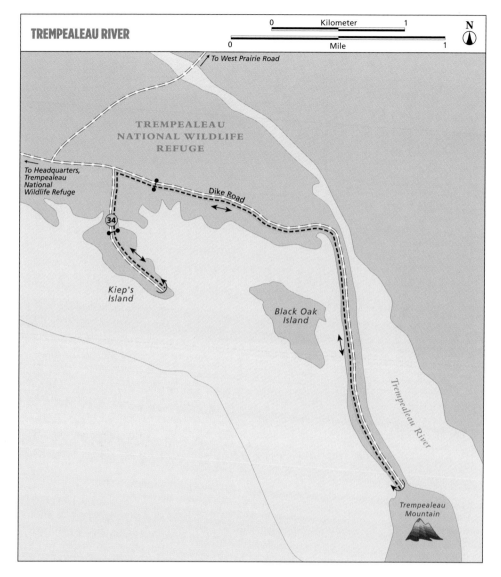

MILES AND DIRECTIONS

0.0 Hike south from the trailhead near the boat landing.

0.4 Turn around at the south end of Kiep's Island.

1.1 Turn right (east) at the intersection of the road to the boat landing and Dike Road.

3.4 Turn around at the south end of Dike Road.

5.7 At the road to the boat landing, turn left (south).

5.9 Arrive back at the trailhead near the boat landing.

35 PERROT RIDGE

Start with a steep climb to the top of Brady's Bluff and along Perrot Ridge for some nice views of the Mississippi River. The hike descends again through open woods, bringing you to a path along the river and railroad tracks back to where you started.

Start: From the trailhead across from West Brady's parking lot
Distance: 4.0-mile loop
Hiking time: About 2 hours
Difficulty: Difficult
Trail surface: Dirt, steps
Best season: April–October
Other trail users: None
Land status: State park
Nearest town: Trempealeau
Canine compatibility: Leashed dogs permitted

Fees and permits: State park vehicle sticker required
Schedule: Daily, 6 a.m. to 11 p.m.
Maps: Perrot State Park trail map, USGS Trempealeau quad
Trail contact: Perrot State Park, W26247 Sullivan Rd., Trempealeau, 54661; (608) 534-6409; https://dnr.wi.gov
Camping: Perrot State Park has 102 drive-in sites 0.5 mile north of the trailhead.

FINDING THE TRAILHEAD

From Trempealeau, take Perrot State Park Road west 3.0 miles to the Brady's Bluff (West) trailhead. GPS: N44 1.259' / W91 29.243'

The riverside segment of the hike runs parallel to busy railroad tracks.

The Perrot Ridge Trail uses steps to negotiate a steep climb up the bluff. PREAMTIP SATASUK

THE HIKE

Location matters, and this hike has it. Make the effort to make two 500-foot climbs to the heights of Perrot State Park, and your reward will be views of the Mississippi River that are among the best in Wisconsin.

Others before us favored this spot. Early Native Americans were here as long as 7,000 years ago, and hundreds of Indian mounds, some the work of the famous Hopewell Culture, dotted the area at one time. European presence began with Nicholas Perrot, who wintered here in 1685, the beginning of a French vanguard that led to the building of a fort in 1731. The story of the human history of this area is the subject of an exhibit in the park's nature center. It is a work in progress. Our understanding of many parts of the history is incomplete.

Begin your hike by walking east from the parking area, across the park road, to the marked trailhead of the Brady's Bluff West Trail. The trail immediately ascends a beautiful ravine and then doubles back above its south wall, a mossy sandstone cliff, before continuing a relentless climb to the top. Wood and stone steps ease the way, and several lookouts provide distraction. The path reaches the summit, containing a shelter and the junction with the Brady's Bluff North and East Trails, at mile 0.5.

Broad views stretch along the river bluffs to Winona in the west and the mouth of the Black River to the east. After savoring the views, walk east through the bluff-top dry prairie, a State Natural Area that features more than one hundred plant species. Long views linger as the path, the Brady's Bluff East Trail, descends to the first trees and then a beautiful oak forest. At mile 1.2 bear left at the junction with the Perrot Ridge Trail.

Turn left (northeast) and walk up the Perrot Ridge Trail, ascending through scrubby woods. Pause and turn around for the views across the river of the Minnesota bluffs and the mouth of the Big Trout Creek Valley as the lane climbs a large, sloping meadow. Pay attention at mile 1.6 as the Perrot Ridge Trail jogs right (northeast) on a ski trail for a

PERROT RIDGE

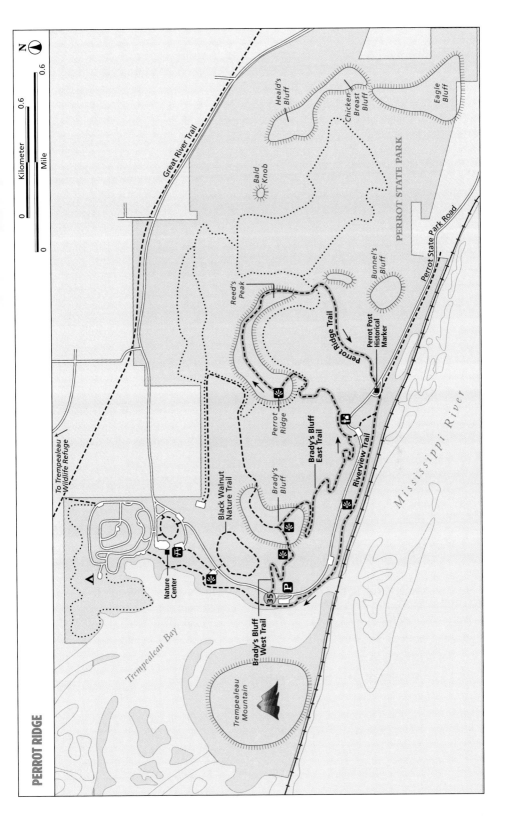

N

Kilometer
0   0.6

Mile
0   0.6

To Trempealeau
Wildlife Refuge

Great River Trail

PERROT STATE PARK

Heald's
Bluff

Chicken
Breast
Bluff

Eagle
Bluff

Bald
Knob

Reed's
Peak

Bunnel's
Bluff

Perrot Post
Historical
Marker

Perrot Ridge Trail

Perrot
Ridge

Brady's Bluff
East Trail

Black Walnut
Nature Trail

Brady's
Bluff

Riverview Trail

Mississippi River

Perrot State Park Road

Nature
Center

Trempealeau Bay

Brady's Bluff
West Trail

Trempealeau
Mountain

35

P

short distance. About 0.1 mile later, after joining the ski trail, turn left (north) as the Perrot Ridge Trail climbs steps to continue its climb to the bluff's summit.

The path tops out in a rocky scramble and continues north, an airy, open ridge walk. Your route continues along the ridgetop for 0.5 mile, but trees soon clog the view, only relenting for one last vista at the crest's end. The Perrot Ridge Trail drops from its namesake, and at a saddle you go straight (south) where the ski trail crosses your path.

Continuing its descent to the southwest, the trail passes through a pleasant, open woodland and down a fern-filled drainage. The trail meets the park road at mile 2.9 and crosses to the Perrot Post historical marker, set within a crescent loop of asphalt just off the park road on the side of the river. A trailhead on the left heads back to town. Find the trailhead for the Riverview and Perrot Ridge Trails on the far side of the half loop, behind the historical marker. The trail offers views of the Mississippi River as well as the active railroad tracks running parallel on your left. At first this is a wide grassy lane, but it soon turns into a well-trod, but sometimes root-filled, path.

Continue walking west, sometimes on the water's edge, but always near the river. The shoreline and the trail swing north where the Trempealeau River joins the Mississippi River. Another quarter mile of walking will complete your loop, bringing you to the boat landing and parking area where the hike started.

Local information: Trempealeau County Tourism, 36245 Main St., Whitehall, 54773; (608) 538-2311; www. co.trempealeau.wi.us

MILES AND DIRECTIONS

0.0 Climb the stairs at the Brady's Bluff West Trail trailhead.

0.5 Bear right at the intersection with the Brady's Bluff East Trail.

1.2 Bear left at the juncture with the Perrot Ridge Trail.

1.6 Bear right a short distance on a ski trail.

1.7 Take the steps to the summit of Perrot Ridge.

2.2 Bear right at the intersection with a ski trail.

2.9 Cross Perrot State Park Road.

3.0 Go west on the Riverview Trail.

4.0 Arrive back at the trailhead.

36 MCGILVRAY BOTTOMS

Seven bridges allow this two-track trail to pass deep into a floodplain of the Black River. Enjoy a mix of rivers, wetlands, and forest on a trail through this wildlife-rich area.

Start: From the trailhead in the parking area
Distance: 5.2-mile out-and-back
Hiking time: About 2 hours
Difficulty: Easy
Trail surface: Dirt
Best season: April–October
Other trail users: None
Land status: State wildlife area
Nearest town: Trempealeau
Canine compatibility: Leashed dogs permitted
Fees and permits: None
Schedule: Daily, from 6 a.m. to 11 p.m.

Maps: Van Loon State Wildlife Area map, USGS Galesville (inc.) quad
Trail contact: Friends of McGilvray Road, www.7bridgesrd.org; Wisconsin DNR, 101 S. Webster St., Madison, 53707; (888) 936-7463; https://dnr.wi.gov
Special considerations: Use caution during hunting seasons. This is a floodplain environment, and high water could be a factor between March 15 and May 1.
Camping: Perrot State Park, 10.0 miles west, has 102 drive-in sites.

FINDING THE TRAILHEAD

From Trempealeau, drive east 7.2 miles on WI 35 and turn left (north) on Amsterdam Prairie Road. Drive north 1.7 miles and turn left (west) into the signed parking area. A box on the bulletin board holds maps. GPS: N44 1.266' / W91 18.383'

The Black River in Van Loon State Wildlife Area is so spread out as to require seven bridges to hike across.

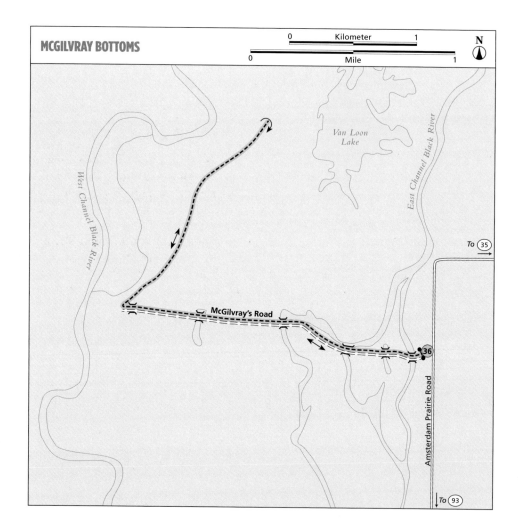

THE HIKE

Alexander McGilvray began a ferry service across the Black River at this site in 1854, but the log drives of the second half of the 1800s blocked operations for months at a time. The first attempt at a solution, construction of bridges on "McGilvray's Road," lasted only until the spring floods of 1895 took out several of the wooden spans.

The next round of construction saw the erection of five steel bridges of the bowstring-arch-truss type around 1908. Part of their design was an unusual hook-clip, invented by Charles Horton, which eliminated the need for rivets and bolts. These five bridges, along with one at Amnicon State Park near Superior and two others, are the only existing examples of this configuration in the state.

Two other bridges, one the main channel structure dismantled in 1948, added to the total, and locals nicknamed the route "Seven Bridges Road." Today it is a pleasant walking route, and McGilvray Bottoms' official name is the Van Loon State Wildlife Area.

Begin your outing by hiking west from the trailhead, down a short slope, on the gated lane that is McGilvray's Road. At the bottom of this incline is the first bridge and the beginning of the vast floodplain ecosystem your route traverses.

A mosaic would be an apt description of the floodplain. Part of the variety comes from its components: river channels, sloughs, hardwood forests, and wetlands. Within those commingling parts, the seasonal ebb and flow of water levels changes the entire landscape. Surging river channels that may threaten to knock out a bridge in the spring can be dry, sandy walking routes in the fall. And sometimes there is the big change, the kind of epic flood that knocked out the 1895 bridges and rearranged river channels at will.

Continue walking west and within a quarter mile pass the second and third bridges. The road has been running due west, and at this point it angles slightly northwest before running due west again. Scenery between the river channels varies between open hardwood forest and expansive wetlands.

The route, an elevated old road, is also an excellent viewing platform to scan this rich ecosystem for wildlife. Turkeys and grouse inhabit the hardwoods, while herons hunt frogs in the marshes. Beaver and otters swim the river channels.

Crossing the fourth and fifth bridges takes you over channels that hold water even in a dry fall. At mile 1.6 you reach the sixth bridge. Twenty yards past that span, turn right (north) on a grassy jeep road that runs northeast. This lane shows up as a broken line on the map at the trailhead bulletin board.

This old road, little more than tire ruts at times, runs northeast through open woods and an occasional meadow-like opening. One pleasant mile from the McGilvray Road it disappears into a jumble of faint paths. This is a good spot to turn around and walk back to the trailhead.

Local information: Trempealeau County Tourism, 36245 Main St., Whitehall, 54773; (608) 538-2311; www. co.trempealeau.wi.us

MILES AND DIRECTIONS

0.0 Hike west from the trailhead on Amsterdam Prairie Road.

1.6 At Bridge 6 turn north on a jeep road.

2.6 At the end of the road, turn around.

5.2 Arrive back at the trailhead.

The views of the confluence of the Wisconsin and Mississippi Rivers from the tops of the bluffs in this state park are unmatched. But this loop, which connects through several of the park's trails, also offers Native American mounds, notable birdwatching, wildflowers, and hardwood forests.

Start: From the trailhead at the Homestead Picnic Area parking lot
Distance: 7.5-mile loop
Hiking time: About 3 hours
Difficulty: Moderate
Trail surface: Dirt
Best season: April–October
Other trail users: Bicycles in some sections
Land status: State park
Nearest town: Prairie du Chien
Canine compatibility: Dogs are not permitted on the nature trail segment, but are allowed on leashes throughout the rest of the hiking trails.

Fees and permits: State park car sticker required
Schedule: Daily, 6 a.m. to 11 p.m.
Maps: Wyalusing State Park trail map, USGS Bagley (inc.) and Clayton (inc.) quads
Trail contact: Wyalusing State Park, 13801 State Park Ln., Bagley, 53801; (608) 996-2261; https://dnr.wi.gov
Special considerations: Parts of the Sentinel Ridge and Bluff Trails are not for acrophobics.
Camping: Wyalusing State Park has 109 drive-in sites.

FINDING THE TRAILHEAD

From Prairie du Chien, drive 7.2 miles southeast on US 18 and turn right (southwest) on CR C. Take that road southwest 3.1 miles and turn right (west) on CR X. Drive 1.3 miles and turn right (north) on the park entrance road. Drive north 0.3 mile and turn left (west) on Homestead Camp Road. In the next traffic circle, take the fourth exit, heading south toward Homestead Picnic Area. Find the trailhead to the right (west) in the picnic area parking lot. GPS: N42 58.468' / W91 07.565'

THE HIKE

Of this entire 7.5-mile loop, there is only a 1.0-mile stretch of trail that I think of as halfway commonplace. Every other mile of trail on this route possesses something special, a telling scene of time and place that I would gladly return to see.

Begin your tour by walking to the west side of the Homestead Picnic Area. The trail, 3 feet wide, eroded, and root-filled, descends through a beautiful open forest of maples and oaks. At about a quarter mile, it meets Sugar Maple Nature Trail (no dogs allowed here). At this juncture, consider going to the right as a short out-and-back of a few hundred feet to see Pictured Rock Cave, a mossy, sandstone hollow in the rock with a small seasonal waterfall. The namesake pictographs, however, are no longer visible.

Return to the main trail and continue the descent, emerging on the park road that leads to the boat landing at mile 0.9. Turn left (west) on the road, walk 30 yards, and you will see the Sentinel Ridge Trail on your right (north). Two reasons justify a delay. First, this area is a top spot for bird-watching, especially colorful warblers, during the spring

A memorial to the passenger pigeon overlooks the Wisconsin River.

migration. Also, the 0.1-mile walk west to the boat landing is worthwhile, a chance to commune with a Mississippi River slough.

Next, walk north on the footpath that is the Sentinel Ridge Trail. It quickly begins a serious ascent, one of two 500-foot climbs on this hike. Wooden steps, views from rock outcrops, and a charming forest setting ease the gain in elevation. The path reaches the top of the bluff and passes a long series of Native American burial and effigy mounds, views over the Mississippi River Valley, and a monument to the extinct passenger pigeon.

Continue walking north and east on the Sentinel Ridge Trail, going straight (east) as the Old Immigrant Trail crosses at mile 2.2. At mile 2.6 turn left (north) on the Bluff Trail where a sign points to Treasure Cave. The Bluff Trail runs precariously east, below a band of cliffs. This stretch, a State Natural Area, is notable for its black walnut and other hardwoods as well as spring wildflowers. A steep set of steps, more ladder than stairs, leads up to the cave. Backtrack from here to the top of the bluff and follow the Sentinel Ridge Trail back to that juncture with the Old Immigrant Trail, taking the latter to the right, down along the Wisconsin River.

Massive boulders dot the woods uphill to your right. A bench offers a spot to linger beside the river before the trail turns inland, meeting the Old Wagon Road Trail at mile 4.4. Bear right and ascend to The Knob and a fabulous Wisconsin River overlook. Backtrack to the Old Wagon Trail to continue another 0.5 mile to the park road. Turn left here, following the road 0.1 mile to the next small parking lot on the right where you can pick up the Walnut Springs Trail heading south, bearing right at the juncture with the Sand Cave Trail.

At mile 6.2 the Walnut Springs Trail, passing through meadows and patchy woods, arrives at another small parking area with marked trailheads for two segments of the

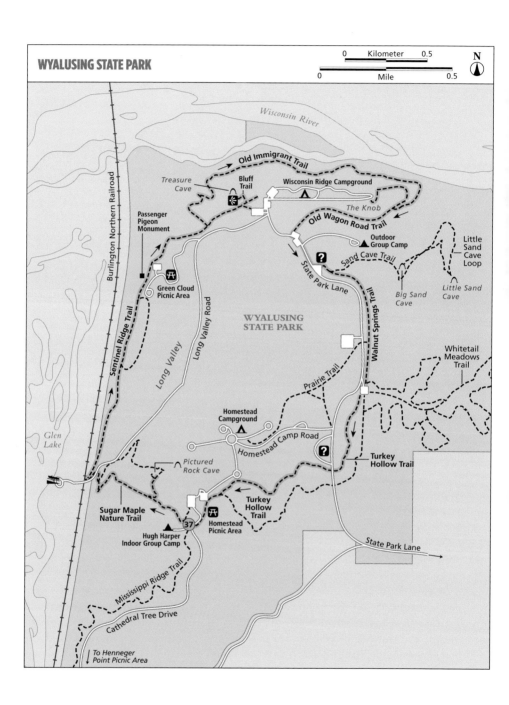

WYALUSING STATE PARK

Kilometer 0 0.5
Mile 0 0.5
N

Wisconsin River

Old Immigrant Trail

Treasure Cave

Bluff Trail

Wisconsin Ridge Campground

The Knob

Old Wagon Road Trail

Passenger Pigeon Monument

Burlington Northern Railroad

Outdoor Group Camp

Little Sand Cave Loop

Sand Cave Trail

?

Big Sand Cave

Little Sand Cave

Green Cloud Picnic Area

Sentinel Ridge Trail

State Park Lane

Walnut Springs Trail

Long Valley Road

Long Valley

WYALUSING STATE PARK

Whitetail Meadows Trail

Prairie Trail

Glen Lake

Homestead Campground

Homestead Camp Road

?

Turkey Hollow Trail

Pictured Rock Cave

Sugar Maple Nature Trail

Turkey Hollow Trail

Homestead Picnic Area

State Park Lane

37

Hugh Harper Indoor Group Camp

Mississippi Ridge Trail

Cathedral Tree Drive

To Henneger Point Picnic Area

A view of the Wisconsin River along Wyalusing State Park right before it meets the Mississippi

Turkey Hollow Trail, an elongated loop, leading south from here. Take the one on the right (nearest the park road). This trail runs south before swinging west to cross the park entrance road. It arrives at the Homestead Picnic Area, the hike's end, at mile 7.5.

Local information: Prairie du Chien Area Chamber of Commerce, 211 S. Main St., Prairie du Chien, 53821; (800) 732-1673; www.prairieduchien.org

MILES AND DIRECTIONS

- **0.0** Head west from the Homestead Picnic Area trailhead.
- **0.9** Pass the boat landing and get on the Sentinel Ridge Trail.
- **2.2** Bear right at the junction with the Old Immigrant Trail.
- **2.6** Turn left (north) on the Bluff Trail.
- **3.0** Backtrack to the Sentinel Ridge Trail and the junction with the Old Immigrant Trail and bear right.
- **4.4** Where the Old Wagon Road Trail meets the Old Immigrant Trail, bear right up toward the overlook of The Knob.
- **5.0.** Return to Old Wagon Road Trail and bear right (south)
- **5.4** Turn left and follow the park road south.
- **5.5** Pick up the Walnut Springs Trail on the left.
- **6.2** Cross the parking lot to Turkey Hollow Trail on the right.
- **6.5** Cross the park road and stay on the Turkey Hollow Trail.
- **7.5** Arrive back at the trailhead.

38 GOVERNOR DODGE STATE PARK

One of the loveliest state parks in the Driftless Area, Governor Dodge offers many miles of trails for hikers, bikers, and equestrians, but this loop of combined trails offers a roundup of the park's finest features: sandstone bluffs, spring creeks, a waterfall, a lake, and a forested canyon. The prairie stretches are full of wildflowers, and the hardwood forest is a glowing treasure in fall.

Start: From the Stephens' Falls trailhead
Distance: 8.3-mile loop
Hiking time: About 3.5 hours
Difficulty: Moderate
Trail surface: Dirt, grass, some asphalt
Best season: April–October
Other trail users: Equestrians, cyclists
Land status: State park
Nearest town: Dodgeville
Canine compatibility: Leashed dogs permitted
Fees and permits: State park vehicle sticker required

Schedule: Daily, 6 a.m. to 11 p.m.
Maps: Governor Dodge State Park trail map, USGS Pleasant Ridge (inc.) quad
Trail contact: Governor Dodge State Park, (608) 935-2315; https://dnr.wi.gov
Special considerations: When snow is on the ground, portions of the trails are groomed for skiing and closed to hikers.
Camping: Governor Dodge State Park has 269 drive-in sites in two campgrounds as well as some backpacking sites.

FINDING THE TRAILHEAD

From Dodgeville, drive 3.5 miles north on WI 23 and turn right (east) on the park entrance road. Drive 0.3 mile northeast on the entrance road, stopping to get a trail map at the park office. At the next intersection, continue straight ahead for 0.8 mile and the Stephens' Falls trailhead is on the right. GPS: N43 01.629' / W90 07.870'

THE HIKE

Many families find Governor Dodge State Park, with its two lakes and miles of trails, an ideal place for a camping vacation. Two of those trails, the Lost Canyon Trail and Stephens' Falls, are near the top of the list of park attractions. By combining many of the park's trails, one can follow a loop around much of the park, taking in lakes, springs, overlooks, falls, sandstone bluffs, and canyons in one hike. This wide variety of terrain and views had no trouble holding my interest throughout the hike.

At 0.1 mile you are already seeing one of the most beautiful sites in the park; a short spur trail takes you to a spring-fed creek tumbling over a cliff down into a small canyon. Stairs give you access to a closer look. Back on the main trail, continue past the springhouse uphill on a mowed trail that crosses into prairie. At the juncture with the Gold Mine Trail, bear left. Cross the park road at 0.5 mile, and at the trail juncture at 0.6 mile, turn right (east), heading through gathering hardwood forest until you reach the

Stephens' Falls

Meadow Valley Trail at mile 1.0 and oak, hickory, and walnut trees become denser. Go left (north) here and follow it along a northerly curve. As it turns south again at mile 1.8, bear right as you pass the equestrian Woodland Trail and pass through sumac and some prairie views.

At mile 2.6 you see the Woodland Trail coming from the left (north). Just across a grassy path is the Cave Trail. Take this uphill, and it passes along the edge of Twin Valley Lake on its turn around this large bluff. A steep spur trail leads up to the referenced cave in the trail name. The Cave Trail continues its course around the bluff with the lake and marshy areas on your left until you come to a trail juncture at mile 3.6. Bear left here and you are back on the Meadow Valley Trail, heading into some prairie openings.

The grassy trail then passes through wildflowers and offers the best view of the lake on this trek and then alternates between woods and prairie patches for the next 0.7 mile. At mile 5.3 you come to a parking lot where there is a concessionaire, restrooms, and water. Bear right along the lot, and the trail enters the woods again, passing the amphitheater on your right, then continue through prairie and aspen colonies until you come to a four-way intersection with spur trails to Twin Valley Campground at mile 5.8. Turn left here and cross the park road. At the next trail juncture at mile 6.0, bear right and the trail takes you to its juncture with the Lost Canyon Trail at mile 6.5. Bear left and Cox Hollow Campground is on your left as you hike to the southern point of the trail before it takes its turn north along a long, mostly shaded canyon with large sandstone rock outcrops. A creek runs through the canyon, and three bridges cross it before you arrive at the trail to Stephens Falls on your right at mile 7.6. Bear left here across a small bridge, and the trail

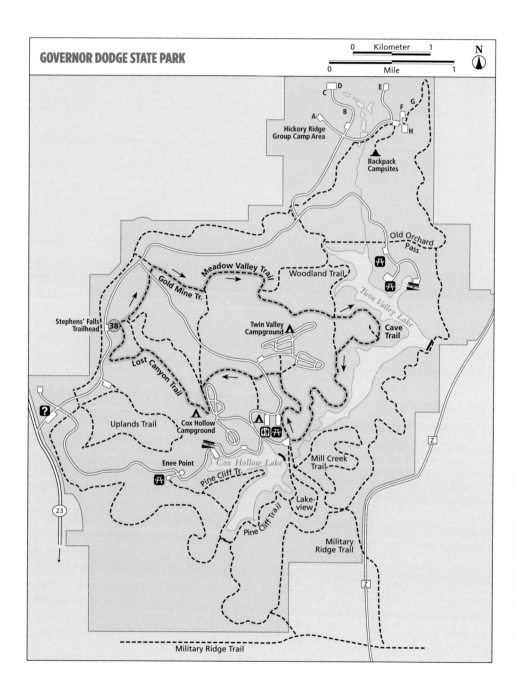

0   Kilometer   1

0   Mile   1

N

Hickory Ridge
Group Camp Area

C
D
E
A
B
F
G
H

Backpack
Campsites

Old Orchard
Pass

Meadow Valley Trail
Woodland Trail

Gold Mine Tr.

Twin Valley Lake

Stephens' Falls
Trailhead
38

Twin Valley
Campground

Cave
Trail

Lost Canyon Trail

Uplands Trail

Cox Hollow
Campground

?

Enee Point

Cox Hollow Lake

Pine Cliff Tr.

Mill Creek
Trail

Lake-
view

Pine Cliff Trail

Military
Ridge Trail

23

Z

Z

Military Ridge Trail

brings you up out of the canyon to the park road at mile 7.9. Turn right and find the trail again into the trees before making the final run through prairie before it returns to that original paved path. Turn left to return to the trailhead at mile 8.3.

Local information: Dodgeville Chamber of Commerce, 338 N. Iowa St., Dodgeville, 53533; (608) 935-5993; www.dodgeville.com

MILES AND DIRECTIONS

0.0 Start east from the Stephens Falls trailhead.

0.1 See Stephens' Falls and continue uphill past the springhouse.

0.2 Bear left at the Lost Canyon Trail/Gold Mine Trail junction.

0.5 Cross the park road and bear right at the trail junction.

0.6 At the Meadow Valley Trail junction, turn left.

1.8 Bear right to stay on Meadow Valley as it meets the Woodland Trail.

2.6 At the trail juncture take a left and a quick right onto Cave Trail.

3.6 Rejoin the Meadow Valley Trail, bearing left (south).

5.3 Bear right at the parking lot and follow the trail north.

5.8 Bear left (west) on the Meadow Valley Trail at the four-way junction with spur trails to Twin Valley Campground.

6.0 Cross the park road and bear right at the trail juncture.

6.5 At the juncture with the Lost Canyon Trail, bear left (south).

7.6 Bear left past the juncture with the trail to Stephens Falls.

8.3 Arrive back at the trailhead.

39 FERRY BLUFF

A local favorite, this short hike climbs high to an exposed rocky cliff and offers the best panoramic view of the Wisconsin River Valley you're going to find.

Start: From the trailhead at the parking area
Distance: 0.8-mile out-and-back
Hiking time: About 1 hour
Difficulty: Easy
Trail surface: Dirt, earth, and wood beam steps
Best season: April–October
Other trail users: None
Land status: State Natural Area
Nearest town: Sauk City
Canine compatibility: Leashed dogs permitted
Fees and permits: None

Schedule: Daily, 6 a.m. to 11 p.m.
Maps: USGS Mazomanie (inc.) quad
Trail contact: Wisconsin Department of Natural Resources, (888) 936-7463; https://dnr.wi.gov
Special considerations: Ferry Bluff is closed from November 15 to March 31 to protect wintering eagles. The viewpoint at the end of the trail is atop a sheer cliff.
Camping: Devil's Lake State Park, 15.0 miles north, has 500 drive-in sites.

FINDING THE TRAILHEAD

 From Sauk City, drive 6.4 miles west on WI 60 and turn left (south) on Ferry Bluff Road. Take that road southeast to mile 7.5, a riverside trailhead. GPS: N43 14.379' / W89 48.600'

THE HIKE

Ferry Bluff features a memorable view of the Wisconsin River Valley. Two hundred feet above the river, a wide sandstone ledge offers broad vistas, stretching to Blue Mounds, 15 miles to the south, and beyond.

Moses and Persis Laws operated a ferry boat landing near the base of the bluff during the late 1800s. Today it is a well-known canoe landing, and the short hike to the bluff-top vistas is a popular one.

From the riverside trailhead walk south on a smooth, constructed trail. When the trail nears the base of the sandstone cliffs, the official trail bears right and begins a steady climb. (The trail down to the left takes you along the base of the bluff to an unimproved canoe landing and is worth an out-and-back walk for some close-up views of the river.) The main trail continues uphill to the north and then swings south to the top of the bluff. The trail continues south toward the river, passing some interpretive signage. A few steps farther the clutter of trees and shrubs drops away and a sweeping panorama greets you. Vultures ride the updrafts along here, and you'll likely see paddlers below on this popular stretch of the river.

Local information: Sauk Prairie Area Chamber of Commerce, 109 Phillips Blvd., Sauk City, 53583; (608) 643-4168; www.saukprairie.com

Baraboo Area Chamber of Commerce & Visitor Center, 600 W. Chestnut St., Baraboo, 53913; (800) 227-2266; https://baraboo.com

Ferry Bluff offers an exceptional view of the
Wisconsin River and neighboring bluffs.

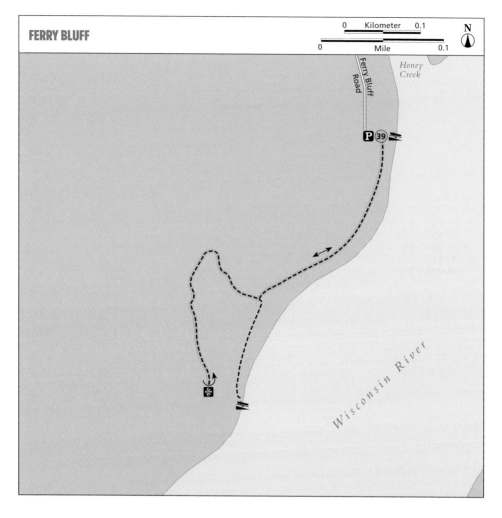

Local event: Bald Eagle Watching Days on a weekend in January in Prairie du Sac. Ferry Bluff Eagle Council, P.O. Box 532, Sauk City, 53583; eagles@ferrybluffeagle council.org; www.ferrybluffeaglecouncil.org

MILES AND DIRECTIONS

0.0 Start from the trailhead.

0.2 At a trail juncture bear right, uphill.

0.4 Arrive at a scenic overlook.

0.8 Arrive back at the trailhead.

40 BLACK HAWK RIDGE

Often you may be the only person in the park as you hike this system of trails through hardwood forest and a good portion of wildflower-filled prairie and climb to the top of a bluff with views of the Wisconsin River Valley.

Start: From the trailhead near Cedar Hills Campground
Distance: 8.3-mile out-and-back
Hiking time: About 3.5 hours
Difficulty: Moderate
Trail surface: Dirt, grass, sand
Best season: April–October
Other trail users: Skiers, equestrians
Land status: State forest
Nearest town: Sauk City
Canine compatibility: Leashed dogs permitted
Fees and permits: None
Schedule: Daily, 6 a.m. to 11 p.m.
Maps: Lower Wisconsin State Riverway, Black Hawk Unit map, USGS Black Earth (inc.) quad

Trail contact: Lower Wisconsin State Riverway, 202 N. Wisconsin Ave., Muscoda, 53573; (608) 739-3188; https://lwr.state.wi.us
Special considerations: Trail maps appear at several intersections on this system. However, these trails do not feature names or markings. I assigned a series of letter designations to intersections to avoid confusion.
Camping: Cedar Hills Campground (608-795-2606), a private facility, is directly south of the trailhead and has forty drive-in sites.

FINDING THE TRAILHEAD

From Sauk City, drive southeast 0.5 mile on US 12 and turn right (south) on WI 78. At mile 5.8 turn left (east) on Dunlap Hollow Road and at mile 6.3 turn left (north) on a dirt road for Cedar Hills Campground. Drive uphill through the private campground to the signed trailhead. GPS: N43 12.795' / W89 44.810'

THE HIKE

In July 1832, Fox and Sac warriors led by Chief Black Hawk ambushed pursuing soldiers on the north end of this state property. That well-executed maneuver gave 1,200 starving Fox and Sac children, women, and elders enough time to escape across the Wisconsin River.

Today, Black Hawk Ridge has a quiet trail system featuring fine views of the Wisconsin River Valley. A private campground at the trailhead offers prime bluff-top campsites, a good base camp for exploring the trails.

Begin your hike by walking north on a gated old-woods road along the crest of the bluff. About 1.0 mile north the trail swings around the western edge of a meadow, turns east, and intersects a north-running connector trail at mile 1.2 (Junction A). Turn left (north) on this trail, entering an oak forest. Almost immediately, turn left (west) again on a trail that quickly loops around to an intersection with a viewpoint spur trail at mile 1.3.

Turn left (northwest) and walk a short distance to a fine lookout, offering long views north to the Baraboo Hills above Devil's Lake. When ready, return to the main trail and walk east, passing another viewpoint offering similar views 0.5 mile later. At mile 2.2 the trail emerges from the oak forest into open old fields near a barn and other structures near the end of Wachter Road. Bear left (northeast) at Junction B, walk to an obvious log

A marshy area between the forest and the meadow high up on Black Hawk Ridge

cabin, and turn right (east) on the two-track remnants of Wachter Road. Walk east from the cabin and turn left (northeast) at mile 2.4 (Junction C).

Follow this trail north on the top of the slope that descends to the west. At mile 2.7 (Junction D), the trail splits. Bear left (north) as the trail descends and swings east to Junction E at mile 2.9. Turn left (northeast), quickly dropping to a saddle. Go straight (northeast), following a path uphill, where the maintained trail turns left.

This path is slightly overgrown, and there are a few briar bushes ahead, but the reward is a broad view of the Wisconsin River Valley, the best of the hike. Follow the path uphill and bear left (northeast) as the path splits. Another split appears as the slope begins to level out. Bear left (north) again at this second split and walk north 100 yards to an open meadow near the top of the bluff's slope. Broad views stretch north and west to Ferry Bluff and beyond.

Return to the maintained trail and retrace your steps to Junction D. Turn left (northeast), walk a little over 100 yards, and turn right (south) at Junction F, at mile 3.7. Hike south through meadows studded with pine trees, going straight where a connector trail enters from the right, then two more from the left. At mile 4.1, Junction G, turn right (west), returning to the barn and other buildings at the end of Wachter Road.

Walk west through the buildings and turn left (south) at Junction B. This trail leads through old fields at the edge of woodlots, across the bluff's plateau-like top. About a mile after Junction B, ignore a connector trail coming in from the north and bear left (west), beginning another swing to the south.

The trail runs south through an oak forest, meanders north before one last, smaller surge to the south, and finally turns north to Junction H at mile 6.7. Turn left (west), following the broad trail through the woods. A short distance farther, bear left (south) at

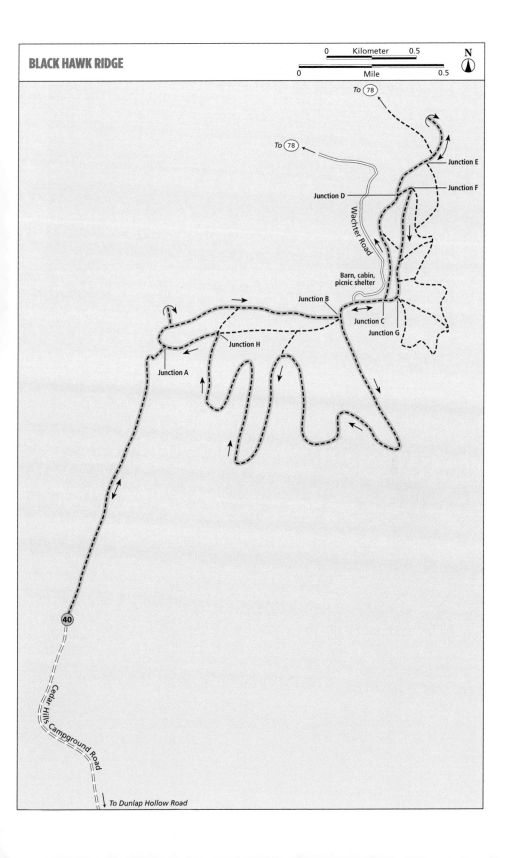

BLACK HAWK RIDGE

To (78)

To (78)

Junction E

Junction F

Junction D

Wachter Road

Barn, cabin,
picnic shelter

Junction B

Junction C

Junction G

Junction H

Junction A

(40)

Cedar Hills Campground Road

To Dunlap Hollow Road

0   Kilometer   0.5

0   Mile   0.5

N

While much of the hike is forest, meadows at the top of the hill are thick with wildflowers in summer.

a small triangular intersection, arriving at Junction A at mile 7.1. From there, retrace your steps south to the trailhead.

Local information: Sauk Prairie Area Chamber of Commerce, 109 Phillips Blvd., Sauk City, 53583; (608) 643-4168; www.saukprairie.com

Local event: Bald Eagle Watching Days on a weekend in January in Prairie du Sac. Ferry Bluff Eagle Council, P.O. Box 532, Sauk City, 53583; eagles@ferrybluffeaglecouncil.org, www.ferrybluffeaglecouncil.org

MILES AND DIRECTIONS

0.0   Hike from the trailhead at Cedar Hills Campground.

1.2   Turn left at Junction A.

1.3   Turn left at the spur junction and a spur to a viewpoint.

2.2   Bear left at Junction B at the end of Wachter Road.

2.4   Turn left (northeast) at Junction C.

2.7   Bear left at the split at Junction D.

2.9   Turn left at Junction E down to a saddle.

3.1   Go straight uphill where the maintained path goes left and bear left at the split for a scenic overlook.

3.3   Return to Junction E.

3.5   Backtrack to Junction D and turn left.

3.7   Turn right (south) at Junction F.

4.1   Bear right (west) toward the barn at Junction G.

4.4   Beyond the buildings at Junction B, turn left (south).

6.7   Turn left (west) at Junction H.

7.1   Bear left to arrive at Junction A.

8.3   Arrive back at the trailhead.

CENTRAL SANDY PLAIN

Ten thousand years ago, Wisconsin's mighty glaciers stopped north and east of the Central Plain and began to melt. That water formed Glacial Lake Wisconsin. When the lake drained, it left a flat landscape that was a mixture of wetland and low-lying oak savannahs and pine barrens. Here and there, sandstone buttes and mesas, once islands in the glacial lake, punctuate the plain.

Today this is a remarkably quiet landscape, teeming with wildlife. Huge swaths of public land, anchored by the 150 square miles of the Central Wisconsin Conservation Area, cover most of the plain. Large parts of the central sand area are de facto wilderness. Hikers who explore the nooks and crannies of the Central Plain find the same quiet ambiance that has drawn eight packs of wild timber wolves to raise pups here.

Wolves are among the residents in the Black River State Forest near Wildcat Mound (hike 41).

41 WILDCAT MOUND

Enjoy a scenic ridge walk through the home turf of an active wolf pack and reintroduced elk herd, followed by a dry crossing of a wildlife-rich marsh.

Start: From the trailhead at Smrekar parking lot
Distance: 13.6-mile one-way shuttle hike
Hiking time: About 5 hours
Difficulty: Difficult
Trail surface: Dirt
Best season: April–August
Other trail users: Skiers
Land status: State forest
Nearest town: Millston
Canine compatibility: Leashed dogs permitted
Fees and permits: None
Schedule: Daily, 6 a.m. to 11 p.m.
Maps: Black River State Forest map, BRSF skiing and hiking trails map, USGS Hatfield Southeast and Warrens West quads
Trail contact: Black River State Forest, W10235 WI 12, Black River Falls, 54615; (715) 284-4103; https://dnr.wi.gov
Special considerations: The Dike Seventeen Wildlife Refuge (the last 2.8 miles of the hike) is closed from September 1 to December 15. That segment, pleasant and full of birds in early April, can be mercilessly hot in the summer. A compass or GPS device is helpful for the short (0.5-mile) off-trail portion at the north end of the Wildcat Trail. Water is scarce on the ridge ski trails. Note that all directions for walking on ski trail segments of this hike are in the direction of signed ski traffic except for the 1.0 mile of "backward" travel on the North Trails.
Camping: Backpack camping is allowed throughout the forest (except refuge) with a free permit available at the Castle Mound Campground or the Black River Falls DNR Service Center. Pigeon Creek Campground, 3.0 miles west of the trailhead, has thirty-eight drive-in sites.

FINDING THE TRAILHEAD

From Millston, drive 4.7 miles east on CR O. Turn left (north) on Smrekar Road and after another 0.7 mile turn right (east) into the Smrekar trailhead parking lot. GPS: N44 13.329' / W90 33.687'

THE HIKE

Wisconsin wolf biologists made an interesting observation in the mid–1990s: The southernmost breeding pack of wild timber wolves in the lower forty-eight states was here, in the Wildcat Mound area. Unlike the Yellowstone wolves that garnered so much publicity, these wolves didn't require a multimillion-dollar federal transplant program to persuade them to migrate. They walked in on their own. Wolves prospered in the area, and by 2000, biologists counted eight packs in the central Wisconsin forest. This hike will take you through the home turf of the "pioneer" pack, the Wildcat Mound grouping. As if this isn't thrilling enough, in 2015 the DNR introduced a herd of twenty-three elk to the forest. Keep that in mind as you travel down these narrow park roads with its turns and hills.

From the south side of the Smrekar parking lot, walk east on a broad cross-country ski trail toward the Ridge Trail. At mile 0.4 go straight (east) on the Ridge Trail as the

Pine plantation in the Black River State Forest at Wildcat Mound. PREAMTIP SATASUK

Central Trail turns north. You ascend steadily through open oak forest for 0.2 mile before gaining the ridgetop and sampling the ambiance that will characterize much of the first half of this hike. Here, from a vantage point 200 feet higher than the trailhead, scenic views appear through openings in the trees. Benches enhance the viewpoints, and sandstone outcroppings appear by the side of the trail.

At mile 1.9 the trail plunges off the crest. At mile 2.2 make a hard left (south), going "backward" on the North Trail. Ignore a sign that announces "Do Not Enter" for ski traffic purposes, but be aware that mountain bikers use these trails. After a mile of contouring the lower slopes of the ridge, turn right (north) on the connector trail that soon takes you past North Settlement Road and the Wildcat Trail parking lot.

Ascend the Norway Pine Trail on its "out" leg, left (west), and a bench with a view rewards you at the top of the climb. A half mile farther the ski trail plunges to the right (north) and a distinct but narrow path ascends to the west. This path takes you to a charming knoll and returns you to the main ski trail a quarter mile later.

At mile 5.6 the ski trail dips to cross Shale Road. Take the Wildcat Trail to the left (west) on the other side. The ascent, bench, and scenic view pattern repeats itself again and the ski trail swings north. As it rounds Wildcat Mound at mile 6.7, a scenic side trail shoots eastward 0.2 mile on a spur ridge. It leads to a fine view southward, showing much of the ridgeline you just traveled.

Continue north on the Wildcat Trail to mile 8.1 of the hike, the northernmost point of the ski trail, where it swings definitively east and a little south to begin its return route to the Shale Road crossing. This spot is in open oak forest after a small downhill drop and features an arrow and skier sign. Your next destination is the junction of Kling Road

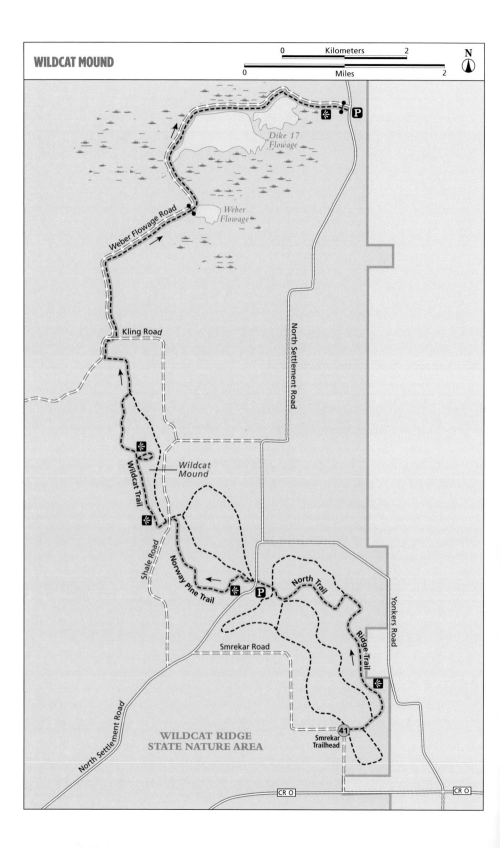

WILDCAT MOUND

0 Kilometers 2
0 Miles 2

N

Dike 17 Flowage

Weber Flowage Road

Weber Flowage

Kling Road

North Settlement Road

Wildcat Trail

Wildcat Mound

Shale Road

Norway Pine Trail

North Trail

P

Ridge Trail

Yonkers Road

Smrekar Road

North Settlement Road

WILDCAT RIDGE
STATE NATURE AREA

41

Smrekar Trailhead

CR O

CR O

and Weber Flowage Road; getting there requires a short and simple exercise in off-trail navigation. Proceed due north; at 130 yards you will find a faint woods road leading north. Follow that faint road north through thickening brush, and after 0.4 mile you intersect another, more distinct, brushy road. Turn left (west) on this road. Turn right (north) on Kling Road, a maintained sandy dirt road, 0.1 mile farther. Follow Kling Road north then east a quarter mile and turn left (north) onto Weber Flowage Road.

Follow Weber Flowage Road north and east 2.0 miles through open oak and pine forest, with abundant grouse and wild turkey, to the small parking lot and gate at Weber Flowage. Round the gate and 100 yards farther on, step into the wide-open expanse of the Dike 17 Wildlife Refuge. Note Saddle Mound, a prominent hill on the east–northeast horizon; under its east end you will see the observation tower near North Settlement Road and the end of the hike.

A grassy road leads northwest through meadows thick with tall grass. As it swings north and northeast, it becomes a dike road with wetlands and abundant wildlife on either side. Ospreys, northern harriers, great blue herons, and sandhill cranes are often present here. A mile after the Weber Flowage gate, the road turns east and follows the northern shore of Dike 17 Flowage. Be sure to ascend the observation tower for a broad view of the wetlands recently crossed as well as the ridge that began your walk.

Options: You can start at Dike 17 and hike south, reversing the route. Another option would be to use the ski trails to create a very elongated loop hike. The ski trails described are part of three loop systems that allow you to return south from the Wildcat system to the Smrekar parking lot with a minimum of backtracking.

Local information: Black River Area Chamber of Commerce, 120 N. Water St., Black River Falls, 54615; (800) 404-4008; www.blackrivercountry.net

MILES AND DIRECTIONS

0.0 Start east from the south side of the Smrekar Road parking lot.

0.4 Stay straight at Ridge Trail junction.

2.2 Make a hard left onto the North Trail.

3.2 Turn right (north) at the connector trail.

3.4 Pass North Settlement Road, Wildcat parking lot.

3.7 Pass Norway Pine Trail junction.

5.6 Cross Shale Road and head left (west) on the Wildcat Trail.

8.1 Arrive at the north end of the Wildcat Trail and go off trail.

8.5 Turn left (west) at an unmarked road.

8.6 Turn right (north) on Kling Road.

8.8 From Kling Road turn left (north) on Weber Flowage Road.

10.8 Pass through the Weber Flowage gate.

13.6 Arrive at Dike 17 observation tower parking lot.

42 NORTH BLUFF

Sandhill State Wildlife Area offers 9,150 acres of preserved wetlands and forest with a 14-mile auto tour around the entire property. Trails and gravel roads crisscross the terrain, taking hikers through prime birding locations and up a tall bluff with an observation tower overlooking it all. The emphasis here is on wildlife.

Start: From the trailhead
Distance: 7.0-mile out-and-back
Hiking time: About 3 hours
Difficulty: Easy
Trail surface: Dirt, gravel
Best season: April–October
Other trail users: None
Land status: State wildlife area
Nearest town: Babcock
Canine compatibility: Leashed dogs permitted
Fees and permits: None
Schedule: Daily, 6 a.m. to 11 p.m. From late October to April, the driving tour road closes, but the gate remains open for hikers.
Maps: Swamp Buck Hiking Trail Map from Sandhill State Wildlife Area, USGS Quail Point Flowage (inc.) quad
Trail contact: Sandhill Wildlife Area, 1715 CR X, Babcock, 54413; (715) 884-2437; https://dnr.wi.gov
Special considerations: Use caution during hunting season. Skiing and hiking are allowed in winter, but the auto tour closes, thus requiring you to hike almost a mile from the gate to the designated trailhead.

FINDING THE TRAILHEAD

From Babcock, drive 0.8 mile southwest on WI 80 and turn right (north) on CR X. After 0.8 mile on CR X, turn left (west) into the entrance area of Sandhill State Wildlife Area. Drive 1.0 mile on the Trumpeter Trail (a graded dirt road) and turn left into the parking area for the Swamp Buck Hiking Trail. Trail maps are in a box at the trailhead. GPS: N44 19.227' / W90 8.135'

THE HIKE

Sandhill State Wildlife Area's abundance of wildlife and open sight lines make this one of the best wildlife viewing spots in the state. As its name indicates, sandhill cranes are a frequent visitor here, but they are far from the only attraction. Wood ducks, herons, teal, and geese are among the seasonal visitors. Otters, beavers, and timber wolves are present all year.

Start your hike by walking south from the trailhead on a gated dirt road. One aspect of the trail's layout is worth noting, a pattern that repeats itself often during the hike. The trail is in the oak and pine woods, but just barely. This routing allows a hiker to scan the open marsh and pond just to the west for birds and other wildlife while remaining hidden in the cover of the trees.

Continue walking south as the trail emerges from the woods and swings west, rounding the south end of the pond on a dike. As you reenter the woods, a sign points you northwest on a wide, grassy trail. At mile 0.8 the trail arrives at a gravel road. Go straight (west) here.

Past the road the trail becomes more of a path, with occasional wood chips in wet spots. About 0.5 mile after the gravel road, the trail reaches a drainage ditch running in a

Long ditches are home to abundant wildlife, especially birds, at Sandhill State Wildlife Area
PREAMTIP SATASUK

A bench overlooking some open water at Sandhill State Wildlife Area PREAMTIP SATASUK

north–south direction. Approach the ditch slowly to improve your odds of seeing musk-rat or other wildlife. A sign points you north on a wide, grassy path on top of the dike bordering the ditch, and at mile 1.5 a bridge takes you to the west side of the ditch. The trail continues north on the ditch's west side for a bit, then turns west, taking boardwalks across wet spots.

As the trail emerges onto dry ground in an oak savannah, a sign points you west onto a grassy dirt road. About a quarter mile farther, the road swings south (ignore a skier sign pointing northwest here), eventually emerging from the woods on a dike heading southwest and intersecting the Trumpeter Trail at mile 2.6. Check the broad marsh to the west, Quail Point Flowage, for sandhill cranes.

Turn right (west), crossing the marsh on a dike. As you reach dry ground, a trail sign points right (north) onto a path. That path heads northwest, nears the road again, and then swings north across a field. At mile 2.9 it turns west and crosses the Trumpeter Trail as it runs along the base of North Bluff.

On the west side of the road, the trail turns southwest in an ascending traverse of the south end of the ridge. It levels out as it reaches the bluff's west side and runs north to a small picnic area. There a trail rising from a parking area to the west leads steeply to the top of the bluff. Turn right (east) and ascend to the top.

An observation tower rises above the trees, offering sweeping views of the central plain. South Bluff's wooded slopes rise 3 miles south and Sugarloaf Mound and other buttes appear 15 miles west. To the southwest, the marshes and woods of the Central Wisconsin Conservation Area seem to stretch forever. When you are ready, retrace your steps to return to the trailhead.

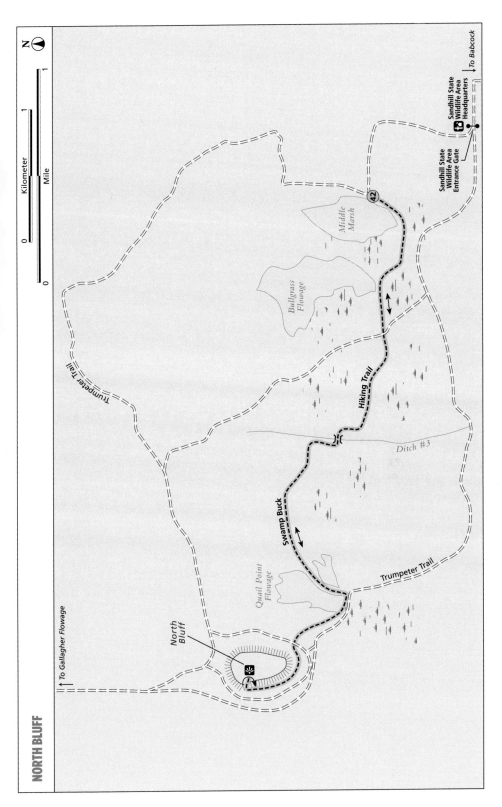

NORTH BLUFF

N

Kilometer
Mile

To Gallagher Flowage

Trumpeter Trail

North Bluff

Quail Point Flowage

Swamp Buck

Bullgrass Flowage

Middle Marsh

42

Ditch #3

Hiking Trail

Trumpeter Trail

Sandhill State Wildlife Area Entrance Gate

Sandhill State Wildlife Area Headquarters

To Babcock

Much of the trail through Sandhill State Wildlife Area is on wide, two-track lanes.
PREAMTIP SATASUK

Local information: Wisconsin Rapids Area Convention & Visitors Bureau, 131 2nd St. N., Wisconsin Rapids, 54494; (800) 554-4484; www.visitwisrapids.com

MILES AND DIRECTIONS

0.0   Head west from the trailhead.

0.8   Go straight across the gravel road.

1.5   Cross a bridge over a ditch.

2.6   Turn right (west) at the Trumpeter Trail, crossing the marsh on a dike.

2.9   Cross the Trumpeter Trail as it runs along the base of North Bluff.

3.4   From the parking lot, take a trail up the bluff.

3.5   Arrive at the top of the bluff.

7.0   Arrive back at the trailhead.

43 LONE ROCK

Approach an isolated sandstone bluff through a secluded State Natural Area and climb to the top for some long views to the horizon.

Start: From the trailhead on 14th Drive
Distance: 6.2-mile out-and-back
Hiking time: About 3 hours
Difficulty: Moderate to the base of the rock, difficult to the top
Trail surface: Dirt, grass
Best season: April–October
Other trail users: None
Land status: State Natural Area
Nearest town: Adams/Friendship
Canine compatibility: Leashed dogs permitted
Fees and permits: None

Schedule: Daily
Maps: USGS Adams (inc.) quad
Trail contact: Wisconsin Department of Natural Resources, 532 N. Main St., Friendship, 53934; (608) 339-3385; https://dnr.wi.gov
Special considerations: Use caution during hunting season. The entire walk traverses a State Natural Area. Treat it well.
Camping: Roche-a-Cri State Park, 8.0 miles north, has forty-one rustic, drive-in sites.

FINDING THE TRAILHEAD

From Adams/Friendship, drive 3.0 miles south on WI 13 and turn right (west) on CR F. Go 1.5 miles west on CR F and turn left (south) on 14th Drive. Drive 1.2 miles south and turn right (west) into the parking area at the trailhead. GPS: N43 54.416' / W89 50.863'

Lone Rock's ridge stands high above the surrounding terrain and is visible from miles away.

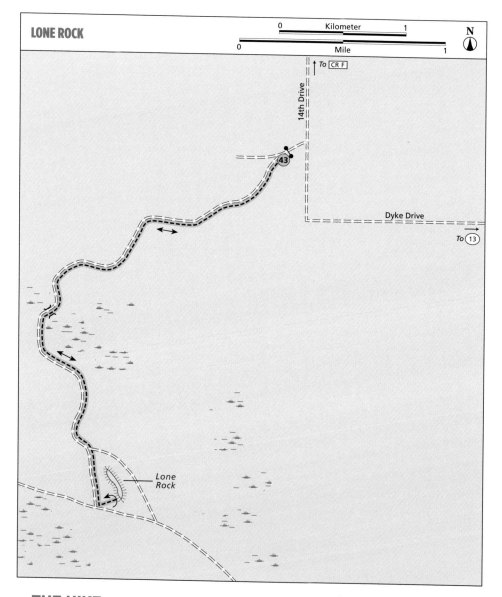

THE HIKE

Lone Rock is an outing with a story line I like. The walk in, through pleasant oak–pine woods, is just long enough to build suspense. When the sandstone bluff finally comes into sight, there is a sense of reward, of compensation for curiosity and effort. The hidden route to the top, and the long views, add to that sentiment.

Most remarkable about those views, stretching across the forested flats and buttes of central Wisconsin, is that few things made by humans are in sight. Bluffs and mounds in Black River State Forest, some 40 miles away, show on the northwest horizon.

The route to Lone Rock is a marked snowmobile trail that makes for fast walking. From the trailhead, walk west past a gate on a wide grassy trail that was once a road. Just past the gate there is a split. An orange arrow points to the choice on the right, a lane going west. Ignore that arrow and take the choice on the left (southwest). This road displays the orange markings of a snowmobile trail.

Follow this road west and south through the forest, along narrow, low fingers of dry land amid wetlands. At mile 1.6 there is a notable change in your route as it turns south. At that point, the older road becomes a snowmobile trail, more of a winding lane.

At mile 1.8, amid a westward jog, the snowmobile trail crosses a wood bridge over a small creek. Resuming its southward march, the trail crosses a power line, and at mile 2.7 the sharp north end of Lone Rock looms above the trees. As the butte comes into sight, there is a split. Ignore an arrow pointing left (east) to the snowmobile trail. Bear right (due south) on a lane that travels the bottom of Lone Rock's western slope. A pine plantation lines this lane to the right (west).

At mile 3.0 this lane stops at a T intersection with a dirt road, apparently untraveled by vehicles, running east–west. This point is west and a little south of the south end of Lone Rock. A lane runs northeast from this point, up the slope and through the open oak woods to the butte.

Follow the lane up to 100-foot-high cliffs. At the base of the cliffs, turn right (southeast) and walk 200 feet to a break in the walls that shows the wear marks of an impromptu path. This break, a charming 30-foot-wide canyon, offers a way to the top that is little more than steep walking. One or two spots require high steps. There is no serious danger on the ascent route, only above, on the cliff tops.

Lone Rock's plateau-like top is pretty darn neat. A path leads around the circumference, with notable viewpoints on the west side and south end. The north end narrows to a catwalk, with sheer drops on either side. Rattlesnake Mound fills a good part of the eastern horizon, and Quincy Bluff is prominent to the southwest. Sandhill cranes bugle in the marsh below Quincy Bluff, and hawks ride the thermals rising from the promontories. When you're ready, hike back along the route you came in on to return to the trailhead.

Local information: Adams County Chamber of Commerce & Tourism, 636 S. Main St., Adams, 53910; (608) 339-6997; www.visitadamscountywi.com

MILES AND DIRECTIONS

0.0 Head southwest from the trailhead, taking the left branch of the trail where it splits.

1.6 The trail follows a snowmobile trail south.

1.8 Cross a wood bridge over a creek.

2.7 At the trail split, bear right (south) on a lane beneath the west slope of Lone Rock.

3.0 At a T intersection west and south of Lone Rock's south end, take a lane left (northeast) to the butte.

3.1 Turn right at the base of the cliff and follow a 30-foot-wide canyon to the top.

6.2 Arrive back at the trailhead.

EASTERN MORAINES AND LAKE MICHIGAN PLAIN

Two glaciers, the Green Bay Lobe and the Lake Michigan Lobe, scoured eastern Wisconsin, leaving plains and low hills in much of their path. The rock debris at what was the boundary between the two ice sheets, the tumbled topography of the Kettle Moraine country, holds renowned samples of glacial landscape forms: kames, eskers, moraines, and kettles. Marshes in the low spots offer valuable habitat for sandhill cranes, beaver, and waterfowl.

To the east, the long swath of Lake Michigan's shoreline runs north to the Door County peninsula, where dolomite bedrock shows in coastal headlands. There lake-effect climate nurtures remnant boreal forests and rare orchids. All of Lake Michigan's shoreline, Wisconsin's east coast, is a vital migration route for raptors, shorebirds, and songbirds.

Hikers can walk the roller coaster–like terrain of the Kettle Moraine or scan for mergansers along Door County's rocky shores. Point Beach's 6.0-mile-long strand makes a fine walking venue for a Lake Michigan treat, a moonrise glistening on the water.

An old resort cabin from the early 1900s in Toft Point State Natural Area, named for the family that settled the point area and opened the resort (hike 49)

44 EAGLE BLUFF

Trek above and below Door County's highest bluff on this fine shoreline ramble with views of Lake Michigan on one side and 150-foot dolomite cliffs rising above you on the other. The final stretch passes along the bluff top through hardwood forest.

Start: From the Eagle Bluff trailhead
Distance: 2.1-mile loop
Hiking time: About 1 hour
Difficulty: Difficult
Trail surface: Dirt, rock
Best season: April–October
Other trail users: None
Land status: State park
Nearest town: Ephraim
Canine compatibility: Leashed dogs permitted
Fees and permits: State park vehicle sticker required
Schedule: Daily, 6 a.m. to 11 p.m.
Maps: Peninsula State Park trail map, USGS Ephraim (inc.) quad

Trail contact: Peninsula State Park, 9462 Shore Rd., Fish Creek, 54212; (920) 868-3258; https://dnr.wi.gov
Special considerations: Parts of this trail are steep and rough. Stay on the trail, both for safety reasons and to protect the fragile bluff ecosystem. Check out the park's 60-foot bluff-top Eagle Tower and its 850-foot-long accessible ramp completed in 2021.
Camping: Peninsula State Park has 468 drive-in campsites 2.0 miles west of the trailhead.

FINDING THE TRAILHEAD

From Ephraim, drive 1.4 miles southwest on WI 42 and turn right (northwest) on Shore Road. Drive north on Shore Road 1.0 mile and turn right (north) into the Eagle Bluff trailhead and parking area. GPS: N45 09.70146' / W87 12.122'

THE HIKE

Peninsula State Park's Eagle Bluff Trail is a small package with a large impact. In its 2.1-mile length, it loops above and below the cliffs of Door County's highest bluff and samples the shoreline of Eagle Harbor. For a finale, it strolls through charming grassy glens in a beech–maple forest with birch trees scattered throughout.

Start your hike at the signed trailhead at the north end of the Eagle Bluff parking area. The trail, steep and rough at times, switchbacks its way down the slope to the north, passing birch trees, ferns, and a cliff band. At mile 0.2 the Minnehaha Trail enters from the left (west). Turn right (east) and begin a 1.0-mile-long traverse at the bottom of the bluff.

As the trail heads east, the steep slope of the bluff above becomes a dolomite cliff. Because of the curve of the shoreline and cliff here, as well as vegetation, you never quite see the cliff as a whole here. Rather, a series of smaller scenes develops: small caves and hollows, arches, shady nooks, and a flowing spring.

Eventually the cliffs end, the slope lessens, and the trail turns west to make its ascent. Before you start up, sample the shoreline just to the east. It's rocky but welcoming and a good place to practice the fine art of Lake Michigan gazing.

From the shore, the trail swings west and then north, ascending past rock bands to Eagle Terrace. This constructed terrace was a quarry around 1900 and later a tourist site.

Towering rocky cliffs
at Eagle Bluff
DOORCOUNTY.COM/
DOOR COUNTY
VISITOR BUREAU

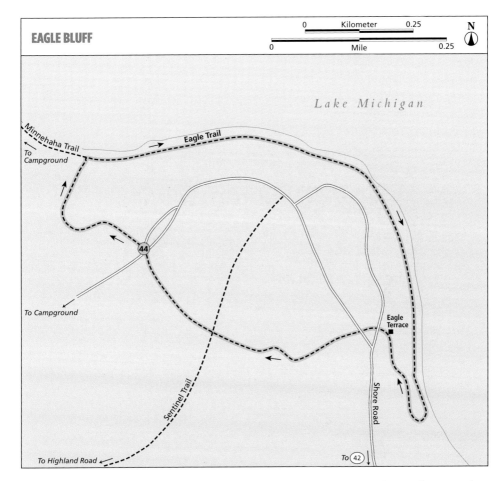

Ascend the steps on its west side and continue west across the parking lot to Shore Road beyond at mile 1.5.

The trail is now on the plateau-like top of the headland and continues west through a pleasant hardwood forest. Go straight (northwest) as the Sentinel Trail crosses at mile 1.9 before returning to the trailhead at mile 2.1.

Local information: Door County Welcome Center, 1015 Green Bay Rd., Sturgeon Bay, 54235; (920) 743-4456; www.doorcounty.com

MILES AND DIRECTIONS

0.0 Start from the Eagle Bluff trailhead.

0.2 Turn right (east) at the Minnehaha junction.

1.5 Go west across the parking lot and cross Shore Road.

1.9 Stay straight (northwest) at the Sentinel Trail intersection.

2.1 Arrive back at the trailhead.

45 DOOR BLUFF HEADLANDS PARK

This short trek is nice at the end of a hiking day, as it takes you cliff-side for a sunset vista.

Start: From the trailhead at the turnaround
Distance: 0.5-mile out-and-back
Hiking time: About 30 minutes
Difficulty: Easy
Trail surface: Dirt
Best season: April–October
Other trail users: None
Land status: County park
Nearest town: Ellison Bay
Canine compatibility: Leashed dogs permitted

Fees and permits: None
Schedule: Daily, half hour before sunrise to 11 p.m.
Maps: USGS Ellison Bay (inc.) quad
Trail contact: Door County Parks, 421 Nebraska St., Sturgeon Bay, 54235; (920) 743-5511; www.co.door.wi.gov
Special considerations: Be careful near the sheer cliff at the viewpoint.
Camping: Peninsula State Park, 12.0 miles south, has 468 drive-in sites.

FINDING THE TRAILHEAD

From Ellison Bay, drive north 2.2 miles on Garrett Bay Road. At mile 2.3 turn left (west) on Door Bluff Park Road, then immediately turn right (north) at the county park sign. Continue 0.8 mile on this gravel road and park at the turn-around inside Door Bluff County Park at mile 3.5. GPS: N45 17.82798' / W87 03.663'

Door Bluff juts out into Green Bay on Lake Michigan.
DOORCOUNTY.COM/DOOR COUNTY VISITOR BUREAU

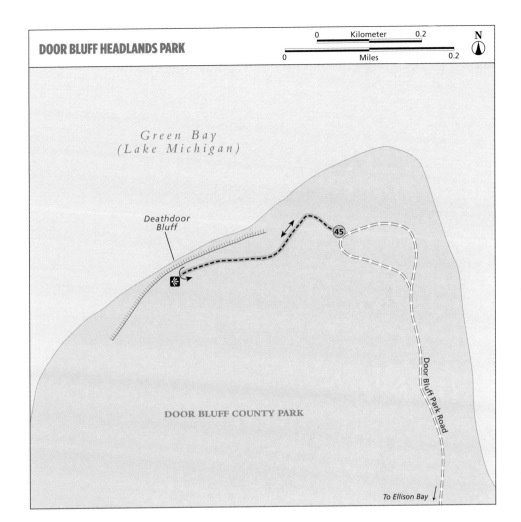

Green Bay
(Lake Michigan)

Deathdoor
Bluff

45

DOOR BLUFF COUNTY PARK

Door Bluff Park Road

To Ellison Bay

0   Kilometer   0.2

0   Miles   0.2

N

THE HIKE

Central to this 155-acre county park is Door Bluff, also referred to as Deathdoor Bluff for its view out toward the strait between the islands and the Door County peninsula's end, Porte des Morts or Death's Door. But the vista from the trail looks out at Green Bay to the west, making it a classic place to be at sunset. Better yet, the short walk back to the trailhead makes lingering to the end of the show, and a twilight retreat, reasonable. The park is undeveloped and notable for its rocky cliffs as well as an unusual stand of old white cedars.

A rough, well-worn trail starts at the northwest corner of the parking loop. Follow this path northwest, first level, then descending, for ninety paces. At that point you will find yourself on the top of a small cliff band. Turn left (southwest) on a trail that soon ascends to the west. Numerous exposed roots and rocks demand your attention as you walk up this slope. To your north a steep slope becomes a cliff and an opening in the trees offers splendid north and west views across Green Bay to the Michigan shore, some 20 miles away.

DEATH'S DOOR

Off the northern tip of the Door Peninsula and south of Washington Island lies a strait known as Death's Door or Porte des Morts. The narrow straits, the jagged shoals, Lake Michigan gales, and the less maneuverable sailing ships of old made a rather deadly combination here, and many are the wrecks in sailing history. But the foreboding moniker likely finds its origins in Native American lore.

Perhaps the most favored story pertains to a battle between tribes. The Ho-Chunk, often referred to in older texts as the Winnebago, moved from the southwest into what is now the Door Peninsula, pushing the Potawatomi tribe out to Washington Island. The Potawatomi planned to attack the Ho-Chunk and sent three scouts to the peninsula who would then find a safe place for their canoes to land and light a fire to guide the attacking army. The Ho-Chunk captured these scouts. Two allegedly died while the third gave up the plan. The Ho-Chunk then had a plan of their own. First, they would lure the attackers to a part of the coastline—below the high bluff—where they wouldn't be able to land and could thus be attacked while still in their canoes. At the same time, the Ho-Chunk would set out in their own canoes and attack the undefended villages.

The Potawatomi took to the lake in calm waters. As they were approaching the false beacon, however, the water started getting rough. They fell right into the trap and were caught between the prepared Ho-Chunk warriors above and the angry lake around them. All were lost. But no one was a winner here. Halfway to the vulnerable island, the Ho-Chunk also found themselves in a stormy lake and perished in the waves. From this, the passage between the mainland and Washington Island became known as the doorway to death. Modern Ho-Chunk dispute the story's veracity, arguing the Potawatomi were the aggressors. But the name Death's Door lives on, bolstered by the many shipwrecks that followed.

Local information: Door County Welcome Center, 1015 Green Bay Rd., Sturgeon Bay, 54235; (920) 743-4456; www.doorcounty.com

MILES AND DIRECTIONS

0.0   Depart west from the trailhead.

0.25 Turn around at Deathdoor viewpoint.

0.5   Arrive back at the trailhead.

46 ROCK ISLAND

Two ferry trips are required to reach this vehicle-free island state park. A mostly wooded trail circles the entire island and shows views of Lake Michigan and wanders past historical pioneer attractions and a lighthouse. Camping is wonderful if you get the chance.

Start: From the trailhead at the dock and boathouse
Distance: 5.2-mile loop
Hiking time: About 2.5 hours
Difficulty: Moderate
Trail surface: Crushed rock, dirt, mowed grass
Best season: June–October
Other trail users: None
Land status: State park
Nearest town: Gills Rock
Canine compatibility: Leashed dogs permitted
Fees and permits: Nightly mooring fee for private boats. Ferries to Washington and Rock Islands both require fees, but a state vehicle admission sticker is not required for the Rock Island ferry parking lot.
Schedule: Daily, 6 a.m. to 11 p.m.
Maps: Rock Island State Park trail map, USGS Washington Island Northeast (inc.) quad
Trail contact: Rock Island State Park, 1924 Indian Point Rd., Washington

Island, 54246; (920) 847-2235; https://dnr.wi.gov
Special considerations: If not arriving by private boat, the only way to Rock Island is on the passenger ferry *Karfi*. That service (800-223-2094) runs several times a day between late May and early October, connecting Washington Island's Jackson Harbor and Rock Island. Round-trip combination tickets for both ferries are recommended and can be purchased at the Northport Car Ferry booth, which is the only one of the ferry points that accepts credit cards. Motor vehicles and bicycles are prohibited on Rock Island.
Camping: Rock Island has thirty-five walk-in campsites within 0.5 mile of the dock and a loaner cart for moving your gear. Five designated backpack campsites are 1.0 mile from the dock, along the island's southeast corner.

FINDING THE TRAILHEAD

Rock Island is in the far northern end of Door County. From Gills Rock, take the Washington Island Ferry (800-223-2094; www.wisferry.com). On Washington Island, drive north, then east about 7.5 miles on CR W to Jackson Harbor. Turn left (north) on Indian Point Road, drive 0.1 mile, and then turn right (east) into the Rock Island ferry parking lot. Cross to the dock, and the trail begins behind the boathouse. GPS: N45 24.579' / W86 49.747'

THE HIKE

State maps and common wisdom portray Rock Island as the end of the line. A small island off the tip of Door County, it is the ultimate weekend getaway and a prime place to watch the moon rise from a watery Lake Michigan horizon.

Turn the clock back 300 years, and travel patterns, as well as the way humans viewed Rock Island, were significantly different. Both Native Americans and voyageurs saw Rock Island not as the end but rather as a middle point in the trading route known as the Grand Traverse. This course allowed freighter canoes to travel from what is now Door County to Upper Michigan's Garden Peninsula. The string of islands in between,

A view north along the shore near the Rock Island trailhead also shows the park office.

including Rock Island, guaranteed that the longest open-water crossing would be only about 5 miles. Rock Island was an important rendezvous point for fur traders. Both the Potawatomi and the French had intermittent villages here in the 1700s.

Begin your tour of the island at the dock on its southwest side. Next to the dock is a significant distraction, the spectacular boathouse and great hall of Chester Thordarson. Thordarson, an Icelandic-born electrical inventor, bought most of Rock Island in 1910. The building, with its mythological carvings, is a notable relic of the Thordarson era on the island and well worth a visit. It is also a great place to duck out of the weather while waiting for the ferry back to Washington Island. Thordarson's heirs sold the island to the state in 1964, and it became a state park.

Walk north from the dock along the Thordarson Loop Trail past a ranger residence and up a short hill to a large, arching gate at mile 0.3. Continue walking north on the broad trail, entering the fine hardwood forest that will characterize much of the loop. Bear left (north) at mile 0.7 at the Fernwood Trail junction (west). The Thordarson Loop Trail resumes its course north and arrives at Pottawatomie Lighthouse at mile 1.5. This stone structure, built in 1858, replaced a lighthouse built in 1836. Scan the northeast corner of the lighthouse clearing for a path that leads down stone and wood steps to the rocky beach below.

The historic boathouse on Rock Island

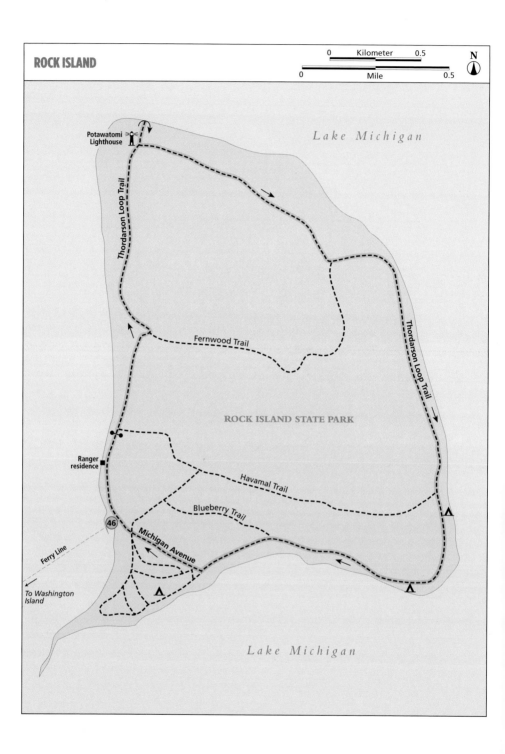

ROCK ISLAND

Lake Michigan

Potawatomi Lighthouse

Thordarson Loop Trail

Fernwood Trail

ROCK ISLAND STATE PARK

Thordarson Loop Trail

Ranger residence

Havamal Trail

Blueberry Trail

46

Ferry Line

Michigan Avenue

To Washington Island

Lake Michigan

0   Kilometer   0.5

0   Mile   0.5

N

When ready, proceed to the southeast corner of the lighthouse clearing where the trail begins its run to the east. A small cemetery is nearby. After about a quarter mile, an opening in the trees offers a long view to the north. On a clear day, Michigan's St. Martin Island and Garden Peninsula are easily seen.

The trail comes to the Fernwood Trail junction (east) at mile 2.4. Turn left (northeast) and descend a short slope on a path with an abundance of rocks and roots. Shortly after, the trail reaches the top of the cedar-lined shoreline cliffs and turns south, along the top of the bluff.

You will reach an old water tower and an open field offering broad lake views just before the Havamal Trail junction at mile 3.7. Bear left (south) at the intersection, following the trail around the island's southeast corner, passing a dark cedar grove as the path swings west.

Bear left (southwest) at mile 4.5 as the Blueberry Trail cuts inland. The trail parallels the sandy shoreline here, leading into the campground area. At about mile 4.9 the trail makes a right (northeast) onto the straight grassy road known as Michigan Avenue. That route leads directly to the dock, and the end of the hike, at mile 5.2.

Visit the Pottawatomie Lighthouse on Rock Island for a nice view of the lake.

During fall migration this island is an important stopover for a wide variety of birds, including hawks and blue jays, which most people seldom think of in flocks. The fall colors are also impressive. By mid-September, especially during the weekdays, far fewer visitors make the crossing, leaving Rock Island about as secluded as it can get.

Local information: Door County Welcome Center, 1015 Green Bay Rd., Sturgeon Bay, 54235; (920) 743-4456; www.doorcounty.com

MILES AND DIRECTIONS

0.0   Depart north from the trailhead at the dock and boathouse.

0.3   Pass through a gate.

0.7   Bear left (west) at Fernwood Trail junction.

1.5   Visit the Potawatomi Lighthouse.

2.4   Bear left (northeast) at the Fernwood Trail junction.

3.7   Bear left (south) on Thordarson Trail at the Havamal Trail junction.

4.5   Bear left (southwest) at the Blueberry Trail junction.

5.2   Arrive back at the trailhead.

47 NEWPORT STATE PARK

Other than perhaps Rock Island, this is the quietest of Door County's excellent state parks. Two of the park's several trails combine to make a sort of dumbbell trek through pristine forest with occasional Lake Michigan shoreline views and access.

Start: From the trailhead at the parking lot
Distance: 12.2-mile dumbbell
Hiking time: About 5 hours
Difficulty: Difficult
Trail surface: Dirt
Best season: April–October
Other trail users: None
Land status: State park
Nearest town: Ellison Bay
Canine compatibility: Leashed dogs permitted
Fees and permits: State park vehicle sticker required
Schedule: Daily, 6 a.m. to 11 p.m.
Maps: Newport State Park trail map, USGS Spider Island (inc.)

and Washington Island Southwest (inc.) quads
Trail contact: Newport State Park, 475 CR NP, Ellison Bay, 54210; (920) 854-2500; https://dnr.wi.gov
Special considerations: The difficult rating reflects the hike's length. Newport's level ground and well-maintained trails make for fast walking. There are dispersed campsites throughout the park. Be considerate of the campers' privacy when near the campsites.
Camping: Newport State Park has seventeen walk-in campsites.

FINDING THE TRAILHEAD

From Ellison Bay, drive north and east 2.5 miles on WI 42 and turn right (south) on Newport Drive. After 2.6 miles turn right (south) onto the park entrance road. Drive 0.9 mile and stop at the entrance gate to get a trail map. Continue another 0.8 mile on the park road to parking lot #3, at the end of the road. GPS: N45 14.279' / W86 59.268'

THE HIKE

When it comes to finding a long walk along the state's Lake Michigan shore, this route is in the running for top honors. Newport State Park gets a thumbs-up for its size, with its 11 miles of shoreline and 20 miles of trail. Best of all, this place has ambiance. The shoreline is a quiet one, and the forest is a notable beauty. Development at the park is minimal and likely to stay that way; the area has semi-wilderness status. This hike's route takes you first to Newport's north end, back past the trailhead, and then to the park's southern part.

Start the hike by walking due east 200 yards from the trailhead toward the lake. In the last low dunes before the beach, a sign indicates where the Europe Bay Trail heads north. Turn left (north) and follow that broad route north into the woods. At mile 1.3 take the right (north) choice as the trail splits into a narrow loop.

Bear right (north) at mile 2.0 as the trail's two branches rejoin. Cross Europe Bay Road at mile 2.1 and walk north. The trail skirts the edge of the woods just off the beach for a short distance then runs slightly inland. It then returns to the shoreline for a scenic 0.5-mile-long stretch, a fitting ending for its northward leg. A bench with prime lake views and small rock ledges decorate the shoreline stretch.

An aerial view of Newport State Park shows its sandy shoreline where trails and campsites are quite close to the water. DOORCOUNTY.COM/DOOR COUNTY VISITOR BUREAU

The sandy beach along Lake Michigan at Newport State Park
DOORCOUNTY.COM/DOOR COUNTY VISITOR BUREAU

Just after a small rock chasm, the Europe Bay Trail turns west (inland) and then south. Bear right (southwest) on the Hotz Loop Trail at mile 3.7. The Hotz Loop Trail travels south, ascending and descending small ridges along the eastern shore of Europe Lake.

At mile 5.1 the Hotz Loop Trail passes beneath a charming stone archway, part of a constructed gate from a previous landowner, next to Europe Bay Road. Turn left (east) there at mile 5.1 and walk 50 yards east on the road to meet the Europe Bay Trail. Turn right (south) on the Europe Bay Trail to return to the trailhead to begin the second half of the hike. Just south of Europe Bay Road, bear right (south), taking the westward option of the trail loop on your return trip.

From the trailhead at mile 7.2 of the hike, walk south on the broad Newport Trail. Bear left (south) as the Newport Trail splits at mile 7.5. Fifteen feet south of that first split you come to another intersection. Turn left (east) there at the sign that reads "Sand Cove, Duck Bay." Follow that trail as it winds around rocky points and small coves to an intersection with the Newport Trail at mile 8.5. Turn left (south) on the Newport Trail, walking first near the lake then inland as the trail cuts across a small peninsula.

Bear left (south) at an intersection with the Ridge Trail at mile 9.6. Continue walking south and turn right (north) at mile 10.0 at an intersection with the Rowley's Bay Loop Trail. The Rowley's Bay Loop Trail and Newport Trail share a common path as they leave that intersection and roll north through a beautiful maple forest. Bear right (north)

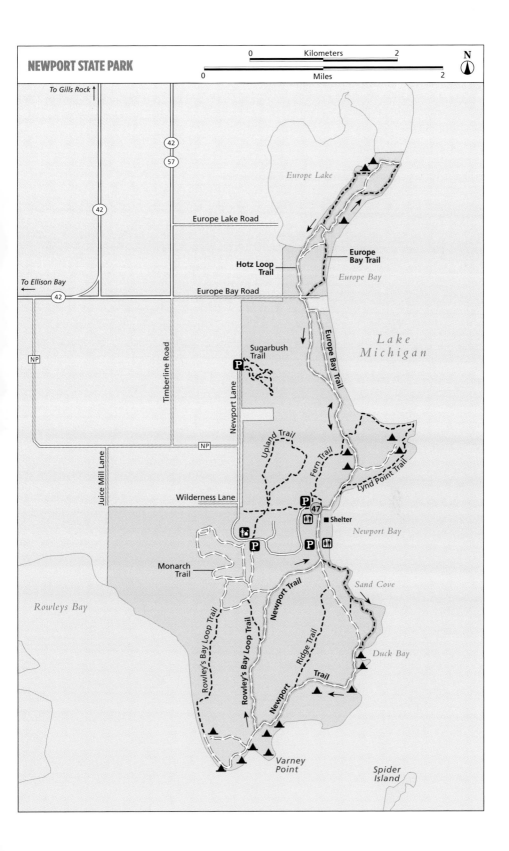

NEWPORT STATE PARK

0   Kilometers   2

0   Miles   2

N

To Gills Rock

42

57

42

Europe Lake

Europe Lake Road

To Ellison Bay

42

NP

Hotz Loop Trail

Europe Bay Trail

Europe Bay

Europe Bay Road

Timberline Road

Sugarbush Trail

P

Newport Lane

NP

Lake Michigan

Upland Trail

Fern Trail

Europe Bay Trail

Lynd Point Trail

Juice Mill Lane

Wilderness Lane

P

47

Shelter

Newport Bay

P

P

Monarch Trail

Rowleys Bay

Rowley's Bay Loop Trail

Rowley's Bay Loop Trail

Newport Trail

Newport Trail

Ridge Trail

Sand Cove

Duck Bay

Varney Point

Spider Island

as the two trails split at mile 10.7 and follow the Newport Trail northeast to a junction at mile 11.9. Bear left (north), retracing your steps of the first part of the southern leg of the hike, back to the trailhead at mile 12.2.

Options: The north and south segments of the recommended hike are fine outings on their own. The northern hike is 7.0 miles long, and the southern route is 5.0 miles in length. Add the Lynd Point Trail to either one or to the whole for an extra 1.5 miles of shoreline.

Local information: Door County Welcome Center, 1015 Green Bay Rd., Sturgeon Bay, 54235; (920) 743-4456; www.doorcounty.com

MILES AND DIRECTIONS

0.0 Start from parking lot #3 trailhead.

0.1 Take the Europe Bay Trail left (north).

1.3 Bear right (north) where the Europe Bay Trail splits.

2.0 Bear right again where the Europe Bay Trail rejoins.

2.1 Cross Europe Bay Road.

3.4 Europe Bay Trail turns inland.

3.7 Bear right (southwest) at the Hotz Loop Trail junction.

5.1 Turn left on Europe Bay Road to pick up the trail south.

7.1 Return to the beach area.

7.2 Cross to the south and pick up the Newport Trail.

7.5 Bear left (south) as the Newport Trail splits and then turn left (east) at the sign that reads "Sand Cove, Duck Bay."

8.5 Turn left (south) on the Newport Trail.

9.6 Bear left (south) at the Ridge Trail junction.

10.0 Turn right (north) at Rowley's Bay Loop Trail junction.

10.7 Bear right (north) where the Rowley's Bay Loop Trail splits and follow the Newport Trail.

11.9 Turn left (north) at the Newport Trail junction to return to the trailhead.

12.2 Arrive back at the trailhead.

48 **THE RIDGES**

This nature sanctuary protects fascinating ridges that mark changes in the lakeshore over thousands of years and offers trails and boardwalks that crisscross throughout. Unusual plant and insect life proliferates amid the swales and overgrown sandy ridges, and you can still see a couple of range lights that sailors once used to navigate the nearby harbor.

Start: From the trailhead at the nature center
Distance: 2.1-mile lollipop
Hiking time: About 1 hour
Difficulty: Easy
Trail surface: Dirt, boardwalks, some sand
Best season: April–October
Other trail users: None
Land status: Private nature sanctuary, open to the public
Nearest town: Baileys Harbor
Canine compatibility: Pets are prohibited
Fees and permits: A $5 trail fee for adults
Schedule: Daily. Nature center daily 9 a.m. to 5 p.m. with extended hours in summer.

Maps: Trail Guide ($2) from the Nature Center; USGS Baileys Harbor East (inc.) quad
Trail contact: The Ridges Sanctuary, 8166 WI 57, Baileys Harbor, 54202; (920) 839-2802; www.ridgessanctuary.org
Special considerations: This is a private nature sanctuary protecting rare habitat and plants. Treat it well. Stop at the nature center, register, and read the rules. Snowshoe rentals are available in winter.
Camping: There are 468 drive-in sites at Peninsula State Park, 7.0 miles northwest.

FINDING THE TRAILHEAD

From its intersection with CR F in Baileys Harbor, drive 0.2 mile north on WI 57; the Ridges Sanctuary's Cook-Albert Fuller Nature Center is on the right. Park at the center and stop for optional nature guides and other information. The trailhead is north of the building at the edge of the woods. GPS: N45 04.088' / W87 07.432'

THE HIKE

Lake Michigan's influence seems to be everywhere at the Ridges. The lines of the landscape itself, the "Ridges," are crescent-shaped linear sand dunes, arranged in chronological order. Thirty in number, they also took an average of thirty years each to form. Between the dunes is a series of swales, narrow wetlands paralleling the sand ridges. This is all part of a habitat so notable that it became Wisconsin's first State Natural Area in 1967. Thirteen rare plant species are present. More than twenty-five native orchids bloom here, a primary motivation in the original preservation drive.

Lake Michigan still holds the key to the Ridges ecosystem. The Ridges boreal forest has an effective moat in Baileys Harbor. The chilly waters protect the flora, remnants from a cooler era, from hot southern breezes.

Begin with the nature center, opened in 2015. A trail guide available here provides an educational angle to your experience. Find the trailhead to the left side of the front of the building. The hike begins on a 0.3-mile out-and-back spur across boardwalks, which takes

A creek passes under the boardwalk at the Ridges Sanctuary.

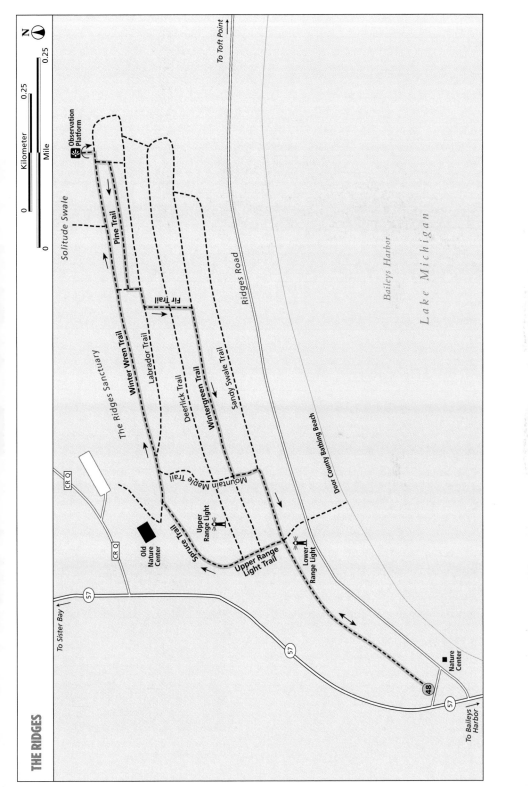

THE RIDGES

The Ridges Sanctuary

Solitude Swale

Pine Trail

Winter Wren Trail

Labrador Trail

Fir Trail

Deerlick Trail

Wintergreen Trail

Sandy Swale Trail

Mountain Maple Trail

Spruce Trail

Upper Range Light

Upper Range Light Trail

Lower Range Light

Old Nature Center

Door County Bathing Beach

Observation Platform

Ridges Road

Baileys Harbor

Lake Michigan

Nature Center

CR Q

CR Q

To Sister Bay

To Baileys Harbor

To Toft Point

48

57

57

N

Kilometer
0   0.25

Mile
0   0.25

you to the rows of trail segments that lie atop the ridges. The route described here takes in the highlights of the sanctuary, but one could spend much more time lingering and wandering, hunting for wildflowers and bird-watching. At 0.3 mile turn left (north) on the boardwalk, and it takes you up to the Upper Range Light, one of two of the original range lights that sailors used to safely navigate the rocky waters into the harbor. Here you will turn right and follow the Spruce Trail 0.1 mile to the original entry trail from where the old nature center was. Go right here, continuing east, and you will pass the Mountain Maple Trail on your right before coming to a trail split where you bear left to follow Winter Wren Trail.

Stop at each of the two observation points on the left for views into Solitude and Winter Wren Swales, where you are bound to find wildlife. From the observation platform, backtrack and bear left on the Pine Trail, passing through pines, of course, until you find the Fir Trail. Stay on this as it crosses the Labrador Trail then the Deerlick Trail until it ends at Wintergreen Trail. Go right (west) here until the next crossing trail on your left, which follows a boardwalk across Sandy Swale to the Sandy Trail. Go right (west) here, and the trail becomes sandier. Watch through here for the rare dwarf lake iris in May and June.

When the trail arrives at the range light boardwalk, turn left and follow it to the Lower Range Light. Cross Ridges Road to the beach, and you are standing on the youngest ridge. When you are ready to continue, hike back to the trail system, using the Upper Range Light as your guide, and turn left on the entry trail to get back to the trailhead.

Local information: Door County Welcome Center, 1015 Green Bay Rd., Sturgeon Bay, 54235; (920) 743-4456; www.doorcounty.com

MILES AND DIRECTIONS

0.0   Start from the nature center trailhead.

0.3   Turn left (north) on the boardwalk toward Upper Range Light.

0.4   Turn right (east) on the Spruce Trail.

0.5   Bear right (east) to stay on the Spruce Trail and the spur trail to the old parking area.

0.6   Bear left to take the Winter Wren Trail at the split for the Labrador Trail.

0.9   Go left on the boardwalk out-and-back to the first observation platform.

1.0   Go left onto the observation deck.

1.1   Backtrack, turning right (west) on Winter Wren Trail, and take a quick left (south) on the Pine Trail.

1.2   Turn left (south) on the Fir Trail and stay on it until it dead-ends at the Wintergreen Trail.

1.3   Turn right (west) on the Wintergreen Trail.

1.5   Turn left (south) on the boardwalk to cross to the Sandy Trail and turn right (west).

1.7   Turn left (south) on the boardwalk and head toward the Lower Range Light.

1.8   Turn around at the Lower Range Light or beach.

2.1   Arrive back at the trailhead.

One of the park's rare plants is the dwarf lake iris.

49 MOONLIGHT BAY

Offering first the woods and then the magnificence of Lake Michigan, this hike is a less-traveled trek in Door County as you trace the edge of a point, following along the rocky shore.

Start: From the trailhead at the gate
Distance: 5.4-mile loop
Hiking time: About 2.5 hours
Difficulty: Moderate
Trail surface: Dirt, grass, rock
Best season: May–October
Other trail users: None
Land status: Non-DNR-owned State Natural Area
Nearest town: Baileys Harbor
Canine compatibility: Leashed dogs permitted
Fees and permits: None
Schedule: Daily
Maps: USGS Baileys Harbor quad

Trail contact: Cofrin Center for Biodiversity, UW–Green Bay, 2420 Nicolet Dr., Green Bay, 54301; (920) 465-5032; biodiversity@uwgb.edu
Special considerations: The off-trail, shoreline segment of this hike can be hazardous under adverse conditions (storm surges, high water, or shore ice). If water levels are high, rounding the two bays described as dry might require some bushwhacking. Toft Point is a State Natural Area. Treat it well.
Camping: Peninsula State Park has 468 drive-in sites, 7.0 miles northwest of the trailhead.

FINDING THE TRAILHEAD

From Baileys Harbor, drive north then east on Ridges Road. After 1.5 miles (where Ridges Road starts to turn south), turn left (northeast) on a shaded dirt and gravel lane. Go 0.2 mile to a gate and sign for the Toft Point State Natural Area. Pullouts here will accommodate about six vehicles. GPS: N45 4.424' / W87 5.835'

THE HIKE

Few moderate loop hikes can match this walk for its combination of intimate forest and views of Lake Michigan. Most of this hike takes place within the Toft Point State Natural Area, a 700-acre preserve owned by the University of Wisconsin–Green Bay and the Wisconsin Chapter of The Nature Conservancy and notable for its remnant boreal forest of balsam fir and white spruce as well as its shoreline. As I strolled through the whispering trees, the peace was broken by a murder of crows chasing an eagle back and forth above the treetops. An auspicious start to a day of hiking.

Walk past the gate (northeast) on a smooth, shaded dirt road. After 0.5 mile you will see an opening to the north as a broad sedge meadow appears and extends to the edge of Moonlight Bay. Shortly after that, the first buildings of the old Toft resort come into sight amid an overgrown meadow area. Past the last of the cabins, the road reenters the woods and stops at the rocky eastern shore of the peninsula. As you step through the trees to the water's edge, you will see the beginning of the shoreline route you will follow for the next 3.0 miles.

The open lake is a striking sight after traversing the forest. Certainly the woods are charming in their own quiet sense, and a short distance inland mossy rocks mark an

The edge of Moonlight Bay on Lake Michigan

ancient shoreline. But here, next to the blue water of Lake Michigan, your senses leap from the foreground to the horizon amid wind, waves, and wildflowers.

If there is one outstanding characteristic of this hike, it is this: the juxtaposition of the micro and the macro. The relationship between forest and lake begins that theme, and the intricate shoreline continues it with style. Broad lake views are constantly in sight, while the convoluted texture of the coast leaves you constantly wondering what is around the next bend.

Two possible routes offer a choice for the next segment. A path just inside the shoreline trees leads south for 0.5 mile. You can follow that trail or stay on the rocky bench that is the shore. Many of the individual rocks on the shoreline are flat, and the footing varies from remarkably smooth to occasionally tedious.

Either way, 0.5 mile farther south you meet a north-facing bay, just as the path ends. I found the bay a dried-out flat, half sand and half dry mud, easy and pleasant travel. With higher water, you may have to bushwhack a little to get around to the north-facing peninsula on the east of the bay, your next goal. Its northern tip is mile 1.9 of the hike.

As you proceed south, Moonlight Bay broadens into the open water of the lake. Far to the northeast, Cana Island Lighthouse, looking like a faint white candle on the horizon, comes into view.

Another bay, this one facing east, has a bottom as dry as the last but with considerably more rocks to assure passage. Your route continues south and at mile 2.9 turns to the west with the shoreline. The lake is rowdier here, reflecting your position on the end of the Toft Point peninsula.

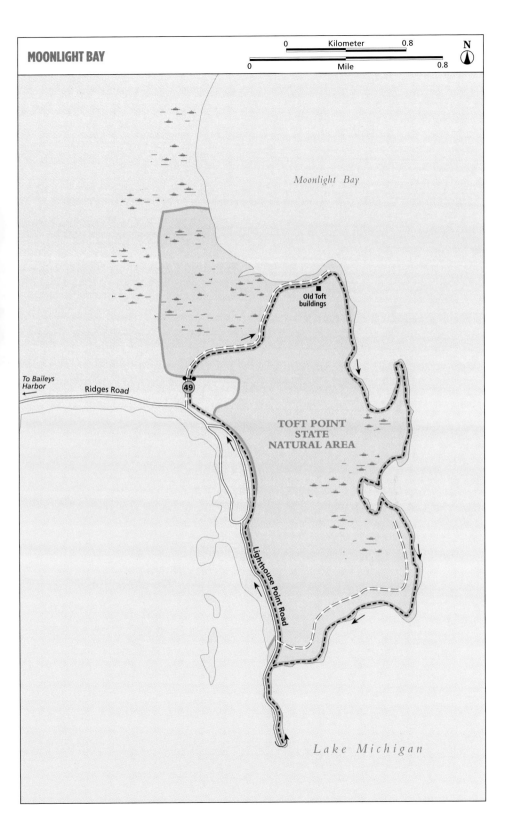

MOONLIGHT BAY

Moonlight Bay

Old Toft
buildings

To Baileys
Harbor

Ridges Road

49

TOFT POINT
STATE
NATURAL AREA

Lighthouse Point Road

Lake Michigan

N

Kilometer
0   0.8

Mile
0   0.8

To the southwest a narrow spit of rocks, shrubs, and trees sticks a quarter mile out into the lake and is well worth visiting. Since you left the forest, you have been traversing a domain that changes hands often, sometimes land, sometimes water. Now you arrive literally at land's end, a culmination of your shoreline journey. When you sit on the tip of this peninsula, little more than a gravel bar, water almost surrounds you.

Just northeast of where this subpeninsula joins the mainland is a small parking lot east of a house. Turn north here and pick up Lighthouse Point Drive/Ridges Road where it changes from paved to gravel (at mile 4.2). Walk 1.0 mile north and make a right turn (northeast) into the shady lane you parked on; the gate is less than a quarter mile farther. Halfway along this road walk, Lighthouse Point Drive becomes Ridges Road.

Options: The 2.0-mile round-trip from the gate to the old Toft buildings and the scenic shoreline beyond is an outstanding, easy out-and-back hike. Accessing any of the southern shoreline of Toft Point from Ridges Road/Lighthouse Point Drive is also an excellent outing.

Local information: Door County Welcome Center, 1015 Green Bay Rd., Sturgeon Bay, 54235; (920) 743-4456; www.doorcounty.com

MILES AND DIRECTIONS

0.0 Depart from the trailhead at the gate near the "Toft Point State Natural Area" sign.

0.8 Pass the old Toft resort buildings.

1.9 Round the tip of the small, north-facing peninsula.

2.9 Turn west at the southeast point of the shoreline.

3.8 Come around at the southern tip of Toft Point peninsula.

4.2 Join Ridges Road and walk north.

5.4 Arrive back at the trailhead at the gate.

50 **POINT BEACH**

A partial segment of the Ice Age National Scenic Trail traverses the Point Beach State Forest ski trails, along forested sand ridges and amid swales, before crossing a creek and its wetlands and dunes to arrive at the shore of Lake Michigan. It's a long hike with shorter options, but the miles of undeveloped beach as well as the ecosystem created by the dunes are worth the extra time.

Start: From the Ice Age Trail trailhead at the park road
Distance: 8.9-mile reverse lollipop
Hiking time: About 3.5 hours
Difficulty: Moderate
Trail surface: Grass, dirt, some cordwalk and crushed limestone
Best season: April–October
Other trail users: Skiers, bicycles in some segments
Land status: State forest
Nearest town: Two Rivers
Canine compatibility: Leashed dogs permitted except during ski season

Fees and permits: State park vehicle sticker required
Schedule: Daily, 6 a.m. to 11 p.m.
Maps: Point Beach State Forest trail map, USGS Two Rivers (inc.) quad, Ice Age Trail Atlas Point Beach Segment Map #96
Trail contact: Point Beach State Forest, 9400 CR O, Two Rivers, 54241; (920) 794-7480; https://dnr.wi.gov
Camping: There are 127 drive-in sites just north of the trailhead.

FINDING THE TRAILHEAD

From Two Rivers, take CR O north 5.1 miles. Turn right (east) into Point Beach State Forest. Park just past the entrance station. Toilets and water are nearby. GPS: N44 12.695' / W87 30.678'

THE HIKE

Nowhere else on Wisconsin's Lake Michigan shoreline is there anything quite like Point Beach State Forest. Here 6 scenic miles of undeveloped sand beach border a quiet forest accented with string bogs. A well-marked system of hiking trails offers routes of different lengths through the shade of the woods, while the wide-open spaces of the shore beckon beachcombers. The beach segment of the hike may be mercilessly hot in the middle of a summer day. Conversely, it makes a splendid evening or moonlight walk.

From the entrance station, walk west 140 yards on the entrance road. At that point turn left (south) on a narrow, rustic footpath clearly marked as the Ice Age National Scenic Trail. Enter a grove of cedars and notice the marshy area to your right, a swale.

At 0.7 mile bear left (east) at the trail juncture with the Red and Blue Trails, two of three ski loops that make up the Ridges Trails. The system is named for the series of sandy ridges created by lake levels long ago. In between are swales similar to the ones you'll find at the Ridges sanctuary hike. Continue along the yellow-blazed Ice Age Trail, and at 0.8 mile you come to a curve south where a spur trail continues east, straight over the dunes to the beach and past a kayak/Ice Age Trail campsite. Have a peek at the lake if you prefer, then continue south through the woods on the Ice Age Trail/Blue Loop.

Cordwalk crosses the dunes where the Ice Age Trail then connects to a segment along the Lake Michigan shoreline south to Two Rivers.
PREAMTIP SATASUK

SANTA SAILS NO MORE: THE CHRISTMAS TREE SHIP

Herman E. Schuenemann was born in Ahnapee, Wisconsin (now Algoma), and in the late nineteenth century he became a ship captain, plying the waters of Lake Michigan. But the people and papers of Chicago came to know him as Captain Santa. His ship, a three-masted schooner called the *Rouse Simmons*, was well-known for its late-season deliveries of Christmas trees to the port in Chicago each year.

The ship set sail from Thompson, Michigan, on November 23, 1912, with a full load of Christmas trees destined for the Windy City, but the winds of November intervened. A lighthouse attendant in Kewaunee spotted its distress flag when a notorious November gale took the *Rouse Simmons* to a watery grave 6 miles northeast of Rawley Point, where Point Beach State Forest is today. Captain Santa and another captain, plus at least nine sailors, were lost. However, some Northwoods lumberjacks, who some claim had hitched a ride on the ship, may have more than doubled that count. Trees washed up on shore for days, months, then years, and the lake even gave up the captain's wallet in 1924.

But the wreck itself remained lost until Kent Bellrichard, a diver from Milwaukee—searching for the 1887 wreck of the steamship *Vernon*—came across the Christmas Tree Ship instead. She lay at 170 feet with hundreds of trees still onboard, many with the needles still on them, preserved by the cold waters.

Since the wreck, the reports were of an outrageous snowstorm, of layers of ice on the ship, of conditions that made it impossible to see. But the historical record shows visibility of at least at 6 miles and the actual snowstorm not beginning until later in the evening after the Christmas Tree Ship was gone. The gale surely didn't help, but some sources dug up by the Wisconsin Historical Society claim the massive load of trees piled on the decks and in the hold left the ship barely a foot above the waterline.

Today the *Mackinaw*, a Coast Guard cutter, commemorates the *Rouse Simmons* by delivering a load of several hundred Christmas trees to Chicago, all of which are donated to economically disadvantaged families.

At 1.5 mile bear left as you join the Yellow Trail, and after another 0.4 mile the trail crosses a park road that connects to the group camp on your left (east). Stay straight across this and continue through the woods until at 2.5 miles you get your first look at Molash Creek through the trees on the left. A bench sits on the bank overlooking the still waters, broad and marshy. The path swings to a more southwesterly direction.

Bear left at the return path for the Yellow Loop at 2.8 miles, saving it for your return, and left again where the Ice Age Trail joins the crushed rock of the bike path at mile 3.0. From here the trail ascends a short hill and enters into open, grassy terrain until mile 3.4, where you pass a spur trail to a parking area on your right as you bear left on the Ice Age Trail as it enters the woods again, crossing Molash Creek on a wide wooden bridge 100 feet later.

Pass another spur trail on the right out to the road, and at mile 3.5 the bike path splits off to the right, while you bear left on the clearly marked Ice Age Trail, a rustic footpath once again. The trail goes back into deep woods, and as you get closer to the as yet invisible lake, the path skirts the edge of Molash Creek's marshy edge. When the backs of the dunes become visible, the Ice Age Trail takes a turn south through pine plantation before making the turn east over the dunes on a cordwalk. Here you find a bench with a magnificent view from the top of the last dune before the waves of Lake Michigan. This is the turnaround point, but it's unlikely you will be in a hurry to leave.

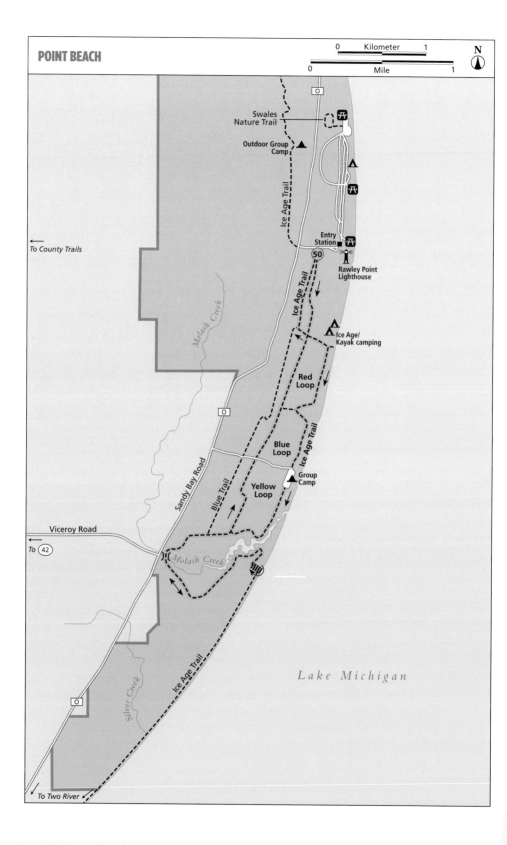

POINT BEACH

0   Kilometer   1

0   Mile   1

N

Swales
Nature Trail

Outdoor Group
Camp

Ice Age Trail

To County Trails

Molash Creek

Entry
Station

Rawley Point
Lighthouse

Ice Age Trail

Ice Age/
Kayak camping

Red
Loop

Blue
Loop

Ice Age Trail

Sandy Bay Road

Blue Trail

Yellow
Loop

Group
Camp

Viceroy Road

To 42

Molash Creek

Silver Creek

Ice Age Trail

Lake Michigan

To Two River

Stay on the path or the beach to avoid damaging the fragile dune environment, home of rare plants. This is a good spot to contemplate the ebb and flow of Point Beach's topography. Both the forest you recently left and the beach you stand on owe their defining characteristics to the cumulative effects of the wind, waves, and sand of Lake Michigan.

When you are ready, backtrack along the Ice Age Trail, crossing the bridge and passing the bike trail juncture in the woods until you come to the Yellow Trail juncture. This time, bear left (north) and follow it all the way back to the park road. Within 0.6 mile of the end, the bike trail joins from the left and you walk crushed limestone all the way out. At the park road turn right (east) and you can see the trailhead 100 feet away.

Options: Rather than backtracking from the turnaround point, you could head north 2.5 miles along the beach all the way back to the lighthouse and park entry station to complete a long loop and reduce the hike mileage by 1.5 miles. However, this would require crossing Molash Creek. This might mean traversing a narrow strip of sand between standing water and the lake or fording the mouth of a creek in water higher than your boots. The conditions may change relatively quickly. Another option is to remain on the Ridge Trails and complete the loop of the Red/Blue/Yellow Trails for an even 5.0 miles. Also, a return along the bike path offers an easier, level surface.

Local information: Manitowoc Area Visitor and Convention Bureau, 4221 Calumet Ave., Manitowoc, 54220; (800) 627-4896; www.manitowoc.info

MILES AND DIRECTIONS

0.0 Start south from the trailhead.

0.7 Bear left on the Ice Age Trail.

1.5 Bear left (south) at the Blue/Yellow Trails juncture.

1.9 Cross the road to the group camp.

2.5 Pass a bench overlooking Molash Creek as the trail bends southwest.

2.8 Bear left at the return trail of the Yellow Loop.

3.0 Turn left as the Ice Age Trail joins the bike trail heading south.

3.4 Cross the Molash Creek bridge.

3.5 Bear left where the Ice Age Trail leaves the bike trail.

4.8 Cross the dunes on a cordwalk to the beach (turn around).

6.1 Cross Molash Creek.

6.7 Bear left at the Yellow Trail junction.

8.9 Arrive back at the trailhead.

51 EMMONS CREEK

A segment of the Ice Age National Scenic Trail passes through Hartman Creek State Park and offers a fine hike through oak forest and along the clear waters of a trout stream.

Start: From the Ice Age Trail trailhead at Windfeldt Lane
Distance: 6.8-mile lollipop
Hiking time: About 3 hours
Difficulty: Moderate
Trail surface: Dirt
Best season: April–October
Other trail users: None
Land status: State park
Nearest town: Waupaca
Canine compatibility: Leashed dogs permitted
Fees and permits: State park vehicle sticker required
Schedule: Daily, 6 a.m. to 11 p.m.

Maps: Ice Age Trail Atlas Hartman Creek and Emmons Creek Segments Map #48, Hartman Creek State Park trail map, USGS Blaine (inc.) and King (inc.) quads
Trail contact: Hartman Creek State Park, N2480 Hartman Creek Rd., Waupaca, 54981; (715) 258-2372; https://dnr.wi.gov. Ice Age Trail Alliance, 2110 Main St., Cross Plains, 53528; (800) 227-0046; www .iceagetrail.org.
Camping: Hartman Creek State Park has 103 drive-in sites adjacent to the trailhead.

FINDING THE TRAILHEAD

From Waupaca, drive 5.0 miles west on WI 54 and turn left (south) on Hartman Creek Road. Drive 2.0 miles south to the Hartman Creek State Park entrance station. Obtain a trail map there and continue south another 0.5 mile to Windfeldt Lane. Turn right (west) and drive 0.5 mile to where the Ice Age Trail crosses the road. Park in the far southwest corner of the campground just to the northeast of this trail crossing. GPS: N44 19.405' / W89 13.429'

THE HIKE

Hartman Creek State Park, with its quiet lakes, is a popular spot for weekend and vacation camping. This hike takes you away from the well-known areas of the park into its quiet southwest corner and on to the Emmons Creek Fishery and Wildlife Area. It's a pleasant walk through an oak forest sprinkled with an occasional pine plantation or meadow-like old field to the star of the show, Emmons Creek. That clear-running stream brightened my day. A bench, dedicated to Aldo Leopold, aids contemplation.

Begin the hike by walking south from Windfeldt Lane on the Ice Age Trail. It is a wide trail and marked with yellow paint blazes as it winds through an open oak forest dotted with pines. Almost immediately two left turns, first south, then east, bring the trail onto an overgrown field. The field gives way to a patch of woods, and another field follows.

Two intersections in this open stretch feature maps. Go straight (south) at the first one and right (west) at the second one, leading to a low knoll featuring a bench that could seat twenty hikers. This spot, shown on park maps as High Point, offers views of the surrounding fields and meadows. Hawks circle above, scanning for their next meal.

Resume walking southwest on the well-marked Ice Age Trail, now in woods. A short distance farther, go straight (south) at an intersection with a ski and bike trail. This junction, complete with map, is the last of the cluster of trails just south of Windfeldt Lane.

Emmons Creek in Emmons Creek
Barrens State Natural Area
PREAMTIP SATASUK

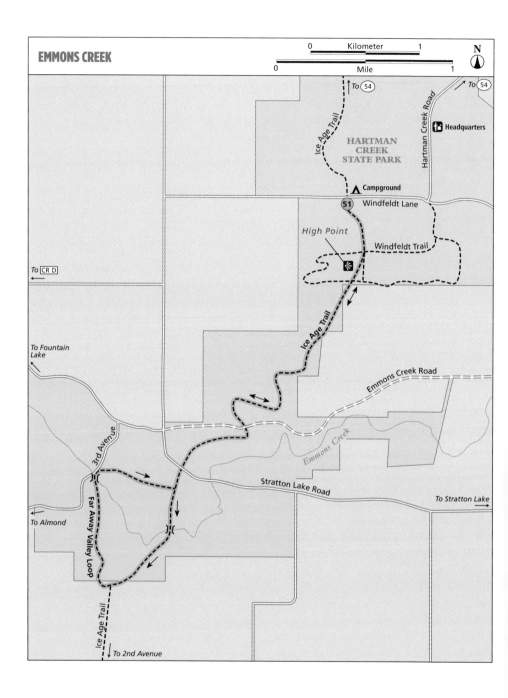

EMMONS CREEK

0 — Kilometer — 1
0 — Mile — 1

N

To 54
To 54

Ice Age Trail

HARTMAN
CREEK
STATE PARK

Hartman Creek Road

Headquarters

Campground

51 Windfeldt Lane

High Point

Windfeldt Trail

To CR D

Ice Age Trail

To Fountain
Lake

Emmons Creek Road

Emmons Creek

3rd Avenue

Stratton Lake Road

To Stratton Lake

To Almond

Far Away Valley Loop

Ice Age Trail

To 2nd Avenue

The trail, now a 2-foot-wide path, winds south through open oak forest, passing a sign that announces the Emmons Creek Fish and Wildlife Area near a short stretch of pine plantation. A grove of older white pines sits on the top of a short, sharp rise. At mile 1.8 the trail crosses Emmons Creek Road and shortly after that swings west on top of a ridge. The trail, a grassy old road here, runs through pine plantations before descending southward to Stratton Lake Road at mile 2.4.

Walk south across the road and through the open meadows and fields beyond. Watch for harriers here. Harriers, unlike other members of the hawk family, do not circle and scan from on high. They cruise close to the ground, taking their prey by surprise.

The trail reaches the Far Away Valley Loop north junction at mile 2.5. Bear left (south) here, continuing on the main Ice Age Trail to the bridge over Emmons Creek at mile 2.7. A bench here makes an appealing break spot.

Emmons is a beautiful, clear stream, 10 feet wide and running between grassy hummocks and marsh marigolds blooming in April. Trout, rising for insects, dimple the surface. A boardwalk takes the trail southwest, slightly away from the creek.

The stream is again close to the trail a quarter mile farther on and 100 feet down a slope to the northwest. It's well worth dodging a few bushes to make your way down to the creek and soak in the scene. Seeps and springs are abundant at the bottom of the slope, so be careful to step on the solid grass hummock areas.

When you are ready, continue walking southwest on the Ice Age Trail, reaching the Far Away Valley Loop south junction at mile 3.1. Turn right (west), following the green blazes of that trail as the Ice Age Trail (yellow blazes) goes south. The Far Away Valley Loop meanders northwest, through scrub oaks and occasional lichen.

The creek appears again on your right (east), and a moment later you reach 3rd Avenue and a bridge over Emmons Creek at mile 3.8. Turn right (northeast), crossing the bridge, and a moment later turn right (east) on a marked path. Walk east, passing through a pine plantation and then the open fields leading to the Far Away Valley Loop north junction at mile 4.3. At that intersection you join the main Ice Age Trail (yellow blazes) by turning left (north) to retrace your steps back to Windfeldt Lane.

Local information: Visit Waupaca County, www.visitwaupacacounty.com

MILES AND DIRECTIONS

0.0   Start at the trailhead south of Windfeldt Lane.

0.5   Pass High Point.

1.8   Cross Emmons Creek Road.

2.4   Cross Stratton Lake Road.

2.5   Bear left (south) at Far Away Valley Loop north junction.

2.7   Cross the Emmons Creek foot bridge.

3.1   Turn right (west) at Far Away Valley Loop south junction.

3.8   Cross the Emmons Creek bridge at 3rd Avenue.

4.3   Turn left (north) onto the Ice Age Trail at Far Away Valley Loop north junction.

6.8   Arrive back at the trailhead.

52 HORICON MARSH

Bring your binoculars for this massive wetlands of international importance and bird-watching hot spot. Follow a boardwalk along cattails and near open water, visit an island of nesting birds, and climb a hill with a view out over the entire marsh. While there are some forested segments here, much of the hike is level with the water on crushed rock paths circling impoundments where waterfowl gather.

Start: From the trailhead next to the visitor center
Distance: 4.9-mile loop
Hiking time: About 2 hours
Difficulty: Easy
Trail surface: Crushed rock, dirt, grass
Best season: Spring through fall, especially during bird migration
Other trail users: None
Land status: State park
Nearest town: Waupun

Canine compatibility: Leashed dogs permitted
Fees and permits: None
Schedule: Daily, 5 a.m. to 10 p.m.
Maps: USGS Waupun North and South; at the visitor center, posted on the trail
Trail contact: Horicon Marsh State Wildlife Area, N7725 WI 28, Horicon, 53032; (920) 387-7890; www.horiconmarsh.org
Special considerations: Binoculars and field guides are a good idea.

FINDING THE TRAILHEAD

From Milwaukee, take WI 145 north and exit onto US 41/45 north. Follow US 41 for 24 miles and take exit 72 for WI 33. Turn left on WI 33 and go 15.1 miles. Turn right on WI 28/Clason Street and drive 1.9 miles. The visitor center is on the left, and the trailhead is to the left of the building. GPS: N43 28.430' / W88 36.068'

The trail at Horicon Marsh sometimes follows the dikes.

Observation platforms offer sweeping views of Horicon Marsh.

THE HIKE

Any hike should start with a visit to the Horicon Marsh Education and Visitor Center. Two floors of exhibits explain the origins of the marsh, its importance, and its residents (and migrants). The center overlooks the marsh and has a gift shop and an abundance of free information, such as birding checklists and park maps. You can get to the trails right out the back door.

From the parking lot, pass around the visitor center to the left to start on the trail. On your right is Bachhuber Impoundment, an area of open water set off by walkable dikes where you are likely to see a lot of waterfowl. A boardwalk runs parallel to the trail but is deeper into cattails if you prefer. Both come to Indermuehle Island, where you can follow a loop trail through the woods and possibly see nesting birds. A boardwalk trail off the island path connects south to an alternative parking lot along the highway. Complete the loop of Indermuehle, and the crushed-rock trail continues along the impoundment to the center of the park. Here you enter trees and brush, and the path goes to the left up the hill to where the visitor center used to be. At the top of the hill, step off the trail to find observation points giving you a very wide view of the marsh and its enormity. A fixed spotting scope is here if you didn't bring binoculars.

Get back on the trail and continue south along this ridge, heading through brush and descending the hill until the path turns right, crosses the road, and continues on a trail from a parking lot there. This is the last stretch of woods, and the trail delivers you to open grasslands at the bottom of that hill you were just on at the observation point. The park service maintains roads through here, but where you are allowed to go is clearly marked.

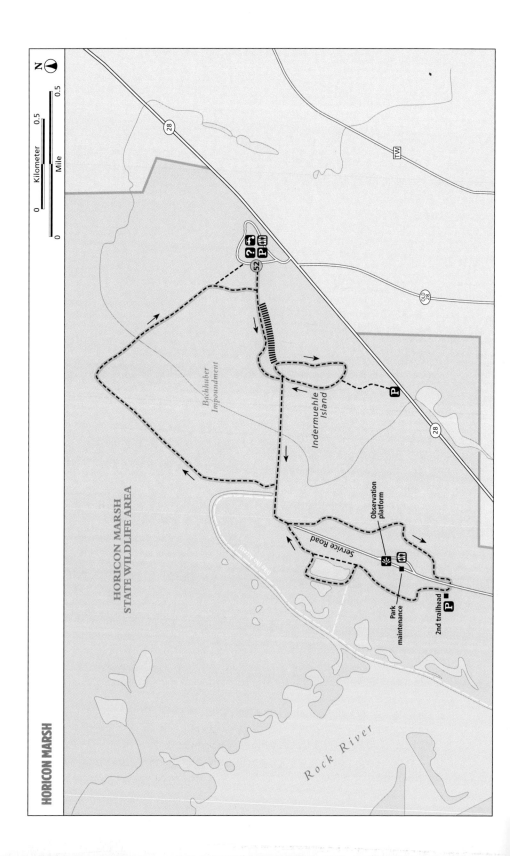

HORICON MARSH

Kilometer
0   0.5
0   0.5
Mile

N

HORICON MARSH
STATE WILDLIFE AREA

Bachhuber
Impoundment

Indermuehle
Island

Observation
platform

Park
maintenance

Service Road

2nd trailhead

Rock River

52

28

OLD
28

TW

THE MAKING OF A MARSH

Before there was a marsh, there was a lake, Glacial Lake Horicon, in fact. First, the ice sheet carved away limestone to create a basin, leaving a few drumlins behind, which you can still see as islands in parts of the marsh. Then, as the Green Bay ice lobe melted, debris was deposited in the form of a moraine. This became the dam that gathered the icy waters. What is now the Rock River drained the lake slowly and wore away that natural barrier, but slowly enough that silt and peat would accumulate and eventually become this 32,000-acre marsh. But that wasn't the end of the story. European settlers came to the area and founded the town of Horicon. A local sawmill needed water power, so a dam was constructed in 1846 to build that marsh back into a lake again. The water levels rose dramatically, and the marsh was no longer. Enter the angry landowners who now needed snorkels if they wanted to see their land. The case went to the Wisconsin State Supreme Court, and in 1869 the court sided with the landowners, and the dam was removed. Soon after, it became apparent that massive amounts of birds were partial to the marsh. Despite some failed efforts to drain out plots of farmland in the early twentieth century, the marsh prevailed, and in 1927 the Horicon Marsh Wildlife Refuge Bill was passed by the state government. Eventually the preserved lands grew to their current size, and now the northern two thirds are managed as a national refuge, while the southern portion is maintained by the Wisconsin Department of Natural Resources. Both the national and state refuges have hiking trails (see Honorable Mentions at the end of the book for the National Refuge), and the latter also offers a paddling trail (see FalconGuides *Paddling Wisconsin*).

Trails venture out into the marsh with water on either side. At the end of the turn through the marsh, take the trail left into the woods. Turn left on a service road and return to the impoundment where you started. This time take a left on the back of the dike and follow that path all the way back around the impoundment to the visitor center. At 4.7 miles a cutoff trail bears left up the hill to the center. Stay right and follow the eastern edge of the impoundment and at the next juncture, turn left to return to the trailhead.

MILES AND DIRECTIONS

0.0 Start from the trailhead and take the path or boardwalk (they run parallel) along the water of the Bachhuber Impoundment.

0.2 Take the loop trail into the trees on Indermuehle Island.

1.1 Arrive back at the main trail and bear left.

1.4 Pass the dike trail coming to you on the right.

1.9 Stop at the observation platform.

2.3 Cross a park service road and a parking lot to find a second trailhead on the right.

2.8 Take the dike trail left out into the marsh.

3.1 Take the trail left at the end of it.

3.2 At a trail juncture in the woods, take the trail left.

3.4 At the corner of the Bachhuber Impoundment, take the dike trail left.

4.7 Bear right at the trail split.

4.9 Arrive back at the trailhead.

53 **NORTH KETTLE MORAINE**

Of all the 60-some miles of Ice Age Trail in the Kettle Moraine State Forest, this is the trail segment with the longest continuous stretch of woods. The woodland ambiance along this hike is a pleasure for the eye, but there is a practical angle here as well. This shady, up-and-down-the-moraine, 10.3-mile route is one of my favorites for a sunny summer day.

Start: From the trailhead at CR V
Distance: 10.3-mile lollipop
Hiking time: About 4.5 hours
Difficulty: Difficult
Trail surface: Dirt
Best season: April–October
Other trail users: None
Land status: State forest
Nearest town: Dundee
Canine compatibility: Leashed dogs permitted
Fees and permits: State park vehicle sticker required
Schedule: Daily, 6 a.m. to 11 p.m.
Maps: Ice Age Trail Atlas Parnell Segment Map #88 and #89, Kettle

Moraine State Forest Trail Map, USGS Cascade quad
Trail contact: Kettle Moraine State Forest Northern Unit, Forest Headquarters, N1765 Hwy. G, Campbellsport, 53010; (262) 626-2116; https://dnr.wi.gov. Ice Age Trail Alliance, 2110 Main St., Cross Plains, 53528; (800) 227-0046; www.iceagetrail.org.
Camping: Shelter #4 with permit from Kettle Moraine State Forest, reservations required. Call (888) 947-2757. Long Lake, 3.0 miles west of the trailhead, has 200 drive-in sites.

FINDING THE TRAILHEAD

From WI 67 in Dundee, drive 3.0 miles east on CR F and turn left (north) on Pine Road. Drive 1.2 miles north and turn left (west) on CR V. Drive 0.3 mile west. Park on the wide shoulder on the south side of the road as it descends into an open area. GPS: N43 40.00290' / W88 07.439'

THE HIKE
Begin by following the broad Ice Age Trail north from CR V as it follows the crest of the moraine. A broad marsh begins to the west, while the first of a series of small wetlands appears in a bowl to the east. About 0.5 mile north the trail skirts an open field for a quarter mile, reenters the woods, and ascends the moraine in a short, steep climb. On a fine spring day, the kettle wetlands along this stretch will be noisy with the chorus of spring peepers, frogs rejoicing in the warm weather. During the summer, watch for tiny frogs, the size of your smallest fingernail, along the trail.

The Ice Age Trail continues northeast, with minor wetlands on either side, and crosses Scenic Drive at mile 1.3. Follow the trail north as it dips and rolls through a pleasant hardwood forest. At about mile 2.8 the path passes through a notably pleasant glade featuring a grassy forest floor beneath widely spaced trees, before crossing CR U at mile 3.1.

North of CR U the trail ascends to a junction with the Parnell Tower Trail at mile 3.4. Bear left (northwest), following both the blue blazes of the Ice Age Trail and the yellow blazes of the Parnell Tower Trail for the next quarter mile. The combined path descends an eroded slope to the west before swinging north to a junction at mile 3.7, where the

Glacial drumlins visible in the distance

two trails split. Trail shelter #4 is nearby to the east. Bear right (northeast) at that split, following the yellow blazes of the Parnell Tower Trail north.

After a little more than a mile, the path, a loop route, begins a swing east and then south. Keep walking south as the trail, at times a rock garden, ascends the higher part of the moraine and arrives at the Parnell Observation Tower at mile 6.3. The view from the top, taking in large parts of southeastern Wisconsin on a clear day, is well worth the climb. A water pump and toilets are southeast of the tower in a parking and picnic area.

When you are ready, locate the continuation of the trail, just south of the tower. The path runs southwest slightly and then turns west, rejoining the Ice Age Trail at mile 6.9. This is the same intersection you saw at mile 3.4 of the hike. Turn left (south) and retrace your steps on the Ice Age Trail to return to CR V.

The 60-foot Parnell Tower provides views of glacial formations otherwise not visible from close up.

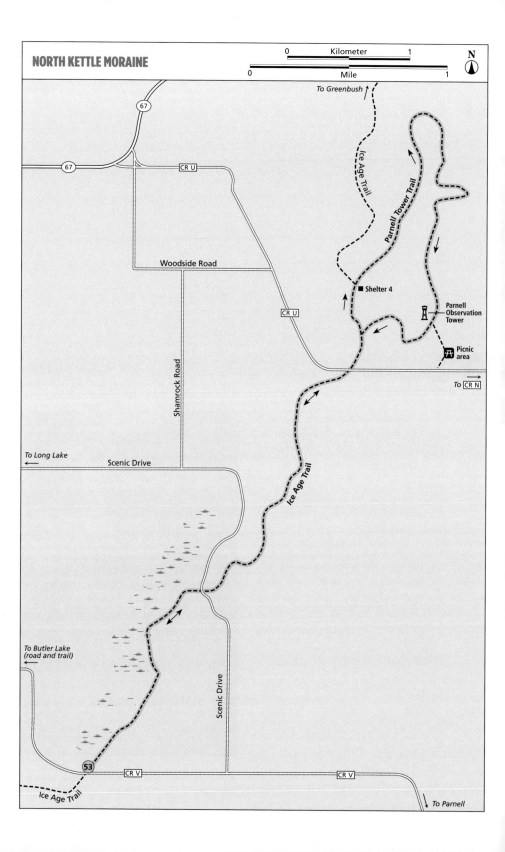

0   Kilometer   1

0   Mile   1

N

To Greenbush ↑

67

67   CR U

Ice Age Trail

Parnell Tower Trail

Woodside Road

CR U

■ Shelter 4

Parnell
Observation
Tower

Picnic
area

To CR N →

To Long Lake
←

Scenic Drive

Shamrock Road

Ice Age Trail

To Butler Lake
(road and trail)

Scenic Drive

53   CR V   CR V

Ice Age Trail

To Parnell ↓

A trail shelter along the Ice Age Trail in Kettle Moraine State Forest
PREAMTIP SATASUK

MILES AND DIRECTIONS

0.0   Start north from CR V.

1.3   Cross Scenic Drive.

3.1   Cross CR U.

3.4   Bear left (northwest) at the Parnell Tower Trail junction.

3.7   At the trail split at the Parnell Tower Trail junction, turn right (northeast) and pass shelter #4 on your right.

6.3   Arrive at Parnell Tower.

6.9   Bear left at the Parnell Tower Trail junction as you backtrack to the trailhead.

10.3   Arrive back at the trailhead.

54 ICE AGE TRAIL: CEDAR LAKES LOOP

Hike along the forested Polk Kames. Thanks to a white-blazed alternative trail on the other side of the kames, you can hike this segment of the Ice Age Trail round-trip without repeating too much ground. A couple of short stretches pass through rolling farmland, but most of it is in thick forest of oak, maple, and beech, and follows the glacial formations.

Start: From the trailhead by the parking area
Distance: 3.8-mile lollipop
Hiking time: About 1.5–2 hours
Difficulty: Easy to moderate, due to rustic trail surface
Trail surface: Dirt
Best season: April–October
Other trail users: None
Land status: State land
Nearest town: Slinger

Canine compatibility: Leashed dogs permitted
Fees and permits: None
Schedule: Open daily, year-round
Maps: USGS Hartford East; Ice Age Trail Atlas Cedar Lakes Segment Map #85; in a box at the trailhead
Trail contact: Ice Age Trail Alliance, 2110 Main St., Cross Plains, 53528; (800) 227-0046; www.iceagetrail.org

FINDING THE TRAILHEAD

From Milwaukee, take WI 145 north and exit onto US 41/45 north. Follow US 41 to WI 144 and take exit 66 for WI 144. Go north (right) on WI 144 for 0.3 mile and turn right on CR NN/Arthur Road. Continue 0.7 mile, and the parking lot is on the right. The trailhead is at the lot. GPS: N43 21.175' / W88 16.267'

THE HIKE

This trail begins by heading south on a two-track lane along the edge of a field, but by 500 feet you are into the trees. Watch for a narrow, rustic footpath on the right marked with the yellow blazes of the Ice Age National Scenic Trail. Take this trail into the woods over gently rolling terrain through tall stately hardwoods with sparse understory. A footbridge at 0.2 mile traverses a low soggy spot at the edge of a small marshy area on your left. The roll of the terrain starts to become a bit more strenuous, but never more than moderately so.

At 0.4 mile the trail comes alongside a ridge on your left and then angles slightly left between it and the next ridge. These are kames, glacial deposits formed at the bottom of downward-flowing water from a glacier, and you will see several throughout the hike. These are the Polk Kames and the largest collection of them in Wisconsin. At 0.5 mile cross through an agricultural field—the trail is usually clear, but watch for the posts with yellow blazes—and after a row of trees, follow the trail as it angles left through more farmland before turning due east and returning to the forest. Be aware of thorny creeping plants along the trail; they like to scratch skin or snag clothing.

The trail follows a curve north and all the way around until it heads south at the 1.0-mile mark. The ground slopes left as you traverse another kame. Smaller trees are

Boardwalks traverse some low points amid the kames along the Cedar Lakes Segment of the Ice Age Trail. PREAMTIP SATASUK

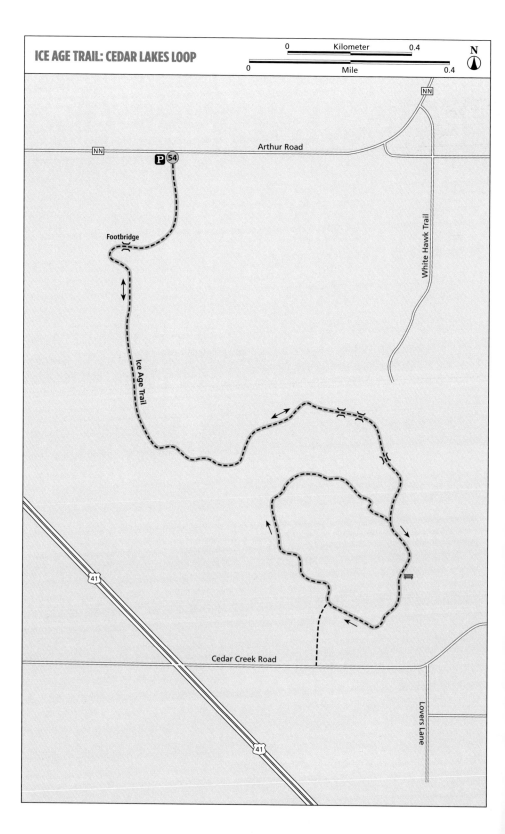

ICE AGE TRAIL: CEDAR LAKES LOOP

0   Kilometer   0.4

0   Mile   0.4

N

NN

Arthur Road

NN

P 54

White Hawk Trail

Footbridge

Ice Age Trail

41

41

Cedar Creek Road

Lovers Lane

overshadowed by towering oaks. Climb over another kame and come down to a footbridge over a low intermittent stream at 1.2 miles. Another footbridge follows. The thin understory allows you to really see the lay of the land, including a rather tall kame on the right. Pass along the southern edge of the kame and marshy area on your left, cross another footbridge, and you come to a trail juncture and map board at 1.4 miles. The trail on the right is marked with white blazes, an alternative trail, but still officially the Ice Age Trail. Go left here on the yellow-blazed path. (You can go either way, though; they come together again less than a half mile later.)

The trail passes higher along the ridges, and you pass a bench and an interpretive sign about how a kame is formed. Cross a boardwalk at 1.7 miles, and 0.1 mile later come to the next juncture with the white-blazed trail. If you go straight, the Ice Age Trail continues 0.1 mile to Cedar Creek Road, which connects it west to the Slinger Segment. Take the white-blazed trail to the right and cross a boardwalk bridge. Highway noise becomes more apparent on the west side of the kames. Cross a farmers' access road to a field tucked into the woods on the right, and pass a rock wall that bears south from the edge of the trail. The trail comes out of the trees and hugs the line between farm field and forest—shaded in the morning, exposed in the afternoon. Hike a short distance to a bench and map board. Take the trail back into the woods.

Hike through another small clearing, and at 2.3 miles watch for a sign that reads "Entering Sensitive Area." Down to the right is a water-filled kettle. The trail switches back, taking you down for a closer look, then crosses a boardwalk before coming back to the yellow-blazed trail. Take it to the left and backtrack to the parking lot.

MILES AND DIRECTIONS

0.0 Start at the trailhead near the parking area.

0.2 Cross a footbridge along a marshy area.

0.5 Enter an agricultural field.

1.2 Cross a footbridge over an intermittent stream.

1.4 At the trail juncture with the white-blazed trail, go left.

1.8 Go right at a second juncture with the white-blazed trail.

1.9 Skirt an agricultural field.

2.4 Arrive back at the first trail juncture and go left to return to the trailhead.

3.8 Arrive back at the trailhead.

SOUTHERN BLUFFS AND MORAINES

The beauty of southern Wisconsin ranges from dramatic—the rocky bluffs towering over Devil's Lake and the eroded rock bridge at Natural Bridge State Park—to simple elegance—the small sandstone canyon at Parfey's Glen and the reflecting waters of a small kettle at Beulah Bog. The Ice Age National Scenic Trail has taken advantage of this beauty as it wends its way south before making the turn north into eastern Wisconsin.

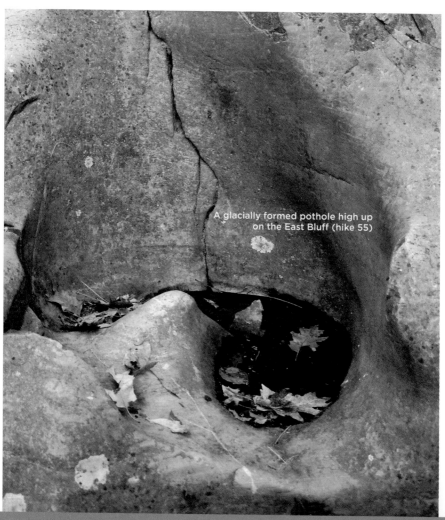

A glacially formed pothole high up on the East Bluff (hike 55)

55 DEVIL'S LAKE EAST BLUFF

One of the more strenuous hikes, this trail climbs the rocky bluff to offer sweeping views of Devil's Lake, notable rock formations, and hardwood forest.

Start: From the East Bluff trailhead
Distance: 4.6-mile loop
Hiking time: About 2 hours
Difficulty: Difficult
Trail surface: Dirt, rock
Best season: April–October
Other trail users: None
Land status: State park
Nearest town: Sauk City
Canine compatibility: Leashed dogs permitted
Fees and permits: State park vehicle sticker required
Schedule: Daily, 6 a.m. to 11 p.m.

Maps: Devil's Lake State Park trail map, USGS Baraboo (inc.) quad
Trail contact: Devil's Lake State Park, S5975 Park Rd., Baraboo, 53913; (608) 356-8301; https://dnr.wi.gov
Special considerations: Trails traverse rock sections that become very slick when wet. This hike is not a good choice for acrophobics. This is the state's most visited park. In peak season, arrive early as parking lots may fill up and close.
Camping: Devil's Lake State Park has 423 drive-in campsites.

FINDING THE TRAILHEAD

From Sauk City, drive north 11.3 miles on US 12 and turn right (east) on Ski Hi Road. Drive 1.3 miles and turn left (north) on South Shore Road. Drive another 1.3 miles to a right turn (east) on Park Road. After 0.2 mile turn right (southeast) into the park. An entrance station 0.8 mile later offers a chance to gather trail maps. Continue 1.0 mile east, past railroad tracks, and turn right (southeast) on a park road that leads to a parking area, with the trailhead directly to the east. GPS: N43 25.7209' / W89 43.602'

THE HIKE

Spring-fed Devil's Lake occupies a scenic gap in the South Range of the Baraboo Hills. With three 500-foot bluffs rising from its shores and notable rock formations on the bluff tops, it has attracted visitors for centuries. This route samples the best that Devil's Lake has to offer, while ascending and descending the spectacular East Bluff twice. These attractive trails are not a secret, and on a fine weekend day you should expect to see many other visitors.

Begin your hike by walking east from the trailhead on the broad dirt road that is the beginning of the East Bluff Trail. The trail immediately swings to the southeast and a split occurs. The dirt road continues southeast as the East Bluff Woods (yellow) Trail. Take the right (south) choice and climb the constructed stone steps and asphalt of the East Bluff Trail (orange) as it ascends through a beautiful hardwood forest.

For the next mile the trail winds between the forest and the rock outcrops that mark the edge of the escarpment while climbing to the top of the East Bluff. Along the way, numerous viewpoints offer broad views of the lake below and the West Bluff on its far shore.

At mile 1.1 the East Bluff Trail intersects the Balanced Rock Trail. Turn right (west) and begin a memorable, steep descent over talus and cemented rock steps. Halfway down, the route passes the trail's namesake boulder.

A view toward the South Bluff from the East Bluff at Devil's Lake

Shortly after the Balanced Rock Trail finally leaves its chaotic rock route for the security of dirt and the valley floor, it intersects the Grottos Trail at mile 1.5. Turn left (east) and take this broad path through an oak forest as it parallels the rock debris at the base of the bluff's slope.

Turn left (north) on the CCC Trail at mile 2.2 as it steeply ascends the bluff on rock steps. Near the top it snakes through several cliff bands before swinging left to follow the top of the escarpment west. At mile 3.0 a short trail to the left (south) leads to one of the most famous rock formations, the Devil's Doorway. The 100-yard spur leads down stone steps and across a broad rock ledge to the best vantage point for viewing this natural stone arch.

Return to the main path and walk west to the intersection with the Balanced Rock Trail at mile 3.3. Turn right (north) on a broad jeep road, a route for emergency vehicles. Shortly after, swing left (north), ignoring the jeep road that goes straight, and follow the yellow markings of the East Bluff Woods Trail.

At first the trail traverses the oak woodlands that characterize the top of the bluff. As the trail descends to the north, a damper climate, maple begins to dominate the forest. At mile 4.6 the trail returns to the trailhead, just a stone's throw past the fork where the East Bluff Trail (yellow) joins the route.

Local information: Devil's Lake State Park Area Visitor Guide, www.devilslake wisconsin.com

MILES AND DIRECTIONS

0.0   Start from the trailhead of the East Bluff Trail (orange).

1.1   Descend right (west) on the Balanced Rock Trail.

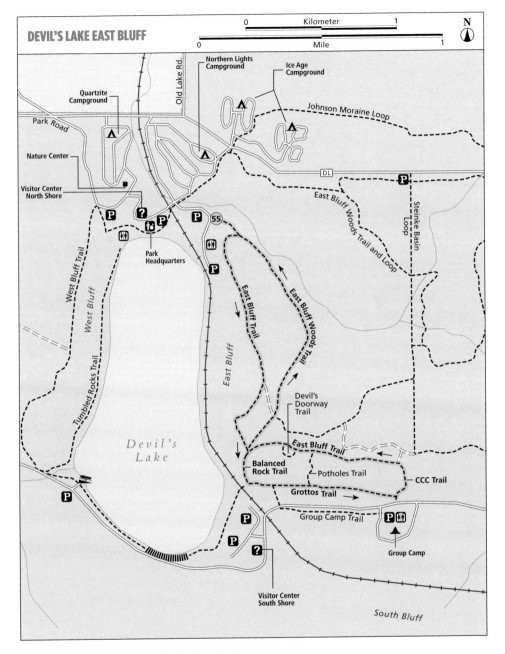

DEVIL'S LAKE EAST BLUFF

0 ——— Kilometer ——— 1

0 ——— Mile ——— 1

N

Quartzite Campground

Northern Lights Campground

Ice Age Campground

Old Lake Rd.

Johnson Moraine Loop

Park Road

Nature Center

Visitor Center North Shore

DL

East Bluff Woods Trail and Loop

Steinke Basin Loop

Park Headquarters

55

West Bluff Trail

West Bluff

East Bluff Trail

East Bluff Woods Trail

East Bluff

Tumbled Rocks Trail

Devil's Lake

Devil's Doorway Trail

East Bluff Trail

Balanced Rock Trail

Potholes Trail

CCC Trail

Grottos Trail

Group Camp Trail

Group Camp

Visitor Center South Shore

South Bluff

1.5   Turn left (east) on the Grottos Trail.

2.2   Take the CCC Trail left (north).

3.0   Go left (south) 100 yards to see Devil's Doorway spur.

3.3   Bear right on the East Bluff Woods Trail (yellow trail, but not Ice Age Trail).

4.6   Arrive back at the trailhead.

56 DEVIL'S LAKE TO PARFREY'S GLEN

Combining state park trails and the Ice Age National Scenic Trail, this thru-hike starts with sweeping bluff-top views at Devil's Lake and ends with the intimate charms of the scenic gorge of Parfrey's Glen.

Start: From the trailhead of the East Bluff Trail
Distance: 8.5-mile point-to-point shuttle hike
Hiking time: About 4 hours
Difficulty: Difficult
Trail surface: Dirt, rock
Best season: April–October
Other trail users: None
Land status: State park
Nearest town: Sauk City
Canine compatibility: Leashed dogs permitted, but prohibited in Parfrey's Glen
Fees and permits: State park vehicle sticker required
Schedule: Daily, 6 a.m. to 11 p.m. (8 p.m. in Parfrey's Glen)

Maps: Ice Age Trail Atlas Devil's Lake and Sauk Point Segments Map #61, USGS Baraboo (inc.) quad
Trail contact: Devil's Lake State Park, S5975 Park Rd., Baraboo, 53913, (608) 356-8301; https://dnr.wi.gov. Ice Age Trail Alliance, 2110 Main St., Cross Plains, 53528; (800) 227-0046; www.iceagetrail.org.
Special considerations: Trails traverse rock sections that become very slick when wet. This hike is not a good choice for acrophobics. Devil's Lake is the state's most visited park. In peak season, arrive early as parking lots may fill up and close.
Camping: Devil's Lake State Park has 423 drive-in campsites.

FINDING THE TRAILHEAD

From Sauk City, drive north 11.3 miles on US 12 and turn right (east) on Ski Hi Road. Drive 1.3 miles and turn left (north) on South Shore Road. Drive another 1.3 miles to a right turn (east) on Park Road. After 0.2 mile turn right (southeast) into the park. An entrance station 0.8 mile later offers a chance to gather trail maps. Continue 1.0 mile east, past railroad tracks, and turn right (southeast) on a park road, and at the second in a series of four roadside parking lots, the trailhead is directly to the east. GPS: N43 25.7209' / W89 43.602'

THE HIKE

Two of the most scenic hikes in south-central Wisconsin, the East Bluff of Devil's Lake and Parfrey's Glen, anchor each end of this route. Along the way, it skirts cliff tops and traverses a hardwood forest at the east end of Devil's Lake State Park. Rolling east, it ascends through old fields and small wood lots to Sauk County's highest point and long views stretching to Blue Mounds, 30 miles to the southwest. Finally, it drops to the valley floor to sample the intimate charms of Parfrey's Glen.

For the first 2.5 miles, this hike's route is the same as the Devil's Lake East Bluff Hike. At mile 2.2 of the hike, the route begins a steep ascent of the East Bluff on the CCC Trail. As the trail reaches the lip of the bluff, it turns sharply west. Just after that turn, at mile 2.5, turn right (northwest) on a narrow path that connects with the Ice Age Trail 90 yards later and continue east on the broad, graveled Ice Age Trail. Go straight (east) 200 yards later at mile 2.7, where the Steinke Basin Trail goes north.

Sandstone embedded with stones
and quartzite at Parfrey's Glen

DEVIL'S LAKE TO PARFREY'S GLEN

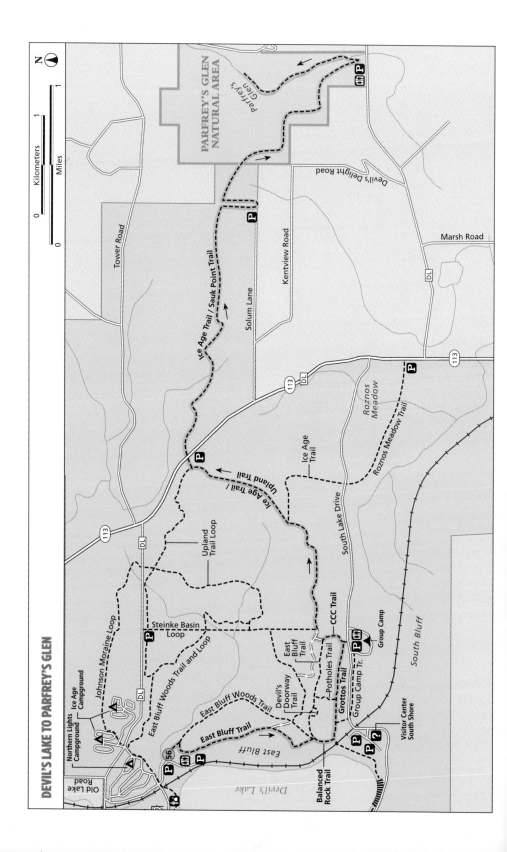

The Ice Age Trail continues east, rising 100 feet onto a high spot on the bluff and running close to the top of the escarpment. Garage-size chunks of granite litter the top of the slope, and quiet hikers can spot turkey vulture flocks roosting in the rock fields. The South Bluff, rising 0.5 mile away across the valley, screens views in that direction, but to the southeast long vistas open up to Lake Wisconsin and beyond.

Swing north, still walking in a fine hardwood forest, and at the Ice Age Trail junction at mile 3.5—where the Ice Age Trail departs southeast toward Merrimac—bear left (north) on the Upland Trail, continuing to another Ice Age Trail intersection on the northeast side of the park at mile 4.4. Turn right (east) on the Ice Age Trail and shortly after cross WI 113 at mile 4.5.

East of WI 113 the trail's route takes on a more pastoral flavor, running through small sections of woods and meadow-like old fields. About 1.25 mile east of WI 113, follow the crest of a broad ridge before turning south in a meadow bordered by scrubby woods. Long views open up to the southwest, across the Wisconsin River Valley, to Blue Mounds and beyond. Hawks work the open spaces, riding the bluff top breezes.

At mile 6.4 the trail passes the eastern end of Solum Lane and swings northeast, beginning a gentle ascent. The radio towers ahead of you mark Sauk Point, the highest spot in Sauk County, a reminder to turn around from time to time and check for views. A meadow offers a view to the south before the trail turns east and begins to descend.

Follow the trail southeast, in and out of woods, as it steadily drops. For the last 0.8 mile the path goes through a pleasant stretch of older maple forest before arriving at the Parfrey's Glen trailhead and parking area at mile 8.5.

Local information: Devil's Lake State Park Area Visitor Guide, www.devilslake wisconsin.com

MILES AND DIRECTIONS

0.0   Start from the trailhead of the East Bluff Trail.

1.1   Descend right (west) on the Balanced Rock Trail.

1.5   Turn left (east) on the Grottos Trail.

2.2   Take the CCC Trail left (north) up the bluff.

2.5   Turn right (northwest) on the Ice Age Trail.

2.7   Stay straight on the Ice Age Trail at its juncture with the Steinke Basin Trail.

3.5   Bear left (north) on the Upland Trail at its juncture with the Ice Age Trail.

4.4   Turn right (east) on the Ice Age Trail junction.

4.5   Cross WI 113.

6.4   Pass the end of Solum Lane and bear left (northeast) on the Ice Age Trail.

8.5   Arrive at the Parfrey's Glen parking area.

57 PARFREY'S GLEN

This is a local favorite for a quick stroll through a natural beauty, Parfrey's Glen. This hike may be short, but the charming sandstone glen, gurgling brook, small waterfall, and unusual species of plants are cause for lingering.

Start: From the trailhead near the parking lot
Distance: 1.4-mile out-and-back
Hiking time: About 30 minutes
Difficulty: Easy
Trail surface: Dirt, rock
Best season: April–October
Other trail users: None
Land status: State park
Nearest town: Merrimac
Canine compatibility: Pets are not permitted.
Fees and permits: A state park vehicle sticker is required.

Schedule: Daily, 6 a.m. to 8 p.m.
Maps: USGS Baraboo (inc.) quad
Trail contact: Devil's Lake State Park, S5975 Park Rd., Baraboo, 53913; (608) 356-8301; https://dnr.wi.gov
Special considerations: Parfrey's Glen is a state scientific area that requires visitors to remain on the trail and within 20 feet of the creek. Visitors are not allowed past the waterfall. Food and pets are not allowed.
Camping: Devil's Lake State Park, 5.0 miles west, has 423 drive-in sites.

FINDING THE TRAILHEAD

From Merrimac, drive north 2.5 miles on Bluff Road and turn left (west) on CR DL. After 0.2 mile turn right (north) into the Parfrey's Glen DNR parking lot. GPS: N43 24.630' / W89 38.210'

Moss grows on the sandstone at Parfrey's Glen, moistened by seeps.

Pay close attention to the little
things at Parfrey's Glen.

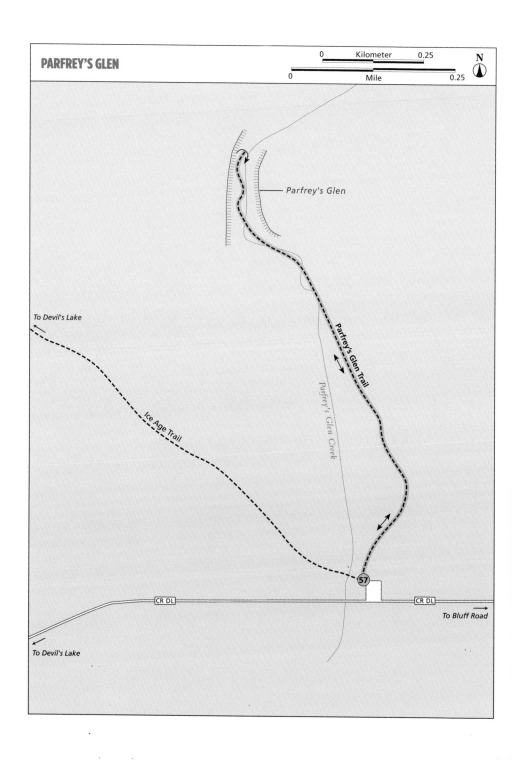

0   Kilometer   0.25

0   Mile   0.25

N

Parfrey's Glen

To Devil's Lake

Parfrey's Glen Trail

Ice Age Trail

Parfrey's Glen Creek

57

CR DL   CR DL

To Bluff Road

To Devil's Lake

THE MERRIMAC FERRY

Possibly the most unusual segment of the Ice Age Trail is the one across the Wisconsin River. Hikers take a load off and let the Merrimac ferry span the water between the Merrimac and Gibraltar Segments of the trail. The river is dammed here, creating the wider Lake Wisconsin.

Created by Chester Mattson and George Grant and opened in 1848, the Merrimac ferry used to cost twenty-five cents to bring a horse across. Today's *Colsac III*—named for Columbia and Sauk, the counties it connects—doesn't even cost a dime. This free ferry, on WI 113 just south of the Parfrey's Glen, runs round the clock and is the only crossing between the bridges of WI 12 in Sauk City to the west and I-94 to the east. Guided by three steel cables, the ferry holds up to 15 vehicles but manages to move 250,000 of them each year from about the end of March to the end of November—the season when the lake is ice-free. If the lines are long in summer, don't worry, there is an ice-cream stand on the Merrimac side.

THE HIKE

Parfrey's Glen, a picturesque, a quarter-mile-long sandstone gorge, cuts through the Baraboo Hills' south slope 5.0 miles east of Devil's Lake. Robert Parfrey, the site's namesake, operated a grain mill near the mouth of the narrow canyon in the 1870s.

Today the glen has state scientific area status to protect its rare plants. The glen is a moist, shaded environment, harboring plants such as white pine, yellow birch, and mountain maple that are more typical of northern Wisconsin.

From the trailhead walk north on a gently ascending lane, first in an old field and then in thickening woods. The road becomes a 4-foot-wide path made of stones and crosses on rocks over Parfrey's Glen Creek. The boardwalk and bridges were washed out by floods in 2008 and 2010, so now visitors are advised to stay on the rustic trail and are not allowed to venture more than 20 feet from the creek or into the area beyond the waterfall at the far point of the hike.

Here the drainage is still a broad ravine, but where the trail ascends stone steps, the canyon begins in earnest. Forty-foot-high walls, sheltering shaded nooks, soon grow to nearly 100 feet in height.

The path continues to a point where a pile of fallen rocks lies on the canyon floor. Just on the other side is the end of the trail, a walled viewpoint. From this spot you can actually see out of the upper end of the gorge, as well as a small, 6-foot-high waterfall some 30 yards in front of you. Due to the fragile nature of the plant life here, hikers are not allowed to explore beyond the trail and pets are not allowed.

Local information: Devil's Lake State Park Area Visitor Guide, www.devilslake wisconsin.com

MILES AND DIRECTIONS

0.0 Head north from the Parfrey's Glen trailhead.

0.7 Arrive at the waterfall and the end of the trail.

1.4 Arrive back at the trailhead.

58 **NATURAL BRIDGE**

Hike up a bluff into the woods with a scenic overlook and a geological wonder: a natural bridge created by erosion. Then cross the highway and explore another forested bluff often passed over by bridge visitors.

Start: From the trailhead near the parking lot
Distance: 2.4-mile loop
Hiking time: About 1 hour
Difficulty: Moderate
Trail surface: Dirt
Best season: April–October
Other trail users: None
Land status: State park
Nearest town: Sauk City
Canine compatibility: Dogs are not permitted.
Fees and permits: A state park vehicle sticker is required.

Schedule: Daily, 6 a.m. to 11 p.m.
Maps: USGS Blackhawk (inc.) quad; posted on the trail; Devil's Lake State Park office
Trail contact: Devil's Lake State Park, S5975 Park Rd., Baraboo, 53913; (608) 356-8301; https://dnr.wi.gov
Special considerations: The rock bridge and archaeological site are fragile areas and behind a fence for a reason; do not touch or climb here.
Camping: Devil's Lake State Park, 5 miles west, has 500 drive-in sites.

FINDING THE TRAILHEAD

From Sauk City, drive north 8.0 miles on US 12. Turn west and drive 10.9 miles west to the park entrance on the right. The trailhead is on the right. GPS: N43 20.72268' / W89 55.790'

THE HIKE

While a bit smaller in scale, this sandstone bridge is reminiscent of the sculpted rock of the American West. While it is visually impressive, one also need consider that a rock shelter near the 35-foot arch shows evidence of human habitation perhaps more than 10,000 years ago. Most visitors go directly to the arch and back out to their vehicles, but a scenic overlook and a trek through the southern portion of the park merit the extra time.

Take the trail that begins to the right of the pit toilets, starting uphill through mixed forest. At 0.2 mile turn left at a trail juncture. The trail coming from the right is your return route for this hike. In another 500 feet turn right and climb to the top of the bluff, where you find views out over the surrounding woods with its intervening tracts of farmland.

Backtrack from this point and turn right on the main trail again. In less than a quarter mile, you come around a turn in the trail and the arch appears. A wood fence keeps visitors back from the rock formation. The erosion that formed the formation continues, and climbing traffic would only hasten its end. To the right and below the bridge is the old rock shelter.

At mile 0.7 turn right (south) to bypass the short return trail to the parking lot. Rather, continue south on an exposed grassy trail. As you approach the county highway, you pass an old cabin and a smokehouse. Cross the highway at mile 1.0 and follow a path through farmland to the wooded bluff south of here. Tall, old hardwoods provide a thick canopy, but much of the understory is low to the ground so that you can see deep into the woods.

Hikers admire the rock arch at Natural Bridge.

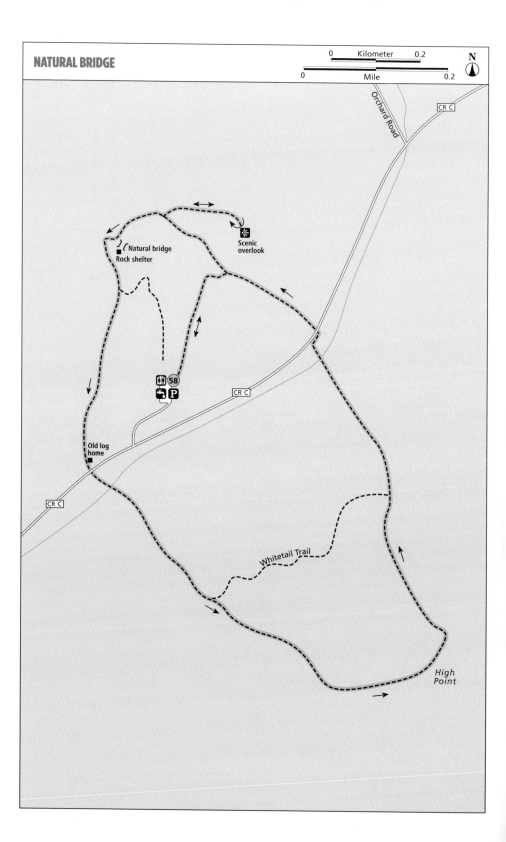

NATURAL BRIDGE

Kilometer
0   0.2

Mile
0   0.2

N

Orchard Road

CR C

Scenic overlook

Natural bridge
Rock shelter

58

CR C

Old log home

CR C

Whitetail Trail

High Point

Natural Bridge

Watch for deer here. At mile 1.2 cross the appropriately named Whitetail Trail (I saw two deer when I passed it), a cutoff path that skips the higher climb. Continue uphill on the main trail. As you come across the high bluff top, the trail starts to descend in switchbacks, crosses the other end of Whitetail Trail on your left at mile 1.8, and continues down out of the forest through a farm field before returning to CR C at mile 2.1. Cross and follow the trail into the woods. At the next juncture turn left and return to the trailhead.

Local information: Sauk Prairie Area Chamber of Commerce, 109 Phillips Blvd., Sauk City, 53583; (608) 643-4168; www.saukprairie.com/explore

MILES AND DIRECTIONS

0.0   Begin at the trailhead near the parking lot.

0.2   Bear left (northwest) uphill.

0.3   Turn right on the trail to the scenic overlook.

0.5   Return from the overlook to the main trail and turn right (northwest).

0.6   Pass the natural rock bridge.

0.7   Bear right (south) at the juncture with the trail to the parking lot.

1.0   Cross CR C.

1.2   Bear right (south) at the juncture with the Whitetail Trail.

1.8   Bear right (north) at the eastern end of the Whitetail Trail.

2.1   Cross CR C.

2.2   Turn left to backtrack to the trailhead.

2.4   Arrive back at the trailhead.

59 LAKE LA GRANGE

Check out a historic pioneer cabin and the remains of a lime kiln before following the southern half of the Blackhawk Segment of the Ice Age National Scenic Trail. This quiet footpath skirts some wetlands before climbing a ridge through mature hardwood forest. Your turnaround point is a peaceful lake and marsh rich in wildlife.

Start: From the blue spur of the Ice Age Trail at Oleson Cabin
Distance: 9.0-mile out-and-back
Hiking time: About 4 hours
Difficulty: Moderate
Trail surface: Dirt, grass
Best season: April–October
Other trail users: None
Land status: State forest
Nearest town: Palmyra
Canine compatibility: Leashed dogs permitted
Fees and permits: State park vehicle sticker required
Schedule: Daily

Maps: Ice Age Trail Atlas Blackhawk Segment Map #79, USGS Whitewater (inc.) and Little Prairie (inc.) quads
Trail contact: Kettle Moraine State Forest Southern Unit, S91 W39091 WI 59, Eagle, 53119; (262) 594-6200; https://dnr.wi.gov. Ice Age Trail Alliance, 2110 Main St., Cross Plains, 53528; (800) 227-0046; www.iceagetrail.org.
Camping: Shelter #3 with permit from Kettle Moraine State Forest. Whitewater Lake, 4.0 miles southwest of the trailhead, has sixty-two drive-in sites.

FINDING THE TRAILHEAD

From Palmyra, drive 3.8 miles south on CR H, which becomes Walworth County Route H. Turn right (west) on Bluff Road and after 1.1 miles turn left (south) on Duffin Road. Park on the wide grassy shoulder at the Oleson Cabin. GPS: N42 49.468' / W88 37.240'

THE HIKE

When you step out of your car at the Oleson Cabin, the quiet ambiance of this hike begins. You won't find any of the crowds here that are at some southern Kettle Moraine trailheads.

A restored two-story log cabin is 100 yards east of the road. Ole Oleson, a Norwegian immigrant, built this home for his family out of tamarack logs hauled from the nearby Scuppernong Marsh in 1846.

Follow the path past the cabin and look for the blue-blazed Ice Age Trail spur marked with a post. Follow this east along the edge of the forest to where it joins the yellow-marked main trail of the Ice Age Trail; follow it to the right (south), and it crosses an optional 0.6-mile spur trail left (east) into the woods to an old lime kiln. Continuing south on the Ice Age Trail through brushy meadows and pine plantations, you come to the spur trail (at mile 0.8) for the #3 shelter (100 yards off the Ice Age Trail). Shortly after that you cross Duffin Road, round a spring-fed wetland, and enter the beautiful hardwood forest you will spend the next hour crossing.

You will receive a quick lesson in the tumbled topography of the Kettle Moraine region as the trail ascends almost 200 feet. At 0.7 mile from the road, the trail passes some large mossy tree trunks lying on the ground and then a large log arranged as a bench,

Lake La Grange at the turnaround point for the hike

capable of seating a dozen. This marks the end of the climb, and it will be another 1.5 miles before you begin the slow descent to Lake La Grange.

Three miles after entering the woods at Duffin Road, the trail emerges into the extensive fields and meadows that border Lake La Grange. The open space is exhilarating after your sojourn in the woods and adds a harmonious balance to the day's outing. Hawks work the tall grass. At mile 4.0 a white-blazed alternative path of the Ice Age Trail heads west and then south to the parking area on US 12; bear right here on the yellow-blazed trail. A small rise offers views of the sparkling lake and the hills beyond.

A little farther on you will notice a bench to the north of the trail, overlooking the lake. This area makes a fine destination for your hike. The shoreline beyond the bench is sandy and pleasant. Fifty yards west is a trail juncture: to the left, the Ice Age Trail continues south toward US 12 and the Whitewater Lake Segment, and to the right, a short spur trail leads north 100 yards to the end of Big Spring Drive (see Options). Retrace your steps on the Ice Age Trail to return to the Oleson Cabin trailhead.

Options: You could walk this hike in the opposite direction, starting from the Lake La Grange area. This alternative might be attractive to backpackers wishing to stay at shelter #3 (permit required). One way to do this is to start from the south end of Big Spring Drive (limited parking). Another choice is to start from US 12, which adds 1.5 miles to the distance of the hike. Unfortunately, this is a noisy trailhead next to a busy highway, but as you walk north along the lake, the road noise fades.

Local information: Jefferson County Area Tourism, PO Box 243, Jefferson, 53549; (920) 674-7148; www.enjoyjeffersoncounty.com

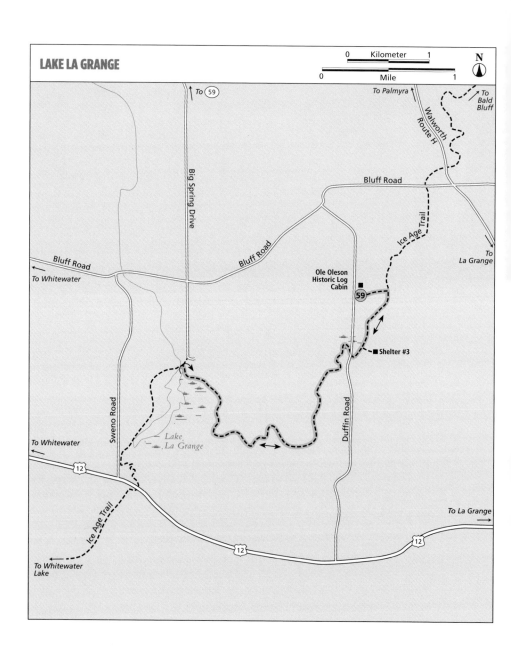

LAKE LA GRANGE

0 Kilometer 1

0 Mile 1

N

To (59)

To Palmyra

To Bald Bluff

Walworth Route H

Bluff Road

Ice Age Trail

To La Grange

Big Spring Drive

Bluff Road

Bluff Road

Bluff Road

To Whitewater

Ole Oleson Historic Log Cabin

(59)

■ Shelter #3

Sweno Road

Duffin Road

Lake La Grange

To Whitewater

12

Ice Age Trail

To La Grange

12

12

To Whitewater Lake

The historic Oleson Cabin PREAMTIP SATASUK

MILES AND DIRECTIONS

0.0   Start from the trailhead at Oleson Cabin.

0.2   Bear right at the junction with the yellow-blazed Ice Age Trail.

0.8   Pass spur trail to shelter #3.

1.0   Cross Duffin Road.

1.7   Pass a log bench at the top of a ridge.

4.0   Bear right at the white-blazed Ice Age Trail juncture.

4.5   Arrive at a bench at Lake La Grange.

9.0   Arrive back at the cabin trailhead.

60 BEULAH BOG

Kettles formed by glacial deposits during the most recent advance of the Ice Age glaciers have turned to bogs, home to a variety of rare plants and some of the most pristine land in this corner of the state. A woodland trail leads to a boardwalk that puts you right in the center of a primeval bog.

Start: At the trailhead in the parking area
Distance: 1.0-mile out-and-back
Hiking time: About 30 minutes
Difficulty: Easy
Trail surface: Dirt, some loose rock, boardwalk
Best season: April–October
Other trail users: None
Land status: State Natural Area
Nearest town: East Troy
Canine compatibility: Leashed dogs permitted
Fees and permits: None
Schedule: Daily

Maps: USGS East Troy quad
Trail contact: Kettle Moraine State Forest Southern Unit, S91W39091 Hwy. 59, Eagle, 53118; (262) 594-6200; https://dnr.wi.gov
Special considerations: Beulah Bog is a State Natural Area. Treat it well. Do not attempt to step off the boardwalk, both for the plants' well-being and yours. During wet periods the boardwalk may be temporarily underwater.
Camping: Pinewoods Campground has 101 drive-in sites, 13 miles north of the trailhead.

FINDING THE TRAILHEAD

From East Troy, drive north 1.0 mile on CR G and turn left on St. Peter's Road. After 0.5 mile turn right (north) on Stringers Bridge Road and drive 1.4 miles to the trailhead parking area on the right (east) side of the road. GPS: N42 49.137' / W88 24.800'

THE HIKE

Name the least-disturbed natural habitat in this corner of the state and it would have to be bogs. Beulah Bog is a good example of these Ice Age relics; its impressive list of credits includes several rare plants and six carnivorous ones. This wetland also features floating mud flats, a bog lake, and a tamarack forest. Best of all, it has a way to get to the middle, a boardwalk. Bogs are neat, intriguing places, but they are inaccessible, too wet to walk and too thick with vegetation to canoe.

Walk east from the trailhead on an unmarked but well-worn trail. This path wanders east and northeast through overgrown old fields and scattered oak trees. At 0.1 mile pass a spur trail on the right that leads a quarter mile southeast to the end of the park in a residential area, passing between two bogs.

Continuing south, pass another spur trail on the right at 0.2 mile and finally come to a turn to the south, descending a wooded hillside on steps, to the bog's north shore. At the bottom of that small slope, at mile 0.4, the boardwalk begins with a 40-foot bridge and continues on a two-plank boardwalk just above the oozing mass below. Continuing its 150-yard run into the bog, the boardwalk passes through a dense stand of tamaracks, with a verdant, mossy carpet below. The boardwalk ends at a small loop with a tiny floating

A boardwalk into tamaracks at Beulah Bog
PREAMTIP SATASUK

The beautiful waters of Beulah Bog

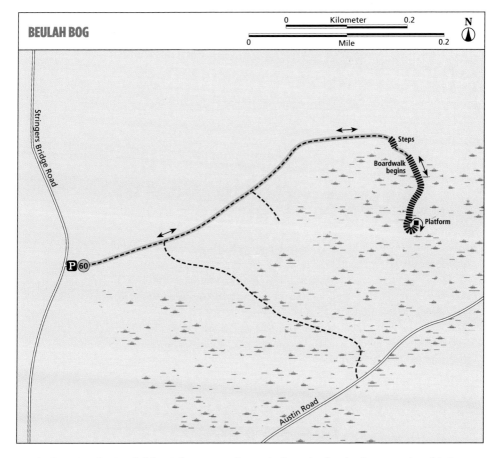

platform in the bog's lake. The tamaracks encircling the kettle that contains this bog make quite an impression. Retrace your steps to return to the trailhead.

Options: The two spur trails offer an additional 0.5 mile of hiking as out-and-backs. The first spur heads southeast along a ridge between two bog-filled kettles. The one on the left (northeast) side is the bog with the boardwalk. Especially when leaves are not present, the view into either bog is impressive. The trail descends to a saddle and, on the climb up the other side, ends in a residential area on Austin Road. The second spur descends a short distance to the edge of the bog.

MILES AND DIRECTIONS

0.0   Begin at the trailhead.

0.1   Pass a spur trail on the right.

0.2   Pass a second spur trail down the hill to the right.

0.4   Follow the boardwalk.

0.5   Arrive at the water's edge and the end of the boardwalk.

1.0   Arrive back at the trailhead.

HONORABLE MENTIONS

KETTLE MORAINE: THRU-HIKES ON THE ICE AGE NATIONAL SCENIC TRAIL

As mentioned before, the Ice Age Trail is a work in progress. Of the 1,200 miles planned for the rustic trail through Wisconsin's most scenic, glacially carved lands, just over 650 miles are complete. The various segments, marked by signs and yellow blazes along the trail, sometimes are contiguous, but in other instances connecting routes or even the trail itself follows country roads and city streets to get to the next stretch of the off-road footpath. The trail is designed for thru-hiking, so with the exception of the occasional loop formed by alternative white-blazed trails, it's an out-and-back trek—unless you thru-hike it. Two excellent long sections lie within the Kettle Moraine State Forest.

A. ICE AGE TRAIL—KETTLE MORAINE STATE FOREST—NORTHERN UNIT

This stretch of rugged footpath only leaves the woods to cross the road less than a couple dozen times in 31 miles, and when it does it is often the Kettle Moraine Scenic Drive. This is the heart of the state forest, and the terrain rises and falls over moraines and eskers and around kettles. The Ice Age Trail passes through or nearby the New Fane Trail, Mauthe Lake's Tamarack Circle Trail, Butler Lake Trail, Parnell Tower Trail, and the Greenbush Trails, all of which are included in greater detail in *Best Hikes Near Milwaukee*. Unlike the Southern Unit, the Northern Unit offers water pumps a reasonable distance from each of the trail's camping shelters. The five backcountry shelters are accessible year-round and offer a roofed structure, fire ring, and pit toilet. No more than ten campers are allowed and only for one night. Get the required permit by calling (888) 947-2757 or stopping in at the state forest headquarters, Ice Age Visitor Center, or Mauthe or Long Lake entrance stations. The 135-site campground at Mauthe Lake Recreation Area is also just off the trail. The trailheads, along CR H in the south and CR P in the north, have parking lots, and a number of lots along the length of this segment offer shorter alternatives for your thru-hike. A general map and a chart showing point-to-point mileage from either trailhead are available on the state forest's website or in the *Ice Age Trail Atlas & Guidebook*.

GPS: N43 29.881' / W88 11.583' (CR H); N43 47.786' / W88 2.102' (CR P)
Kettle Moraine State Forest—Northern Unit, Forest Headquarters, N1765 Hwy. G, Campbellsport, 53010; (262) 626-2116; https://dnr.wi.gov. Ice Age Visitor Center, N2875 WI 67, Campbellsport, 53010; (920) 533-8322; https://dnr.wi.gov.

B. ICE AGE TRAIL—KETTLE MORAINE STATE FOREST— SOUTHERN UNIT

Starting in the Whitewater Lake Recreation Area, the Ice Age Trail meanders north and northeast 30 miles to Pinewoods Campgrounds. In addition to the camping available at Whitewater Lake and Pinewoods, there are three shelters—numbered from 3 to 1 if you are coming from the south—located at the 8.2-, 18.7-, and 26.2-mile marks. Much of the route is hardwood forest and scattered pine plantation, but there are a few prairie areas as well. The southern section is characterized by a lot of moraine hiking as you follow the ridges through the Whitewater Lake Segment and past the mountain bike areas of the John Muir Trail and Emma Carlin Trail. The first shelter is after rounding La Grange Lake and crossing Duffin Road, just before the John Muir Trail. Beyond that lies Bald Bluff with its scenic overlook and the Emma Carlin Trail before you come to shelter #2 not far from the state forest headquarters on WI 59, a good place to get more

An impressive collection of chicken of the woods mushrooms on a tree along the Ice Age Trail
PREAMTIP SATASUK

water. The last stretch crosses a couple of streams and passes spur trails to notable natural features before heading through the Scuppernong Trail system to arrive at Pinewoods Campground. While the two campgrounds are open from mid-May to mid-October, the three backcountry shelters are accessible year-round and offer a roofed structure, fire ring, and pit toilet. No more than ten campers are allowed and only for one night. Get the required permit by calling (888) 947-2757. A number of parking lots for the Ice Age Trail lie along the length of this segment, offering a number of ways to shorten a thru-hike. A general map and mileage chart are available on the state forest's website or in the *Ice Age Trail Atlas & Guidebook*.

GPS: N42 46.860' / W88 41.708' (Whitewater Lake); N42 57.635' / W88 27.266' (Pinewoods Campground)

Kettle Moraine State Forest—Southern Unit, S91 W39091 WI 59, Eagle, 53119; (262) 594-6200; https://dnr.wi.gov

C. KETTLE MORAINE STATE FOREST—LAPHAM PEAK UNIT

Named for Increase Lapham, known as Wisconsin's first scientist, this unit of the state forest is located just off I-94 west of Milwaukee. Its cross-country ski trails are quite popular and well maintained. These same trails are part of the 17 miles of wide paths through woods and prairie, and up and over some glacial terrain. Four miles of the Ice Age Trail pass through the park, and an observation tower at the park's highest point offers amazing views. Maps are available at the park.

GPS: N43 02.461' / W88 24.253'

Kettle Moraine State Forest—Lapham Peak Unit, W329 N846 CR C, Delafield, 53018; (262) 646-3025; https://dnr.wi.gov

D. KETTLE MORAINE STATE FOREST—PIKE LAKE UNIT

Located a short distance west of the Ice Age Trail: Cedar Lakes Loop hike (hike 54), this section of the Kettle Moraine is named for its lake, good for swimming and fishing. But the rest of the park is primarily wooded with several miles of trails up and down a central kame. A short trail climbs steeply to an observation tower with views as far as Holy Hill, a famous church on another kame to the south. The Astronomy Trail shows relative distances between planets, and a boardwalk serves as an accessible option. A segment of the Ice Age Trail also passes through the park.

GPS: N43 19.165' / W88 19.145'

Kettle Moraine State Forest—Pike Lake Unit, 3544 Kettle Moraine Rd., Hartford, 53027; (262) 670-3400; https://dnr.wi.gov

E. HIGH CLIFF STATE PARK

With panoramic views of Lake Winnebago, this state park offers 17 miles worth of trails. Sights within the park include ruins of an old lime kiln, effigy mounds, a statue of Chief Red Bird, and an observation tower. The park rests on the western edge of the Niagara Escarpment, which reveals itself throughout. The 3.4-mile Red Bird Trail touches on the greatest hits.

GPS: N44 10.021' / W88 17.472'

High Cliff State Park, N7630 State Park Rd., Sherwood, 54169; (920) 989-1106; https://dnr.wi.gov

F. HORICON NATIONAL WILDLIFE REFUGE

These 22,000 acres of internationally significant wetlands are the northern two thirds of the same Horicon Marsh showcased in this book, but this section is managed federally rather than by the state. A trail system combines some boardwalk trail and grassy mowed trails for a solid half day in the refuge. The visitor center has more information about what you will see here, and a trip here combined with the state refuge to the south is a full day. Trails start from the point indicated, but there are also bike paths and a paved circle tour of the property.

GPS: N43 37.830' / W88 40.169'

Horicon National Wildlife Refuge, W4279 Headquarters Rd., Mayville, 53050; (920) 387-2658; www.fws.gov

The trail at Horicon Marsh passes close to the water's edge where waterfowl often gather in abundance.

G. KICKAPOO VALLEY RESERVE TRAILS

The Kickapoo River is remarkable for its scenery and its incredibly erratic course on its voyage to the Wisconsin River. Though it is primarily thought of as a paddler's delight (see FalconGuides *Paddling Wisconsin*), hikers may be surprised to know there are miles of trails through woods and meadows and crisscrossing the river itself. Three modest loops are for hikers only, but add to that a 4.5-mile multiuse trail, 14 miles of mowed mountain bike trails, and 37 miles of rougher equestrian trails. Bridges span the water in some places, but in others you may have to ford the river. Half of the twenty-five primitive campsites are accessible by vehicle, but a third can be reached on foot and/or by canoe.

GPS: N43 35.755' / W90 37.528'

Kickapoo Valley Reserve, S3661 WI 131, La Farge, 54639; (608) 625-2960; https://kvr.state.wi.us

H. KOHLER-ANDRAE STATE PARK

The Lake Michigan shoreline has a presence in this book already with Point Beach and several of the Door County hikes, but you will find no better experience of the dunes than at this state park south of Sheboygan. A cordwalk traverses the dunes and the spaces between them, and the park's beach stretches over a mile. But it's not all sand; trails also skirt a fishing pond, marshland, and wooded forest. A family campground and a nature center round out the offerings.

GPS: N43 40.268' / W87 43.101'

Kohler–Andrae State Park, 1020 Beach Park Ln., Sheboygan, 53081; (920) 451-4080; https://dnr.wi.gov

I. MIRROR LAKE STATE PARK

Another great option if you are visiting the Wisconsin Dells area and looking for something closer than Devil's Lake State Park farther south, this park has seventeen named trails open for hikers. Ranging in length from 0.2 to 3.0 miles, the trails can also be combined for much longer hikes. The finest of them skirt along the lobes of the namesake lake with views from both high above and at the shoreline. The woods hold abundant wildlife and stretches of exposed sandstone.

GPS: N43 33.709' / W89 48.435'

Mirror Lake State Park, E10320 Fern Dell Rd., Baraboo, 53913; (608) 254-2333; https://dnr.wi.gov

J. ROCHE-A-CRI STATE PARK

At the center of this state park 1.5 miles north of Friendship is a large rocky mound that was once an island in the middle of Glacial Lake Wisconsin. The sandstone is splendid, and on its surface you can see Native American petroglyphs and pictographs from native peoples centuries ago. The stairway to the top is great around sunset. Short trails lead to the prettier parts of the park, and a 3.5-mile loop circles the entire mound. Camping is also available.

GPS: N44 00.07674' / W89 48.752'

Roche-a-Cri State Park, 1767 WI 13, Friendship, 53934; (608) 339-6881 (summer), (608) 565-2789 (off-season); https://dnr.wi.gov

K. ROCKY ARBOR STATE PARK

Beyond question, the natural beauty of Wisconsin Dells is competing with a lot of commercial tourist attractions, but by no means should one discount it as an outdoors destination. This state park just outside the city offers nice wooded campgrounds and a gorgeous 1.0-mile trek through carved sandstone where the Wisconsin River once flowed. Now overgrown, the rock formations harbor some rare plants and abundant wildlife.

GPS: N43 38.464' / W89 48.124'

Rocky Arbor State Park, N101 US 12/16, Wisconsin Dells, 53965; (608) 254-8001 (summer), (608) 254-2333 (off-season); https://dnr.wi.gov

GLOSSARY

bog A form of wetlands containing peat, often formed by decomposing sphagnum moss, and characterized by acidic waters and often tamaracks; similar to but distinct from a fen. The water source is primarily precipitation, and the bog forms in a depression with no surface outflows.

bottoms A floodplain area, usually a mixture of forest and wetland.

dike An elevated earthen causeway, passing through a wetland or along a river.

dolomite A rock similar to limestone and consisting largely of calcium magnesium carbonate.

drumlin A hill carved into the shape of an egg on its side by the passing of a glacier. The shape reveals the direction the ice was moving.

esker A long, snake-like ridge of gravel and sand left by streams that flow through tunnels under a glacier.

fen A form of wetland that accumulates decomposing plant life to make peat. Unlike a bog, a fen accumulates water primarily from ground sources and the surrounding watershed, and also releases water via outflows on the surface. Watershed terrain affects the chemistry of a fen, resulting in alkaline or acidic water, but when it happens to be acidic, it is not as acidic as a bog.

goat prairie A steep, bluff-top prairie located on dry, south-facing slopes.

kame A round knoll of gravel or sand deposited by vertical streams of glacial meltwater.

kettle A depression formed when a large chunk of ice is trapped under glacial deposits of sand and gravel and then later melts, leaving the "kettle."

marsh A shallow wetland, largely filled with reeds, cattails, and water lilies.

moraine A mound, hill, or ridge created by glacial deposits at the edge of the glacier's advance. A terminal moraine is such a ridge formed at the glacier's farthest advance before it melts away.

outwash plain A wide plain of sand created by streams from melting glacial ice in front of a glacier.

portage A trail used for transporting boats from one body of water to another or around obstacles.

slough A wetland that is part of the floodplain, or a backwater of a river.

swale A depression or lowland area, typically of wetlands, often wet or marshy.

Wisconsinan glaciation The most recent advance of glaciers over North America, which occurred from 85,000 to just over 10,000 years ago. The ice sheets reached their farthest extent during the period between 21,000 and 25,000 years ago.

woods road A dirt road in the woods that is no longer used by wheeled vehicles. Can be in various stages of revegetation.

CLUBS AND TRAIL GROUPS

American Volkssport Association
www.ava.org
This nonprofit association promotes walking for health and has a couple of active chapters in Wisconsin that organize walking events:

Madison
Madison Area Volkssport Assn., 4306 Fox Bluff Ct., Middleton, 53562;
www.dairylandwalkers.com

Niagara
Menominee River Volkssport Club, 1249 Garfield St., Niagara, 54151; www.menominee
rivervolkssporters.webs.com

Badger Trails, Inc.
P.O. Box 210615
(414) 777-3920
www.badgertrails.org
Badger Trails is a nonprofit organization promoting hiking in Wisconsin. It sponsors three events each year.

Ice Age Trail Alliance
2110 Main St.
Cross Plains, 53528
(800) 227-0046
www.iceagetrail.org
Though many segments of this national scenic trail have been created, some are still on the way and the rest are always being maintained. Local chapters organize hikes and trail-maintenance events. This is a great bunch of people and a fantastic hiking trail. Check the website to find local chapters of the Ice Age Trail Alliance throughout the length of the trail.

MeetUp.com
This social-networking group helps you hook up with like-minded locals. Several Wisconsin cities have groups with outdoor interests including hiking.

North Country Trail Association
www.northcountrytrail.org
Wisconsin has three chapters of this organization: the Brule–St. Croix, Chequamegon, and Heritage Chapters. They occasionally schedule special events and are good sources of information on their respective sections of the North Country National Scenic Trail.

Wisconsin Go Hiking Club
(414) 299-9285
www.wisconsingohikingclub.weebly.com
Since its inception in 1924, this club has been promoting outdoor activity. Often there are several hikes each week, in destinations both near and far. Member dues are nominal, and event costs are shared by participants.

FURTHER READING

Dott, Robert H., and John W. Attig. *Roadside Geology of Wisconsin*. Missoula, MT: Mountain Press Publishing Co., 2004.

Ice Age Trail Atlas & Guidebook 2020-2022. Cross Plains, WI: Ice Age Trail Alliance, 2020 (includes e-version).

Mickelson, David M., Louis J. Maher, and Susan L. Simpson. *Geology of the Ice Age National Scenic Trail*. Madison: The University of Wisconsin Press, 2011.

Revolinski, Kevin. *Backroads and Byways of Wisconsin*. Woodstock, VT: Countryman Press, 2009.

Sherman, Eric, and Andrew Hanson III. *Along Wisconsin's Ice Age Trail*. Madison: The University of Wisconsin Press, 2008.

ABOUT THE AUTHORS

Kevin Revolinski is a freelance writer/photographer who writes mainly about travel and the outdoors. He was born and raised in central Wisconsin in a house full of maps, outdoor guides, and hunting and camping equipment. His maternal grandmother inspired his love of bird-watching, and frequent trips to visit his grandparents in northern Wisconsin made him a passionate fan of the Northwoods and Lake Superior country. He is the author of several books, and his work has appeared in the *New York Times*, *Chicago Tribune*, and *Sydney Morning Herald*. He maintains a travel website called "The Mad Traveler" (www.TheMadTraveler.com) as well as his author site, www.KevinRevolinski.com. He is an avid camper, hiker, paddler, and beer drinker. He lives in Madison, Wisconsin.

Other works by Kevin include *Best Easy Day Hikes Milwaukee*, *Best Easy Day Hikes Grand Rapids*, *Best Hikes Near Milwaukee*, *Paddling Wisconsin*, *Best Rail Trails Wisconsin*, *Insiders' Guide Madison*, and a collection of short stories, *Stealing Away*.

Eric Hansen's first recorded hike was an ascent of New York's Bear Mountain at the age of 4. His parents encouraged him to roam the woods with curiosity and confidence, the beginning of a lifelong love of exploration and route finding in the outdoors. Topographic maps were the wallpaper of his childhood bedroom.

He has hiked and backpacked extensively and now divides his time between the mountains and canyons of the West and the woods and waters of the Midwest. Eric's background includes successful climbs of most of the high peaks in Montana's Glacier National Park and over a dozen rim-river-rim treks in the Grand Canyon. After twenty years of exploring Wisconsin's natural areas, he hiked 800 miles to research this guidebook.

Eric is a frequent contributor and gear reviewer for *Backpacker* magazine. His local outdoor writing credits include *Milwaukee* magazine, the *Milwaukee Journal-Sentinel*, and *Shepherd Express*, as well as *Silent Sports* magazine.

THE TEN ESSENTIALS OF HIKING

American Hiking Society

American Hiking Society recommends you pack the "Ten Essentials" every time you head out for a hike. Whether you plan to be gone for a couple of hours or several months, make sure to pack these items. Become familiar with these items and know how to use them.

1. Appropriate Footwear
Happy feet make for pleasant hiking. Think about traction, support, and protection when selecting well-fitting shoes or boots.

2. Navigation
While phones and GPS units are handy, they aren't always reliable in the backcountry; consider carrying a paper map and compass as a backup and know how to use them.

3. Water (and a way to purify it)
As a guideline, plan for half a liter of water per hour in moderate temperatures/terrain. Carry enough water for your trip and know where and how to treat water while you're out on the trail.

4. Food
Pack calorie-dense foods to help fuel your hike, and carry an extra portion in case you are out longer than expected.

5. Rain Gear & Dry-Fast Layers
The weatherman is not always right. Dress in layers to adjust to changing weather and activity levels. Wear moisture-wicking cloths and carry a warm hat.

6. Safety Items (light, fire, and a whistle)
Have means to start an emergency fire, signal for help, and see the trail and your map in the dark.

7. First Aid Kit
Supplies to treat illness or injury are only as helpful as your knowledge of how to use them. Take a class to gain the skills needed to administer first aid and CPR.

8. Knife or Multi-Tool
With countless uses, a multi-tool can help with gear repair and first aid.

9. Sun Protection
Sunscreen, sunglasses, and sun-protective clothing should be used in every season regardless of temperature or cloud cover.

10. Shelter
Protection from the elements in the event you are injured or stranded is necessary. A lightweight, inexpensive space blanket is a great option.

Find other helpful resources at AmericanHiking.org/hiking-resources